China's Foreign Relations since 1949

THE WORLD STUDIES SERIES

General Editor: JAMES HENDERSON, M.A., Ph.D.,
Senior Lecturer in Education with special reference to Teaching of History
and International Affairs, Institute of Education, University of London

Editorial Board: MOTHER MARY de SALES, M.A., Principal Lecturer in
History, Coloma College

JOSEPH HUNT, M.A., Senior History Master, City of London School

JAMES JOLL, M.A., Professor of International History, London School of
Economics and Politics, University of London

ESMOND WRIGHT, M.A., Professor of American History, University
College, University of London; Director of the Institute of United States
Studies

VOLUMES PUBLISHED

Malaysia and its Neighbours, J. M. Gullick.

The European Common Market and Community, Uwe Kitzinger, Fellow
of Nuffield College, Oxford.

The Politics of John F. Kennedy, Edmund Ions, Department of History,
Columbia University, New York.

Apartheid: A Documentary Study of Modern South Africa, Edgar H.
Brookes.

Israel and the Arab World, C. H. Dodd, Department of Government,
University of Manchester, and M. E. Sales, Centre for Middle
Eastern and Islamic Studies, University of Durham.

The Theory and Practice of Neutrality in the Twentieth Century, Roderick
Ogley, Department of International Relations, University of
Sussex.

The Search for Peace, D. W. Bowett, The President, Queens' College,
Cambridge.

Soviet Foreign Policy since the Death of Stalin, H. Hanak, School of
Slavonic and East European Studies, University of London.

Northern Ireland: Crisis and Conflict, John Magee, Department of
History, St Joseph's College of Education, Belfast.

The Rhodesian Problem: A Documentary Record 1923–1973, Elaine
Windrich, University of California, Los Angeles.

China's Foreign Relations since 1949

Alan Lawrance

Department of History,
Balls Park College of Education, Hertford

LONDON AND BOSTON

ROUTLEDGE & KEGAN PAUL

First published in 1975
by Routledge & Kegan Paul Ltd
Broadway House, 68–74 Carter Lane,
London EC4V 5EL and
9 Park Street,
Boston, Mass. 02108, USA
Set in Monotype Baskerville
and printed in Great Britain by
Butler & Tanner Ltd, Frome and London

ISBN 0 7100 8092 1

Contents

	page
GENERAL EDITOR'S PREFACE	xi
VOLUME EDITOR'S PREFACE	xiii
ACKNOWLEDGMENTS	xv
CHRONOLOGY	xvii
ABBREVIATIONS AND NOTE ON TRANSLITERATION	xxii
INTRODUCTION	I

SELECT DOCUMENTS

PART I: THE ERA OF SINO-SOVIET FRIENDSHIP 1949–55

(a) Leaning to one side

1. Extract from Mao Tse-tung, speech of 11 June 1945 — 20
2. Extract from Mao Tse-tung, speech of 30 June 1949 — 22
3. Extract from Dean Acheson's 'Letter of Transmittal', 30 July 1949 — 25
4. Extracts from an article by Soong Ching-ling, 16 January 1950 — 27
5. The Sino-Soviet Treaty, 14 February 1950 — 29
6. Extracts from a report on China's first Five Year Plan to the National People's Congress, July 1955 — 32

(b) Confronting the United States

7. Extract from President Truman's Statement on the status of Formosa, 5 January 1950 — 35
8. 'No Smoke-screen Round Taiwan', from *People's China*, 16 January 1950 — 36

9. Chou En-lai warns the Americans not to cross the 38th parallel, 2 October 1950   39
10. Extracts from 'The Way of the US Aggressor: Korea', 16 December 1950   41
11. Extracts from speech by Wu Hsiu-chüan, 28 November 1950   45
12. Extract from speech by Congressman Dorn supporting award of thanks of Congress to General Douglas MacArthur   47
13. Extract from 'Judgment of Military Tribunal on US Spies . . .', 23 November 1954   48
14. Extract from speech by J. F. Dulles, 29 March 1954   51
15. Extract from 'China Will Liberate Taiwan', *People's Daily*, 5 December 1954   53
16. Extract from speech by Chou En-lai, 30 July 1955   55
17. Extract from K. J. Young, *Negotiating with the Chinese Communists*, 1968   59

PART II: THE SINO-SOVIET RIFT 1956–65

(a) Origins

18. Extracts from 'The Origin and Development of the Differences between the Leadership of the CPSU and ourselves . . .' *People's Daily*, 6 September 1963   70
19. Extract from speech by Mao Tse-tung, 18 November 1957   74
20. Extracts from Statement of eighty-one communist parties, Moscow, November 1960   75

(b) Open conflict

21. Extract from 'The truth about how the Leaders of the CPSU have allied themselves with India against China', *People's Daily*, 2 November 1963   80
22. Extracts from Chinese government statement on Test Ban Treaty, 31 July 1963   83
23. Extracts from CCP's proposal, 14 June 1963   86
24. Extracts from *Voennaya mysl'* (Military Thought), October 1963   89
25. Extract from H. C. Hinton, *Communist China in World Politics*, 1966   91

26. Extract from 'Why Khrushchev fell', *Red Flag*, 21 November 1964 — 95

27. Extract from 'Refutation of the New Leaders of the CPSU on "United Action" ', *People's Daily*, 11 November 1965 — 100

28. Extract from Vice-Premier Chen Yi's answers to questions put by Japanese paper *Akahata*, 30 December 1965 — 102

29. Extract from Liparit Kyuzajhyan, *The Chinese Crisis*, 1969 — 104

PART III: CHINA AND ITS ASIAN NEIGHBOURS

(a) China's borders

30. Map of 'The Old Democratic Revolutionary Era (1840–1919) . . .' — 115

31. A statement on border policy, *People's Daily*, 8 March 1963 — 116

(b) The Himalayan frontier

32. Extracts from correspondence between India and China concerning the border, 1958–9 — 117

33. Treaty of friendship . . . between the People's Republic of China and the Union of Burma, 28 January 1960 — 126

34. Extracts from Vice-Premier Chen Yi's television interview with Mr Karlsson, 17 February 1963 — 128

35. Extract from 'New Delhi returns evil for good!', *Peking Review*, 25 January 1963 — 133

(c) Indochina

36. Extract from H. C. Hinton, *Communist China in World Politics*, 1966 — 135

37. Extracts from Arthur Lall, *How Communist China Negotiates*, 1968 — 138

38. Extracts from 'Escalation means getting closer and closer to the grave', *People's Daily*, 24 April 1965 — 141

(d) Outer Mongolia

39. Extract from 'Kuriles must be returned to Japan', *Sekai Shuhu*, 11 August 1964 — 144

40. Extract from Foreign Minister Chen Yi's press conference, 29 September 1965   145

(e) Japan

41. Foreign Minister Chen Yi's statement on Japanese-US Security Treaty, 19 November 1958   146
42. Extract from Foreign Minister Chen Yi's press conference, 29 September 1965   148

PART IV: CHINA AND THE THIRD WORLD

(a) The Chinese example

43. Extracts from 'China's Revolution and the Struggle Against Colonialism', *People's China*, 16 February 1950   155
44. Extract from Lu Ting-yi, *People's China*, 1 July 1951   158

(b) Peaceful co-existence

45. Extract from Joint Statement by the Prime Ministers of India and China, 28 June 1954   160
46. Extract from speech by Chou En-lai, Bandung, 19 April 1955   161
47. Extracts from speech by Chou En-lai, Bandung, 23 April 1955   165

(c) The Intermediate Zone: the evolution of a policy?

48. Extracts from 'Apologists of Neo-colonialism', *People's Daily* and *Red Flag*, 25 October 1963   168
49. Extracts from Chou En-lai's speech at Mogadishu, 3 February 1964   171
50. Extract from Foreign Minister Chen Yi's press conference, 29 September 1965   175
51. Extract from B. D. Larkin, *China and Africa 1949–1970*, 1971   177
52. On the Intermediate Zone. Extract from *People's Daily*, 21 January 1964   180
53. Extracts from Lin Piao, 'Long Live the Victory of People's War', *People's Daily*, 2 September 1965   181

(d) Indonesia

54. Extracts from 'People of Indonesia, Unite and Fight

to Overthrow the Fascist Regime', *Red Flag*, July
1967   186

PART V: FOREIGN RELATIONS DURING THE CULTURAL
REVOLUTION

55. Extracts from R. L. Walker, 'Peking's Approach to
the Outside World', *Communist China, 1949–1969. A
Twenty Year Appraisal*, 1970   193
56. Extracts from 'The Great Cultural Revolution is an
Issue of Prime Importance . . .', *Liberation Army
Daily*, 6 June 1966   195
57. Poem by Mao Tse-tung to the melody 'The Full
River is Red'   197
58. *Peking Review* on an incident in Portland Place, 14
July 1967   198
59. 'Mob Burns British Mission in Peking', *Guardian*, 23
August 1967   199
60. Extract from 'Down with the New Tsars', Peking,
1969   202

PART VI: FOREIGN RELATIONS SINCE THE CULTURAL
REVOLUTION

(*a*) *Rapprochement* and recognition
61. Extract from 'Confession in an Impasse', *People's
Daily*, 27 January 1969   207
62. A conversation between Chairman Mao and Edgar
Snow, December 1970   210
63. 'Don't Lose Your Head, Nixon', *People's Daily*, 20
February 1971   212
64. Opposing a 'Two Chinas' solution, *People's Daily*,
4 May 1971   214
65. Extract from speech by Chiao Kuan-hua at Plenary
Meeting of 26th session of UN General Assembly, 15
November 1971   216
66. Joint Communiqué agreed by the Chinese and US
sides in Shanghai, 27 February 1972   219

(*b*) Bangladesh

67. Extracts from statement of the Government of the People's Republic of China, 16 December 1971   223
68. Extract from speech by Chiao Kuan-hua at 27th session of UN General Assembly, 3 October 1972   226

(*c*) Post-recognition policies

69. Joint Statement of the governments of the People's Republic of China and Japan, 29 September 1972   228
70. The Two Intermediate Zones. Extract from *Red Flag*, November 1972   231
71. 'China invites Taiwan to Talks on Reuniting Nation', 'Taiwan Snubs Offer', *Guardian*, 2–3 March 1973   232
72. 'Freed American Spy Looks Back on More Than 20 Years Wasted in a Chinese Prison', *The Times*, 14 March 1973   234
73. 'Soviet Revisionist Spies Caught Red-Handed', *Peking Review*, 1 February 1974   236

PART VII: INTERPRETING CHINA'S FOREIGN POLICY:
A SELECTION OF VIEWS

74. Extracts from A. Huck, *The Security of China*, 1970   240
75. Extract from J. D. Simmonds, *China's World, The Foreign Policy of a Developing State*, 1970   243
76. Extract from I. C. Ojha, *Chinese Foreign Policy in an Age of Transition: The Diplomacy of Cultural Despair*, 1969   244
77. Extract from Neal Ascherson, 'The Great Leap Backwards?', *Observer*, 5 March 1972   248

CONCLUSION   251

SELECT BIBLIOGRAPHY   253

INDEX   255

MAPS

1. Chinese view of American forces, 11 February 1966   62
2. American view of Chinese forces, 7 March 1966   63

General Editor's Preface

The World Studies Series is designed to make a new and important contribution to the study of modern history. Each volume in the Series will provide students in sixth forms, Colleges of Education and Universities with a range of contemporary material drawn from many sources, not only from official and semi-official records, but also from contemporary historical writing from reliable journals. The material is selected and introduced by a scholar who establishes the context of his subject and suggests possible lines of discussion and inquiry that can accompany a study of the documents.

Through these volumes the student can learn how to read and assess historical documents. He will see how the contemporary historian works and how historical judgments are formed. He will learn to discriminate among a number of sources and to weigh the evidence. He is confronted with recent instances of what Professor Butterfield has called 'the human predicament' revealed by history; evidence concerning the national, racial and ideological factors which at present hinder or advance man's progress towards some form of world society.

In this timely volume Dr Lawrance provides an introductory analysis of China's foreign relations since the establishment of the People's Republic. He then proceeds to supply the documentary evidence from which students can draw their own conclusions regarding China's foreign policy in relation to the United States, the Soviet Union and other powers, not least to those constituting the Third World. If, as Eastern wisdom teaches, enlightenment consists in the capacity to see things differently, then the material so skilfully marshalled and ordered in the following pages should enlighten many readers, who are striving to understand the place of China in the modern world.

JAMES HENDERSON

Volume Editor's Preface

The main topics covered in this book are China's relations with the USA and the USSR, China's role in Asia, and China's approach to the countries of the Third World. Particular attention is given to the dramatic *rapprochement* between China and the West which has taken place since the Cultural Revolution.

The fundamental objectives of modern China's foreign policy have been to find security on its borders, to recover Taiwan and to take its place in the United Nations. Peking has also been credited with the aim of exporting its own brand of revolutionary communism and with seeking hegemony in Asia. This collection of documents should help the reader to make his own judgment.

The extracts chosen include not only a selection of the most obviously significant documents but also reports and descriptions which add colour and detail. Most of the material is from Chinese sources. If this book has a bias it is towards presenting the Chinese view which has been frequently neglected and sometimes misinterpreted in the West.

Inseparable from a study of China's foreign relations is an understanding of China's domestic development. In the commentary on the documents brief reference is made to the main events in China's recent history. The reader's attention is drawn to the list of general works in the bibliography.

Acknowledgments

In the preparation of this book I have been indebted to many: to the Principal and Governors of Balls Park College for a year's study-leave; to members of the Department of Chinese Studies at Leeds University, and to the staff of the Brotherton Library, for friendly guidance and assistance; to Dr Richard Spence for his comments on the manuscript and to Loretto Lynch, Denise Franklin and Pat Alderton for help in its preparation. I am particularly grateful to my father Albert Lawrance for collecting newspaper cuttings and to April Carter for painstaking criticism which has made this book better than it would have been. Its remaining faults are my responsibility.

The author and publishers also wish to thank the following for kind permission to print in this volume extracts from the works cited:

Allen & Unwin, *In Two Chinas, Memoirs of a Diplomat* by K. M. Panikkar. Document 9.

McGraw-Hill, *Reminiscences* by General of the Army Douglas MacArthur, © 1964 Time Inc. Document 12.

McGraw-Hill, *Negotiating with the Chinese Communists* by K. J. Young, Copyright © 1968 by the Council of Foreign Relations. Document 17.

Praeger, *Sino-Soviet Military Relations* by R. L. Gartoff, © 1966. Document 24.

Macmillan, London and Basingstoke, and Houghton Mifflin Company, Boston, *Communist China in World Politics* by H. C. Hinton. Documents 25, 36.

Columbia University Press, *How Communist China Negotiates* by Arthur Lall. Document 37.

Hoover Institution Press, *Territorial Claims in the Sino-Soviet Conflict: Documents and Analysis* by Dennis J. Doolin, Copyright © 1965 by the Board of Trustees of Leland Stanford Junior University. Documents 30, 39.

The *New York Times*, report, 25 April 1955, Copyright © 1955 by the New York Times Co., reprinted by permission. Document 47.

The Regents of the University of California, *China and Africa 1949–1970* by Bruce D. Larkin. Originally published by the University of California Press. Document 51.

New York University Press, *Communist China, 1949–1969: A Twenty Year Appraisal* by F. N. Trager and W. Henderson, Copyright © 1970 by New York University. Document 55.

Reuters, Documents 59, 71, 72.

Hutchinson and Random House, Inc., *The Long Revolution* by Edgar Snow, Copyright © 1971, 1972 by Lois Wheeler Snow. Document 62.

Chatto & Windus and the International Institute for Strategic Studies, *The Security of China* by A. Huck. Document 74.

Columbia University Press and Australian National University Press, *China's World. The Foreign Policy of a Developing State* by J. D. Simmonds. Document 75.

Beacon Press, *Chinese Foreign Policy in an Age of Transition*, Copyright © 1969 by Ishwer C. Ojha. Document 76.

The *Observer*, 'The Great Leap Backwards?', by Neal Ascherson. Document 77.

Chronology

1949
1 October   People's Republic of China proclaimed in Peking

1950
January   Britain gave *de facto* recognition to CPR but maintained relations with the KMT regime
February   Sino-Soviet Treaty signed
June   Korean War began
             Land Reform law to redistribute wealth of landlords
October   Chinese forces entered North Korea
             China began to move troops into Tibet

1951
May   Tibet effectively incorporated in CPR
July   Korean armistice negotiations began
November   Launching of 'Three-Anti' movement against corruption, waste and bureaucracy among government employees

1952
February   Launching of 'Five-Anti' campaign against economic corruption
December   USSR returned Central Manchuria Railway to China

1953
January   First Five Year Plan inaugurated
March   Death of Stalin

July   End of Korean War
December   Resolution on formation of Agricultural Co-opera-
              tives

1954
April–July   Geneva Conference
June   Nehru and Chou En-lai issued Five Principles of
              Co-existence
July   Crisis over Taiwan and the off-shore islands
September   First Constitution of CPR adopted
              First bombardment of Quemoy
September–October   Khrushchev in Peking
December   US Defence Pact with Chiang Kai-shek

1955
April   Bandung Conference of Asian and African States
August   Sino-American ambassadorial talks began at
              Geneva
October   Drive for collectivization began

1956
February   Khrushchev denounced Stalin at Twentieth Party
              Congress
May   'Hundred Flowers' movement instigated
October   At Geneva talks China proposed cultural exchanges
              with the US
              China supported Soviet intervention in Hungary

1957
May–June   'Hundred Flowers' movement at height
August   Soviet Union tested intercontinental ballistic mis-
              sile
October   Sputnik launched
              Sino-Soviet nuclear testing agreement signed
November   Mao visited Moscow for 1957 Conference of
              Communist Parties

1958
February   'Great Leap Forward' announced
July   First communes formed. Established throughout
              China by end of year

August   Shelling of Quemoy

December Mao resigned as Chairman of CPR while remaining
              Chairman of CCP

1959

March   Tibetan Revolt. Dalai Lama fled to India

April   Liu Shao-chi became Chairman of CPR

June   USSR abrogated agreement to share nuclear
              weapons

August   Sino-Indian border clashes

September Khrushchev's meeting with President Eisenhower
              Lin Piao replaced Peng Teh-huai as Minister of
              Defence

1960

May   Breakdown of Paris summit conference after U2
              incident

June   Bucharest Meeting of leaders of Communist
              countries in Europe and Asia

August   Soviet technicians withdrawn from China

November Conference of Communist Parties in Moscow

1961

January   Modification of 'Great Leap Forward' policy

May   Geneva Conference on Laos opened

November Khrushchev attacked Albania at Twenty-second
              Party Congress

1962

July   CPR recognized the independent Republic of
              Algeria, under Ben Bella

October   Cuban crisis

October–November Sino-Indian War

1963

July   Test Ban Treaty signed by USA, UK, and USSR

1964

December (1963)–February Chou En-lai's tour of Africa

January   China exchanged full diplomatic recognition with
              France

August	Gulf of Tonkin crisis
October	Khrushchev ousted from power
	China's first nuclear bomb

1965

February	US bombing of North Vietnam
June	Chinese army ranks theoretically abolished
	Ben Bella overthrown. Proposed Afro-Asian Conference postponed
July	US sent additional 50,000 troops to Vietnam
September	Publication of Lin Piao's 'Long Live the Victory of People's War!'
October	Failure of pro-Communist coup in Indonesia
November	'First bugle call' of the Cultural Revolution

1966

March	China refused to attend the Twenty-third Party Congress in Moscow
	Nkrumah ousted from power while in Peking
June	Cultural Revolution in the universities
August	Red Guards formed

1967

April	Foreign Minister Chen Yi criticized by Red Guards for his 'revisionist' foreign policy
June	China's first hydrogen bomb
September	China agreed to build Tanzania–Zambia railway

1968

| May | Sino-American ambassadorial talks suspended |
| September | Revolutionary Committees established throughout China. Red Guards disbanded |

1969

March	Chinese and Soviet forces clashed on the Ussuri River
	President Nixon first hinted via De Gaulle that he would like to visit China
May	Beginning of the return of ambassadors to China's embassies abroad

1970

February	Ambassadorial talks resumed briefly
April	First Chinese satellite in orbit
October	China established diplomatic relations with Canada (and with thirty other Western and Third World countries by the end of 1971)
November	Overall majority vote for seating CPR in UN

1971

February	US supported invasion of Laos by South Vietnam
April	US table tennis team invited to China
June	China rejected Soviet proposal for Five Power Conference on nuclear disarmament
July	Dr Kissinger visited Peking
October	CPR replaced Taiwan regime in UN
December	Indian troops in Bangladesh

1972

February	President Nixon visited Peking
March	China and Britain agreed to exchange ambassadors
September	Sino-Japanese agreement to re-establish relations

1973

February	CPR and USA agreed to set up reciprocal liaison offices in Washington and Peking
August	Tenth Party Congress

1974

January	Trade agreement between CPR and Japan calling for most-favoured nation treatment
	CPR resisted Vietnamese claim to Hsisha Islands
November	Chiao Kuan-hua appointed Foreign Minister of CPR

Abbreviations and Note on Transliteration

CCP (or CPC)	Chinese Communist Party
CENTO	Central Treaty Organization
CPR (or PRC)	Chinese People's Republic
CPSU	Communist Party of the Soviet Union
DRV	Democratic Republic of Vietnam
ICC	International Control Commission
KMT	Kuomintang
KPA	Korean People's Army
MPR	Mongolian People's Republic
NCNA	New China News Agency
NEFA	North-east Frontier Agency
NPC	National People's Congress
PKI	Indonesian Communist Party
PLA	People's Liberation Army
PRC (or CPR)	Chinese People's Republic
SEATO	Southeast Asia Treaty Organization
UAR	United Arab Republic

In the documents the spelling follows the form used in the source. In the parts of the book written by myself I have used, for Chinese names, the standard Wade-Giles system but without the diacritical marks.

Introduction

'Do not forget that China is a large country, full of Chinese' was the advice given by De Gaulle to a French diplomat leaving for Peking. It is well to begin with the most fundamental considerations. China is indeed big, bigger than the continental United States, its people are numerous, approximately 700 million at the last count, and they are homogeneous, over 93 per cent Chinese by race. Moreover China is unique, not only in its long historical traditions as a civilization distinct from Europe and, more recently, as a revolutionary state with its own brand of communism, but also because it has long stood apart from the community of nations.

When in the early nineteenth century the expansionist powers of Europe forced China to open its gates to Western trade, it was an uneven match. Not only was the Ching dynasty (1644–1912) on the decline but the traditional outlook of isolation and self-sufficiency, which had characterized China as the 'Middle Kingdom', was to prove ineffectual against the aggressive Western states. From the time of the Opium War (1839–42) China has been unable to ignore the force of the West and the impact of Western ideas.

The evolution of the Western nations took place within the framework of the interstate rivalries of Europe, within a states-system in which the balance of power was recognized and diplomacy was refined. The Chinese state has been resurrected after the collapse of the old Empire, which in its time recognized no peers and was superbly self-confident in its own civilization. Yet the new China has in some respects broken dramatically with its past. The national leaders, Kuomintang and Communist alike, have sought inspiration from the West, and inevitably have been influenced by outside pressures and the interaction of world events.

The proclamation of the People's Republic of China on 1 October 1949 marked the ending of a civil war which had originated more than two decades earlier. The success of the Chinese Communists owed virtually nothing to foreign help. During the course of the Civil War the Soviet Union continued to recognize the Kuomintang regime (the Nationalists) while American aid flowed freely to Chiang Kai-shek, only to be dissipated by his corrupt and inefficient generals. The Communist victory was largely a moral victory, and it was widely accepted as a nationalist victory, the Nationalist Party being discredited by their ineffectual liaison with their American backers. Much of the misery of China in the past hundred years was associated with foreign exploitation and while Chiang Kai-shek's regime had made some progress towards creating a unified and genuinely independent state it had, in the end, been destroyed by its failure to deal with the need for internal reforms, the determined opposition of the Communists, and the fact of the Japanese invasion. The Communists offered the distressed and disillusioned people of China effective leadership and freedom from both domestic and foreign exploitation. In September 1949 with victory assured Mao Tse-tung was able to proclaim 'Our nation will never be insulted again. We have stood up.'

FUNDAMENTAL OBJECTIVES

The Communists have been careful not to compromise their hard-won independence. They have consistently insisted on their minimum national aims, i.e. the recovery of 'lost' territory (Tibet and Taiwan) and recognition among the community of nations (admission to the UN). Mindful of the past century of exploitation through unequal treaties they have committed themselves to foreign agreements only on terms of mutual benefit, or more often, on terms seen as ultimately beneficial to China. The CPR has entered into only two formal military alliances, one with the Soviet Union in 1950 and one with North Korea in 1961. It has been reported that an alliance with North Vietnam was proposed in 1961 but was rejected by

Hanoi. In the case of both North Korea and North Vietnam China was competing with Soviet interests in areas vital to her own security. Both examples are exceptions confirming the rule that China gives priority to maintaining her freedom of action.

From the time of the *Amethyst* incident in April 1949 when Chinese batteries drove the last British gunboats from the Yangtse River, the Chinese Communists have stood up against any challenge to the national interest and dignity of China. The most obvious affront has been the continuance, with American support, of an alternative regime in Taiwan. This has been a major stumbling block in the CPR's negotiations to establish diplomatic relations with other states and in the question of the China seat in the United Nations, held until 1971 by the Republic of China, i.e. the government of Taiwan.

As a rule the CPR has insisted as a pre-condition for full diplomatic relations that the other country concerned should sever any links with the Taiwan regime. In the case of Britain, which recognized the People's Republic in January 1950, the CPR tolerated the continued maintenance of a British consulate in Taipei, at least to the extent of accepting a British Chargé d'Affaires in Peking in 1954. In the case of France the agreement in 1964 to exchange ambassadors was conceived as an ambiguous arrangement, which provided for reciprocal recognition without specific French renunciation of its existing relations with Taiwan. The CPR seems to have expected that the Taiwan regime would itself sever relations with France. When the expected reaction did not materialize the CPR publicly reminded the French that recognition of the new government of a country naturally implies ceasing to recognize the old ruling group overthrown by the people of that country. To escape the impasse De Gaulle stated publicly that France recognized only one China, and the Taiwan regime was provoked into cutting its diplomatic ties. Nevertheless France retained limited consular representation in Taipei. When Britain pressed for full ambassadorial relations in 1972 China reiterated that the Taipei consulate must be closed; in Chou En-lai's words 'Britain must chop off that tail'. The most likely explanation for the greater tolerance shown to the French is that Peking saw Britain as essentially an American lackey, which France clearly was not.

When relations were established between Canada and the

3

CPR in October 1970 they agreed upon a formula which has since been used with a number of other countries. The joint communiqué stated 'the Chinese Government reaffirms that Taiwan is an inalienable part of the territory of the People's Republic of China. The Canadian government takes note of this position of the Chinese government.' It may be noted that Britain had to pay a higher price for ambassadorial relations in agreeing in March 1972 that the Chinese government was the 'sole legal government of China'.

The CPR's admission to the United Nations was initially opposed by the United States, but in any case the CPR would not consider joining unless the Republic of China were to withdraw. A rise in the number of nations recognizing Peking caused the Americans in 1961 to introduce a procedural motion declaring the matter of China's representation to be an important question and therefore requiring a two-thirds majority in the Assembly. In the recurring votes on the China seat a simple majority for the CPR was achieved for the first time in November 1970, but it was not until October 1971, in the wake of Dr Kissinger's Peking visit, that the matter was finally decided by an overwhelming majority, and the expulsion of the delegates from Taiwan.

Once admitted, the People's Republic has shown considerable enthusiasm for the United Nations Organization (see, for example, Document 65). Previously the Chinese attitude to the organization had been equivocal. They condemned it as an American tool while citing the charter with approval and they have also propounded wide-ranging proposals for its reform. In 1965, for example, after Indonesia had withdrawn from the UN and after the CPR had been disappointed in its hopes of a favourable vote for admission, they elaborated the conditions under which they would join to include the expulsion of all 'imperialist puppets'. Peking's subsequent willingness to drop its more extreme conditions no doubt reflects its conviction that a number of important aims can be served by working within the UN. Not least the seating of the CPR has demoralized the Taiwan regime, while the UN assembly provides a sounding board for Chinese propaganda and is clearly an appropriate arena for parading the rights of medium and small countries against the super-powers.

4

China's pride and sense of prestige as well as her concern for security and independence have determined the Chinese policy on nuclear weapons. From 1957–8, in spite of Mao's well-known aphorism, 'the atom bomb is a paper tiger', the Chinese were determined to build their own nuclear weapons. They did so with remarkable speed, testing their first atomic bomb in 1964 and their first hydrogen bomb in 1967. Bitterly opposed to the Anglo-American-Soviet nuclear test-ban treaty in 1963 (see Document 22), the Chinese have pressed instead for a comprehensive world-wide agreement to prohibit nuclear arms and destroy existing stocks, while stating that China will never be the first to use nuclear weapons. A rationale for the Chinese position was given by Foreign Minister Chen Yi in 1962 when he said 'We are working to develop an atomic bomb of our own for the sole reason that the capitalists consider us under-developed and defenceless so long as we lack the ultimate weapon.' Subsequently China has frequently reiterated, in the course of criticizing super-power politics, that her nuclear policy is essentially defensive (see Document 65).

THE GREAT POWER TRIANGLE

The circumstances of China's renaissance in 1949 have done much to determine her attitudes and policies towards the USA and USSR. At the same time as they were driving out the remnants of the KMT from the mainland and beginning the immense task of restructuring government and society, the Chinese found themselves in a potentially hostile world. The outbreak of the Korean War and the American decision to use its naval power to forestall the liberation of Taiwan emphasized the need for Soviet help and reinforced Mao's decision in 1949 to 'lean to one side'. It would be an easy misunderstanding to assume that China's ideological comrades were bound to give unqualified support. But a brief examination of the facts shows that at no time before Liberation had the CCP received substantial aid from the Soviet Union, while Soviet diplomatic support to the KMT throughout the Civil War was given. Perhaps Stalin hoped that the KMT if successful would implement the Yalta Agreement to restore pre-1904 Russian privileges in Manchuria. The CPR's initial weakness did not hide the fact that it was potentially a great power and Stalin was wary. In the long term the Sino-Soviet Treaty of 1950 may be seen as an aberration dictated by the circumstances of the Cold War, and by China's desperate need for technical and material assistance.

It was no coincidence that moves towards a *détente* between the USA and the USSR after 1958 saw a simultaneous weakening of the Sino-Soviet ties. The Chinese considered that the defensive umbrella of the Soviet Union should serve to protect China until it reached a fully independent position of strength. For the Soviets extending patronage to China was attractive as long as China remained a junior partner subservient to Soviet world interests. The decision of the Soviet Union under Khrushchev to work towards a balance of shared dominance with the United States clashed inevitably with China's ambitions. Understandably one of the first breaks in the Sino-Soviet accord was the withdrawal of Soviet assistance to the Chinese nuclear arms programme (in 1959) while the Soviet-American nuclear testing agreement in 1963 occasioned the open and irreconcilable breach. Similarly it is no coincidence that the armed frontier clashes and threatening military postures of China and the Soviet Union since 1969 have been accompanied by Chinese willingness to seek their own *détente* with the United States.

In this triangular relationship the United States has tended to set the pace. The United States has recently become aware of the limitations of its intransigence, particularly because of the failure of its Vietnam policies, and has begun to put aside Cold War ideologies in return for greater flexibility of action and in response to the actualities of a world where Soviet-American condominion is no longer feasible.

It may well be asked why it has taken so long for the United States to revise its China policies. Apart from the inveterate anti-communism of America's leaders an explanation can be found in the fear that China is a potential colossus with no limits on its ambitions. Such fear has undoubtedly been fed by China's tactics on the world stage, by its apparent role as a revolutionary leader of the Third World, and even by China's use of military force in the border dispute with India.

THE TERRITORIAL BOUNDARIES

Opinion concerning the extent of China's territorial ambitions has varied but it is safe to say that the 'threat' of China has been more apparent than real. It can be argued from historical precedent that China is not an expansionist power and does not wish to extend her frontiers, apart from relatively minor boundary adjustments for militarily defensive or political reasons. The most dramatic example of a border dispute, the Sino-Indian War (see Documents 32, 34) can be explained in such terms. For the greater part of her history since the Han Dynasty China has been content with the boundaries of the Great Wall, the coast and certain islands including Taiwan, and the Himalayas. Her relationship with her neighbours, the former 'tributary states', such as Korea, Vietnam and Nepal, has been aimed, it can be argued, primarily at maintaining friendly regimes as a guarantee of Chinese security. The fact that since the late 1950s China has signed a number of treaties of friendship and non-aggression with its immediate neighbours does not necessarily indicate a desire to dominate them, although the Chinese motives have been questioned (see introduction to Part III). Undoubtedly those agreements have had the effect of diminishing American influence.

Both the Communists and the KMT regime agree on what constitutes the territorial limits of China. Both have rejected concepts of 'two Chinas', 'one China and one Taiwan', and arguments for an 'independent Tibet'. They concur in claiming Chinese sovereignty over the Hsisha islands (the Paracels). Moreover it appears that the leaders of the CPR are prepared to recognize the territorial agreements of their predecessors in cases which were 'freely' negotiated. The Chinese Communists have condemned in principle the 'unequal' treaties, which they define as those concluded under unequal conditions (coercive) or containing unequal provisions (exploitative). Nevertheless the CPR has announced that 'pending future negotiation, the *status quo* should be maintained'. (Document 31.) In practice the CPR has not specifically repudiated the terms of some treaties which were clearly unequal and which it has named as such. For example the Treaty of Nanking (1842), the Convention of Peking (1860) and the Convention of 1898 are the legal basis for

7

the British position in Hong Kong, which for the present the CPR is pleased to tolerate.

CHINA AS A REVOLUTIONARY POWER

China's image has been coloured by the problems of its own continuing internal revolution. There is in retrospect no clear evidence that the processes (sometimes apparently extreme) of political and economic change in China constituted a direct threat outside its borders. Nevertheless pronouncements and slogans intended essentially for home consumption have sounded alarming to foreign ears. Lack of understanding of what really motivates the Chinese combined with uncertainty aroused by the factional divisions among the Chinese leadership have contributed to foreign unease notably during the period of the Cultural Revolution. The continuing revolution in China has not been smooth and internal difficulties have affected the pattern of foreign relations.

So far this analysis has ignored the single most important factor in the motive force of modern China, the faith and spirit of its leaders and the temperament of its people. It can be argued that the Chinese Communists have been first and foremost Chinese and that they have successfully adapted Marxist-Leninist theories to Chinese realities. It can be shown that there is much in common between the traditional Chinese acceptance of Confucian authority and compliance with the demands of a Communist state. Nevertheless the political and economic organization, the visionary enthusiasm and dedication of the leaders and their appeal to the 'masses' have created a new and distinctive political force.

It is perhaps obvious to state that the influence of Mao Tse-tung has been predominant in Chinese affairs. Mao was Head of State (Chairman of the Republic) only from 1949–59 but he has been Chairman of the Party since 1935. He is an outstanding and complex personality. In the transition from revolutionary leader to statesman, Mao has remained a visionary, a romantic sometimes carried away by his own enthusiasms. He has upset his more moderate colleagues, and has often been a nightmare to the serving bureaucrats. It is possible to chart the history of China since 1949 as the waxing and waning of Mao's enthusiasm and influence. In Chinese politics there has been a component which can be identified as Maoist which emphasizes ideology and continuing revolution. It is radical, fervent and puts faith before works. In contrast, and sometimes in opposition, there has been a moderate, less overtly enthusiastic, intellectual, official element. Today this might be called the Chou-ist. Before the Cultural Revolution it was associated with Liu Shao-chi and it has been labelled Revisionist. (More recently Rightist-Revisionist in contrast to Leftist-Revisionist, the new label for extreme Maoism.)

Detailed examination of Mao's philosophy and the question of its originality would be out of place in this work, but note must be taken of the theory of contradictions which appears as a fundamental tenet of the thought of Mao Tse-tung. Mao has stressed the practical importance of contradictions theory. In his terminology it is important to be able to distinguish the 'principal contradiction', or principal 'aspect' within a contradiction, in a particular situation at any one time. It is also important to be able to identify and exploit the contradictions in the enemy camp.

'On contradiction', said to have been written in 1937, was published in 1952. Stripped of its jargon the theory does not appear particularly profound. Mao cites as an example of a principal contradiction the Japanese invasion of China, which at the time took precedence over the contradiction between Communists and KMT. Recognizing this priority the Communists joined in a United Front against the Japanese.

Subsequently in a speech published in 1957 'On the correct handling of contradictions among the people', Mao distinguishes two types of contradictions: 'Antagonistic contradictions . . . between hostile classes and hostile social systems' which can only be resolved by force (not necessarily war); and non-antagonistic contradictions which exist within the Socialist society and which can be resolved through the process of 'uniting, criticizing and education'. In effect it is by identifying and categorizing contradictions that the leadership determines the line which is to be followed. Party workers and cadres then organize and develop public opinion to create through group and personal involvement the 'mass line'.

The distinction between antagonistic and non-antagonistic

contradictions has had implications both internally (for example in 1957 in the controversy centred on the Hundred Flowers Movement) and externally in the ideological debates in the international communist movement. The ideological controversy continued into the 1960s. In late 1963 and 1964 a public debate centred on the theory of 'uniting two into one'. This was condemned by the Maoists as propagating the idea of conciliation. In contrast the slogan 'One divides into two' was the formula for sustained struggle. This polemic against 'revisionism' at home was an early manifestation of the debate at the heart of the Cultural Revolution. It had also clear implications in the Sino-Soviet dispute, and was extended into an attack on 'revisionist' policies towards the Third World.

In 1963 Chinese official pronouncements on the contemporary world situation avoided identifying a principal contradiction and instead distinguished four 'fundamental contradictions', i.e. between the socialist and imperialist camps, between proletariat and bourgeoisie in capitalist countries, between certain imperialist nations, and between the 'oppressed' nations and imperialism. By 1965 greater emphasis was put on the anti-imperialist struggle. In a major policy speech in Indonesia in May, Peng Chen declared that the contradiction between the 'oppressed nations' of Asia, Africa and Latin America and US imperialism had become the principal contradiction. Subsequently in October 1965 Lin Piao discussed the implications of this new official position in his famous article 'Long Live the Victory of People's War' (Document 53).

In many of his writings on foreign affairs Mao appears to be exhorting the peoples of other lands, especially those under 'imperialist' (American) or 'revisionist' (Soviet) influence to revolt against their governments. Before and immediately after 1949 he expressed his faith in the revolutionary people of the world, particularly in the emerging areas of Asia and Africa. Later, in 1964 he divided the world excluding the United States and the Soviet bloc (with China) into 'two intermediate zones', the developed and the undeveloped countries. The model for revolution in the former was, he considered, the Paris Commune of 1871, in the latter it was the Chinese revolution. To Mao it has been clear since about 1959 that the Soviet Union could not be relied upon to support revolution in the undeveloped countries, and it has been the duty of the People's Republic to offer support, mainly moral and propaganda support, to revolutionary movements in other countries. In certain cases and particularly where Chinese security has been at stake, as in Vietnam, practical aid has been given in the form of funds, political guidance and arms. At the same time Mao has been convinced that revolutions must be self-reliant, depending essentially on the enthusiasm of the people of the country concerned. This policy which also has the advantage of being less costly to China, helps to explain why, with the exception of the Korean War, Chinese troops have taken no part in foreign conflicts.

In studying China's various approaches to the Third World countries we must take into account the 'moderate' tendency in Chinese politics. For much of his career a faithful follower of Mao, Chou En-lai has nevertheless tended to favour a more conciliatory approach to foreign governments. He was a chief instigator of the 'Bandung spirit'. Later, following his disastrous over-emphasis on revolution in Africa in 1964–5, for which Mao may have been largely responsible, and the almost total breakdown of communications in the Cultural Revolution, it has been Chou who has given priority to diplomacy over propaganda. Chou has, however, often seen fit to encourage opposition movements abroad as a means of bringing pressure to bear on governments he considers hostile. There are examples of this in China's dealings with Japan (see Document 41) and with Thailand.

In contrast to Chou's sophistication, Mao has sometimes appeared to view foreign policy as an extension of domestic policy. For example Mao's belief that the Chinese bourgeoisie was maintaining its reactionary attitudes, especially after the Hundred Flowers experience, reinforced his view that national bourgeois governments abroad (particularly in India) were necessarily reactionary. Conversely, Mao has used external affairs to prepare Chinese opinion for new domestic policies. For example the militancy implicit in the 'East Wind has prevailed over the West Wind' speech (Document 19) and the off-shore island crisis of 1958, coincided with the Great Leap Forward. The war with India in 1962 preceded the Socialist Education campaign, the propaganda support for the

Vietnamese in 1965 had implications for the Cultural Revolution, and the reaction to the apparent threat from the Soviet Union in 1969 helped to restore unity after the Cultural Revolution.

PARTY LEADERSHIP

In constructing the institutional framework for the People's Republic, China's leaders have used the classical communist system of party organization in parallel with government machinery. The party is paramount and the responsibility for decision-making rests with a few men at the top, the Standing Committee of the Politburo. Chou En-lai, Premier of the State Council, has been a key figure in the Politburo. Until 1959 he was Minister of Foreign Affairs. He has been succeeded in that office by Chen Yi (from 1959 to 1971), Chi Peng-fei (since 1971 and acting Foreign Minister since 1969) and Chiao Kuan-hua since 1974, but there is no doubt that Chou En-lai continued to exercise a dominant influence in foreign policy.

In the case of any country it is difficult to speculate profitably on the interrelated roles of the various government departments. In the case of China the problem is complicated by the dearth of public information, and the fact that the institutional structure is not clear. It appears, however, that while the Politburo includes men with different specialist interests they make collectively the major decisions regarding all aspects of home and foreign affairs. On occasion men have been dropped when their policy has been rejected. A shift in the centre of power within the Politburo has its implications for the whole range of domestic and foreign policies.

The process of achieving agreement and acquiescence to a new line involves not only genuine debate among the top functionaries but sustained propaganda among the 'masses'. The extent to which opposition has been physically eliminated by death or imprisonment is disputed but it is agreed that China's leaders have more often than not aimed at conversion by intellectual, psychological and moral pressure. China's policy makers cannot ignore public opinion if only because the process of conversion takes time. The regime has the advantage of control over the organs of information and propaganda. In the case of foreign affairs the Chinese people have virtually no access to independent information. Nevertheless there is the problem of preparing opinion to accept a dramatic change of line which does not jar too viciously on their credulity. Preparing public opinion to accept Nixon's visit is a case in point. That this was apparently achieved successfully after years of violent anti-American propaganda indicates that there is little limit to the powers of official persuasion!

A collection of documents illustrating such a large and complex subject as China's foreign relations must for convenience be divided into sections. But no division of the subject matter can be entirely satisfactory. Documents appearing in one part may be relevant to topics presented elsewhere.

Arranging the documents, either according to periods or by geographical area, risks obscuring the interaction of events and policies. For example, it is indisputable that a significant change of course occurred with the Sino-Soviet rift, and it can be seen that concurrently China embarked on a more independent appeal to the Third World. But this Third World strategy had its origins much earlier and had already appeared as a distinctively Chinese approach at the time of the Bandung meeting in 1955. To take another example, the Great Proletarian Cultural Revolution is undoubtedly a considerable landmark. From the perspective of the 1970s it has fundamental significance in determing China's outlook and the ideological basis of its strategies. Yet the Cultural Revolution was concerned essentially with internal affairs and its effects on foreign relations may be considered as temporarily disruptive rather than as causing a change of direction.

To note two more examples: India is not only a leading Third World nation and joint instigator with China of the 'Five Principles of Co-existence', but also a neighbour with whom border disputes have led to war. Vietnam is not only an area in which China has supported 'revolutionary struggles'; it is also a focal point in Sino-American relations—as the Vietnamese may find to their cost.

This book has been divided according to the following scheme. Appropriate cross-references will be found in the commentary on the documents.

Part I covers the period 1949–55 and specifically examines

China's relations with the Soviet Union and the United States. It illustrates the effect on Sino-American relations of the Korean War, the disputed status of Taiwan and the war in Indochina. It also notes Chinese proposals, in the 'spirit of Bandung', to negotiate with the United States.

Part II examines the origins and development of the Sino-Soviet rift (in the period 1956–65) from the first muted ideological differences to the complete breakdown of agreement on the fundamental matters of economic and military aid, nuclear arms testing, and world-wide strategy. It considers the implications of the fall of Khrushchev and China's failure to come to terms with his successors.

Part III is concerned with the problem of China's borders and her relations with her immediate neighbours in Asia in the period before the Cultural Revolution. Specifically the documents illustrate border disputes and agreements, China's role in the Indochinese settlement and relations with Japan. Underlying questions concern the extent of China's territorial ambitions, and her influence as an Asian power.

Part IV examines China's policy towards the emerging countries of the Third World in three stages: (i) The period immediately after Liberation when strong verbal support was given to the cause of world revolution. (ii) The mid-fifties when peaceful co-existence was propagated. (iii) The evolution of China's Third World strategy in the 1960s.

Part V illustrates the disruptive effect of the Cultural Revolution.

Part VI takes as its central theme the *rapprochement* between China and the United States, China's admission to the United Nations, and the continuing problem of Taiwan.

PART I

The Era of Sino-Soviet Friendship 1949–55

With victory in the Civil War assured, Mao Tse-tung announced in the summer of 1949 that 'there could be no third road' and that China must lean to one side, to the Communist camp in the Cold War (Document 2). In the circumstances there was no alternative for the new and as yet unconsolidated Chinese regime, although Mao was careful not to exclude the possibility of loans 'on terms of mutual benefit in the future' from the capitalist powers. Whether or not Mao envisaged an independent road for China in years to come, he remained ideologically committed and may well have supposed that the Cold War pressures for unity in the Communist bloc could be used to forge a durable working agreement between China and the USSR, in which China would not be a mere satellite and which would also further the Communist cause throughout the world. There was considerable optimism among the Chinese leaders that the Communist movement was soon to triumph in the other under-privileged countries and they may have hoped that the Soviet Union would keep the United States at bay while the forces of socialist liberation in Asia and Africa, inspired by the Chinese example, launched their own struggles for freedom.

Mao, with Chou En-lai and a large party of officials, went to Moscow in December 1949. Prolonged negotiations led to the signing on 14 February 1950 of a new Treaty of Friendship, Alliance and Mutual Assistance (Document 5). The USSR granted credits to China amounting to $300 million over five years at one per cent interest. A few weeks later it was agreed to set up 4 joint-stock companies for the development of Sinkiang's mineral resources, and to establish a Sino-Soviet airline, a shipyard in Dairen, and to provide technical and military advisers. The Communiqué issued with the Treaty referred to the recognition by both governments of the Mongolian People's Republic. In effect this confirmed its inclusion in the Soviet sphere, and was in contrast to Mao's expressed hope (in an interview with Edgar Snow in 1936) that on liberation Outer Mongolia would 'automatically' join China.

TAIWAN AND KOREA

The Communist victory left the Americans divided and uncertain in their attitude to the new regime. The situation was complicated in December 1949 by the arrival of Chiang Kai-shek in Taiwan and the formal establishment of the KMT regime on the island. It was immediately apparent that both sides intended to continue the civil war. The Communists began preparations for an invasion while the KMT announced that in due course it would return to 'liberate' the mainland. In firmly rejecting the possibility of a compromise based on 'two Chinas', the CPR and the KMT both upheld the doctrine which has continued to divide them. In his island stronghold Chiang Kai-shek was a standing challenge to the legitimacy of the Communist regime, and effectively excluded the CPR from a seat in the United Nations. At first the Americans were loath to commit themselves to the continuing support of the Nationalists (Document 7). However, with the signing of the Sino-Soviet Alliance, and the rise in America of Senator Joseph McCarthy there was a hardening of the American attitude towards China. But it was the Korean War which was crucial. The American decision to interpose the Seventh Fleet in the Taiwan Strait meant that Chinese hopes of invading the island were dashed for the time being. The Korean War also put paid to Peking's hopes of taking over the China seat at the United Nations.

The origins of the Korean War have yet to be clarified. There is some evidence that the South Koreans were encouraged to take a belligerent attitude by the Americans. On the other hand it is clear that North Korea was closely identified with Moscow and it is possible that the Soviet Union encouraged, even if it did not actually instigate, the attack across the border which was intended to 'liberate' South Korea. United States pronouncements in January 1950, which had indicated that the Americans did not consider that South Korea was an essential part of the defence perimeter in the Pacific, may have encouraged confidence in a rapid victory by the North over the South.

There is considerable evidence that China was reluctant to enter the Korean War and that it was only provoked into doing so by MacArthur's threat to extend the war to the Manchurian border. It has also become evident that the Chinese were far from satisfied with the amount of aid furnished by the Soviet Union, while China 'stood in the first line of defence of the socialist camp so that the Soviet Union might stay in the second line' ('Two Different Lines on the Question of War and Peace', *Peking Review*, 22 November 1963). By the summer of 1951, when the armies in Korea had reached a stalemate, peace talks were begun which were to last for two years. Ostensibly the question of the repatriation of prisoners of war was the obstacle to agreement. It has also been suggested that Stalin's intransigence helped to prolong the war. This is the view put forward by A. M. Halpern among others (see e.g. 'China in the Postwar World', *China Quarterly*, no. 21). H. C. Hinton maintains that it was the CPR which refused an armistice, pressing for Soviet military aid to break the deadlock (*Communist China in World Politics*, p. 220). Eventually, soon after Stalin's death, Chou En-lai made a statement (30 March 1953) on the prisoner-of-war issue which led to the signing of the armistice in July.

The Americans, bent on containment, had already in February 1953 'unleashed' Chiang Kai-shek, by removing the restraint on Nationalist operations against the mainland. During 1954 additional military aid was sent to the Kuomintang. At the same time as such piecemeal support was given to the anti-Communists, the United States also threatened 'massive retaliation' against Communist advances.

CONFRONTING THE UNITED STATES:
THE EVOLUTION OF THE BANDUNG STRATEGY

Peking's foreign policy began to enter a new phase in 1953, emphasizing the possibility of peaceful co-existence between

Communist and non-Communist countries. The deadlock of the Korean War, the obvious determination of the Americans to maintain a firm perimeter in Asia, and the prospect of viable nationalist, non-Communist regimes emerging in the ex-colonial countries, were all factors contributing to the new policy. The Soviet allies were clearly neither able nor willing to lead a world-wide crusade against American imperialism. It was becoming apparent to the Chinese leadership that China's status as an Asian nation could be exploited by a new initiative based on a conciliatory diplomatic approach. This new line was dramatically demonstrated at the Geneva Conference (convened in 1954 to discuss both Korea and Indochina), where Chou En-lai made a distinguished debut on the stage of world diplomacy (see Part III, Document 36).

The Americans, who were heavily committed to supporting the French-dominated regimes in Vietnam, Cambodia and Laos, were fearful that the Korean armistice would be followed by an increase of Chinese aid and influence in Indochina (Document 14). Secretary of State Dulles was reluctant to include Indochina on the agenda of the Geneva meeting. The United States government did not sign the Geneva Accords but made a separate statement to the effect that it would not disturb the arrangements.

The Americans did not fear open aggression so much as subversion aimed at undermining anti-Communist regimes, particularly in Southeast Asia. It was this fear in particular which led to the setting up of the Southeast Asia Treaty Organization in September 1954, in which the USA, Britain, France, Australia and New Zealand joined with the Philippines, Thailand and Pakistan to form a joint defence system against Communist aggression, either overt or subversive. The system was intended to apply to the region south of Taiwan, Hong Kong and Macao. With Taiwan the United States signed a separate defensive alliance in December.

The consolidation of the American defensive system in Southeast Asia gave impetus to China's policy of seeking a *modus vivendi* with neutralist states. Its position enhanced by the Geneva settlement, the People's Republic took a leading part in a conference of Afro-Asian heads of state at Bandung in April 1955 (see Part IV). At Bandung Chou En-lai sought to dispel any anxiety that China would play an aggressive or subversive role. He publicly offered to negotiate with the United States on the question of Taiwan.

At Bandung Nehru and U Nu suggested that the Sino-American conversations, initiated at Geneva on the question of prisoners of war in Korea, should continue at ambassadorial level. Beginning in August 1955 the meetings did continue intermittently, first at Geneva and then at Warsaw, providing the only means of direct diplomatic exchange between the People's Republic and the USA (Document 17). Notwithstanding an agreement to repatriate civilians (10 September 1955), the United States and China appeared as far apart as ever on essential issues. For a time the Chinese hoped that some progress on the status of Taiwan might be made at the ambassadorial talks, and began a letter-writing campaign to high-placed officials on Taiwan to convince them that an agreement was in the making. Although the United States persuaded the Nationalists to give up the vulnerable Tachen islands, Chiang Kai-shek remained firm in his insistence on the need for American aid. He secured in May 1957 an agreement for the placing on Taiwan of missiles capable of carrying nuclear or conventional war-heads six hundred miles. To the leaders of the CPR the prospect of reuniting their territory appeared as remote as ever. The apparent indifference of the Soviet Union was particularly galling and was an important factor contributing to the decline of Sino-Soviet friendship.

(a) LEANING TO ONE SIDE

The parable in this extract from Mao Tse-tung's concluding speech at the Seventh National Congress of the Chinese Communist Party is well known and frequently cited in China. Mao was speaking at a time when the future of China was still in the balance and it appeared that the Americans would support Chiang Kai-shek in the post-war struggle for power.

DOCUMENT I. EXTRACT FROM MAO TSE-TUNG, 'THE FOOLISH OLD MAN WHO REMOVED THE MOUNTAINS', SPEECH OF II JUNE 1945 (FOREIGN LANGUAGES PRESS, PEKING, 1972)

There is an ancient Chinese fable called 'The Foolish Old Man Who Removed the Mountains'. It tells of an old man who lived in northern China long, long ago and was known as the Foolish Old Man of North Mountain. His house faced south and beyond his doorway stood the two great peaks, Taihang and Wangwu, obstructing the way. With great determination, he led his sons in digging up these mountains hoe in hand. Another greybeard, known as the Wise Old Man, saw them and said derisively, 'How silly of you to do this! It is quite impossible for you few to dig up these two huge mountains'. The Foolish Old Man replied, 'When I die, my sons will carry on; when they die, there will be my grandsons, and then their sons and grandsons, and so on to infinity. High as they are, the mountains cannot grow any higher and with every bit we dig, they will be that much lower. Why can't we clear them away?' Having refuted the Wise Old Man's wrong view, he went on digging every day, unshaken in his conviction. God was moved by this, and he sent down two angels, who carried the mountains away on their backs. Today, two big mountains lie like a dead weight on the Chinese people. One is imperialism, the other is feudalism. The Chinese Communist Party has long made up its mind to dig them up. We must persevere and work unceasingly, and we, too, will touch God's heart. Our God is none other than the masses of the Chinese people. If they stand up and dig together with us, why can't these two mountains be cleared away?

Yesterday, in a talk with two Americans who were leaving for the United States, I said that the US government was trying to undermine us and this would not be permitted. We oppose the US government's policy of supporting Chiang Kai-shek against the Communists. But we must draw a distinction, firstly, between the people of the United States and their government and, secondly, within the US government between the policy-makers and their subordinates. I said to these two Americans, 'Tell the policy-makers in your government that we forbid you Americans to enter the Liberated Areas because your policy is to support Chiang Kai-shek against the Communists, and we have to be on our guard. You can come to the Liberated Areas if your purpose is to fight Japan, but there must first be an agreement. We will not permit you to nose around everywhere. Since Patrick J. Hurley has publicly declared against co-operation with the Chinese Communist Party, why do you still want to come and prowl around in our Liberated Areas?'

The US government's policy of supporting Chiang Kai-shek against the Communists shows the brazenness of the US reactionaries. But all the scheming of the reactionaries, whether Chinese or foreign, to prevent the Chinese people from achieving victory is doomed to failure. The democratic forces are the main current in the world today, while reaction is only a counter-current. The reactionary counter-current is trying to swamp the main current of national independence and people's democracy, but it can never become the main current. Today, there are still three major contradictions in the old world, as Stalin pointed out long ago: first, the contradiction between the proletariat and the bourgeoisie in the imperialist countries; second, the contradiction between the various imperialist powers; and third, the contradiction between the colonial and semi-colonial countries and the imperialist metropolitan countries. Not only do these three contradictions continue to exist but they are becoming more acute and widespread. Because of their existence and growth, the time will come when the reactionary anti-Soviet, anti-Communist and anti-democratic counter-current still in existence today will be swept away.

*

Soviet policy makers did not anticipate the relatively rapid victory of the Chinese Communists in the Civil War. Only the day before the capitulation of Japan, 15 August 1945, the Soviet Union signed a Treaty of Friendship and Alliance with the Chinese Nationalist Government. This confirmed the agreement made at Yalta, in the absence of the Chinese, for the restoration of Soviet interests in Manchuria. Specifically it provided for joint Sino-Soviet control of the Chinese Eastern and South Manchurian Railways and gave the USSR the use of Port Arthur and Dairen. In effect the treaty restored Russian influence in Manchuria which had been lost in 1905, and was in contrast to the 1943 renunciation by Britain and America of their extra-territorial rights in China. The USSR maintained relations with the Nationalists throughout the Civil War and not until the victory of the Communists was almost complete in 1949 did Stalin cease to recognize Chiang Kai-shek as the *de jure* ruler of China. Stalin may have doubted whether a Communist victory in China would benefit the Soviet Union. Certainly Soviet material support for the Communists in the final years of struggle was minimal while the occupation of Manchuria by Soviet troops was deliberately extended to give time for the Nationalist forces to take over. As late as January 1949, when Chiang Kai-shek had formally handed over to Li Tsung-jen as Provisional President, the Soviet Embassy in China drew up a draft agreement with the KMT. In April the Soviet ambassador was the only foreign diplomat to go with the retreating Nationalists to Canton.

Against this background it was appropriate and necessary for Mao to expound the reasons for a policy of 'leaning to one side'.

DOCUMENT 2. EXTRACT FROM MAO TSE-TUNG 'ON THE PEOPLE'S DEMOCRATIC DICTATORSHIP', SPEECH OF 30 JUNE 1949 (*Selected Works of Mao Tse-tung*, 4, FOREIGN LANGUAGES PRESS, PEKING, 1961, PP. 415–17)

Twenty-four years have passed since Sun Yat-sen's death, and the Chinese revolution, led by the Communist Party of China, has made tremendous advances both in theory and practice and has radically changed the face of China. Up to now the principal and fundamental experience the Chinese people have gained is twofold:

(1) Internally, arouse the masses of the people. That is, unite the working class, the peasantry, the urban petty bourgeoisie and the national bourgeoisie, form a domestic united front under the leadership of the working class, and advance from this to the establishment of a state which is a people's democratic dictatorship under the leadership of the working class and based on the alliance of workers and peasants.

(2) Externally, unite in a common struggle with those nations of the world which treat us as equals and unite with the peoples of all countries. That is, ally ourselves with the Soviet Union, with the People's Democracies and with the proletariat and the broad masses of the people in all other countries, and form an international united front.

'You are leaning to one side.' Exactly. The forty years' experience of Sun Yat-sen and the twenty-eight years' experience of the Communist Party have taught us to lean to one side, and we are firmly convinced that in order to win victory and consolidate it we must lean to one side. In the light of the experiences accumulated in these forty years and these twenty-eight years, all Chinese without exception must lean either to the side of imperialism or to the side of socialism. Sitting on the fence will not do, nor is there a third road. We oppose the Chiang Kai-shek reactionaries who lean to the side of imperialism, and we also oppose the illusions about a third road.

'You are too irritating.' We are talking about how to deal with domestic and foreign reactionaries, the imperialists and their running dogs, not about how to deal with anyone else. With regard to such reactionaries, the questions of irritating them or not does not arise. Irritated or not irritated, they will remain the same because they are reactionaries. Only if we draw a clear line between reactionaries and revolutionaries, expose the intrigues and plots of the reactionaries, arouse the vigilance and attention of the revolutionary ranks, heighten our will to fight and crush the enemy's arrogance can we isolate the reactionaries, vanquish them or supersede them. We must not show the slightest timidity before a wild beast. We must learn from Wu Sung on the Chingyang Ridge. As Wu Sung saw it, the tiger on Chingyang Ridge was a maneater, whether irritated or not. Either kill the tiger or be eaten by him—one or the other.

'We want to do business.' Quite right, business will be done. We are against no one except the domestic and foreign reactionaries who hinder us from doing business. Everybody should know that it is none other than the imperialists and their running dogs, the Chiang Kai-shek reactionaries, who hinder us from doing business and also from establishing diplomatic relations with foreign countries. When we have beaten the internal and external reactionaries by uniting all domestic and international forces, we shall be able to do business and establish diplomatic relations with all foreign countries on the basis of equality, mutual benefit and mutual respect for territorial integrity and sovereignty.

'Victory is possible even without international help.' This is a mistaken idea. In the epoch in which imperialism exists, it is impossible for a genuine people's revolution to win victory in any country without various forms of help from the international revolutionary forces, and even if victory were won, it could not be consolidated. This was the case with the victory and consolidation of the great October Revolution, as Lenin and Stalin told us long ago. This was also the case with the overthrow of the three imperialist powers in World War II and the establishment of the People's Democracies. And this is also the case with the present and the future of People's China. Just imagine! If the Soviet Union had not existed, if there had been no victory in the anti-fascist Second World War, if Japanese imperialism had not been defeated, if the People's Democracies had not come into being, if the oppressed nations of the East were not rising in struggle and if there were no struggle of the masses of the people against their reactionary rulers in the United States, Britain, France, Germany, Italy, Japan and other capitalist countries—if not for all these in combination, the international reactionary forces bearing down upon us would certainly be many times greater than now. In such circumstances, could we have won victory? Obviously not. And even with victory, there could be no consolidation. The Chinese people have had more than enough experience of this kind. This experience was reflected long ago in Sun Yat-sen's deathbed statement on the necessity of uniting with the international revolutionary forces.

'We need help from the British and US governments.' This, too, is a naive idea in these times. Would the present rulers of Britain and the United States, who are imperialists, help a people's state? Why do these countries do business with us and, supposing they might be willing to lend us money on terms of mutual benefit in the future, why would they do so? Because their capitalists want to make money and their bankers want to earn interest to extricate themselves from their own crisis—it is not a matter of helping the Chinese people. The Communist Parties and progressive groups in these countries are urging their governments to establish trade and even diplomatic relations with us. This is goodwill, this is help, this cannot be mentioned in the same breath with the conduct of the bourgeoisie in the same countries. Throughout his life, Sun Yat-sen appealed countless times to the capitalist countries for help and got nothing but heartless rebuffs. Only once in his whole life did Sun Yat-sen receive foreign help, and that was Soviet help. Let readers refer to Dr Sun Yat-sen's testament; his earnest advice was not to look for help from the imperialist countries but to 'unite with those nations of the world which treat us as equals'. Dr Sun Yat-sen had experience; he had suffered, he had been deceived. We should remember his words and not allow ourselves to be deceived again. Internationally, we belong to the side of the anti-imperialist front headed by the Soviet Union, and so we can turn only to this side for genuine and friendly help, not to the side of the imperialist front.

*

In August 1949 the US Department of State published the China White Paper which sought to explain the failure of American policy in China, 1944-9. The following extract from the 'Letter of Transmittal' to the President reveals a tendency to view the whole problem in American rather than Chinese terms, for example, in the reference to 'democratic individualism'.

DOCUMENT 3. EXTRACT FROM DEAN ACHESON'S 'LETTER OF TRANSMITTAL', 30 JULY 1949 (*United States Relations with China*, DEPARTMENT OF STATE, WASHINGTON, 1949, PP. XVI–XVII)

It must be admitted frankly that the American policy of assisting the Chinese people in resisting domination by any foreign power or powers is now confronted with the gravest difficulties. The heart of China is in Communist hands. The Communist leaders have fore-sworn their Chinese heritage and have publicly announced their subservience to a foreign power, Russia, which during the last 50 years, under czars and Communists alike, has been most assiduous in its efforts to extend its control in the Far East. In the recent past, attempts at foreign domination have appeared quite clearly to the Chinese people as external aggression and as such have been bitterly and in the long run successfully resisted. Our aid and encouragement have helped them to resist. In this case, however, the foreign domination has been masked behind the façade of a vast crusading movement which apparently has seemed to many Chinese to be wholly indigenous and national. Under these circumstances, our aid has been unavailing.

The unfortunate but inescapable fact is that the ominous result of the civil war in China was beyond the control of the government of the United States. Nothing that this country did or could have done within the reasonable limits of its capabilities could have changed that result; nothing that was left undone by this country has contributed to it. It was the product of internal Chinese forces, forces which this country tried to influence but could not. A decision was arrived at within China, if only a decision by default.

And now it is abundantly clear that we must face the situation as it exists in fact. We will not help the Chinese or ourselves by basing our policy on wishful thinking. We continue to believe that, however tragic may be the immediate future of China and however ruthlessly a major portion of this great people may be exploited by a party in the interest of a foreign imperialism, ultimately the profound civilization and the democratic individualism of China will reassert themselves and she will throw off the foreign yoke. I consider that we should encourage all developments in China which now and in the future work toward this end.

In the immediate future, however, the implementation of our historic policy of friendship for China must be profoundly affected by current developments. It will necessarily be influenced by the degree to which the Chinese people come to recognize that the Communist regime serves not their interests but those of Soviet Russia and the manner in which, having become aware of the facts, they react to this foreign domination. One point, however, is clear. Should the Communist regime lend itself to the aims of Soviet Russian imperialism and attempt to engage in aggression against China's neighbors, we and the other members of the United Nations would be confronted by a situation violative of the principles of the United Nations Charter and threatening international peace and security.

Meanwhile our policy will continue to be based upon our own respect for the Charter, our friendship for China, and our traditional support for the Open Door and for China's independence and administrative and territorial integrity.

*

In December 1949 Mao Tse-tung led a Chinese delegation to Moscow to negotiate an agreement with the Soviet Union. An article written at the time by Sun Yat-sen's widow, later one of the two Vice-Chairmen of the CPR, sought to justify the policy of 'leaning to one side' by reference to recent events.

DOCUMENT 4. EXTRACTS FROM SOONG CHING-LING (MADAME SUN YAT-SEN) 'THE DIFFERENCE BETWEEN SOVIET AND AMERICAN FOREIGN POLICIES', (*People's China*, 1, 2, 16 JANUARY 1950, PP. 5–8)

Chairman Mao Tse-tung, in his now-historic speech on 1 July 1949, pronounced that the new China, the Chinese People's Republic, would lean to one side in all matters, foreign and domestic. That is the side led by the great Soviet Union under the leadership of the mighty Stalin. That is the side of peace and construction. That is the path joyously followed and ardently studied by the overwhelming masses of the Chinese people.

Events in the world have proven, and are everyday verifying, that this is the only side to which progressive countries can lean. For there are merely two choices at hand. One is the Soviet Union. The other is represented mainly by the United States, Great Britain and France. As we have contact with these two sides, through their foreign policies, we quickly see that they are as different as day is from night. One has all the brightness of day and all the warmth of the sun. That is the socialist Soviet Union. The other is as forbidding as a wintry night with all its coldness. This is the imperialist band led by the United States.

By comparing these two choices, it is easy to see why in

actuality, survival and revival of oppressed nations necessitates leaning to the side of the Soviet Union.

What do the imperialists offer?

First they offer Marshall Plan 'aid'. Their method is to 'educate' you on how good it will be for you. This is done in typical, high-pressure, American advertising style. The sales talk is directed to all those who are floundering in the high seas of unplanned economies and who fear changes which use the strength of the people. The American Wall Streeters hold up their concoction as the newest thing in life-savers. 'It is stream-lined,' they say. 'It will pull you through any situation.' Some governments have fallen for this line and have had the 'life-saver' tossed at them. From their experience it is now history that this highly publicized contraption turns out to be but a strait-jacket. It is filled with lead and bound to sink anyone who attempts to use it. . . .

It will mean further and intensified exploitation of the country's raw materials, to the detriment of the people's present welfare and their future constructive efforts. Witness Western Germany today as it serves Wall Street in full colonial capacity. Coal, timber, scrap metal and other raw and semi-finished materials are pouring out of the country into British and American factories. In return, this highly industrialized part of Germany is being made into an importer of finished products. The result is that their manufacturing industry is rapidly deteriorating and they have accumulated a debt of over three billion dollars to the United States. . . .

Now let us examine the policies and practices of the Soviet Union as they appear on the world scene.

To date, this socialist land has made trade arrangements with the following People's Democracies: Czechoslovakia, Rumania, Bulgaria, Albania, Hungary, Poland, Mongolia and China. All of these agreements were made with one, and only one, purpose in mind—to sincerely aid in the development of these countries. There was no pretense, no bait, no 'education'. There was only one question asked: 'What do you need?' Here are a few practical examples of how this worked out.

China, in its liberation, was faced with tremendous problems concerning rail transportation. The reactionary Kuomintang armies had destroyed bridges by the hundreds. The equally reactionary administrations had allowed equipment to be wasted and ill-used, and the roadbeds were in urgent need of maintenance. This had to be remedied immediately, since so much depended on moving supplies from the countryside to the newly captured cities, and in moving the People's Liberation Army to positions for the final strike against the American-supported Chiang Kai-shek.

Among the very first arrivals in China from the Soviet Union were railway technicians. They worked at the complicated questions and rendered support that put the restoration of our rail system months ahead of schedule. They came without benefit of fanfare. They did their job and not one single thing was asked in return.

Likewise, this past summer, the North-eastern provinces of China suffered an epidemic of the plague. We did not have enough doctors and technicians to stem this dangerous disease, so we called on our great neighbor. The medical teams we required were soon on the scene. They came, they gave their help and they were finished, they went home. There were not even thoughts of repayment or concessions to be sought. They did not ask the right to do anything, except to serve the Chinese people. . . .

Thus, our comparison is complete. The imperialist band led by the United States financial groups is a hindering clod in the way of man's progress, both at home and abroad. The Soviet Union, however, lends a helping hand to struggling young nations both within her borders and without, until they can navigate their own way.

DOCUMENT 5. THE SINO-SOVIET TREATY, 14 FEBRUARY 1950 (*Sino-Soviet Treaty and Agreements*, FOREIGN LANGUAGES PRESS, PEKING, 1950, PP. 5–8)

Treaty of Friendship, Alliance and Mutual Assistance Between the People's Republic of China and the Union of Soviet Socialist Republics

The Central People's Government of the People's Republic of China and the Presidium of the Supreme Soviet of the Union of Soviet Socialist Republics, fully determined to prevent jointly, by strengthening friendship and co-operation between the People's Republic of China and the Union of Soviet Republics, the revival of Japanese imperialism and the resumption of aggression on the part of Japan or any other state that may collaborate in any way with Japan in acts of aggression; imbued with the desire to consolidate lasting peace and universal security in the Far East and throughout the world in conformity with the aims and principles of the United Nations; profoundly convinced that the consolidation of good neighbourly relations and friendship between the People's Republic of China and the Union of Soviet Socialist Republics meets the vital interests of the peoples of China and the Soviet Union, have towards this end decided to conclude the present Treaty and have appointed as their plenipotentiary representatives: Chou En-lai, Premier of the Government Administration Council and Minister of Foreign Affairs, acting for the Central People's Government of the People's Republic of China; and Andrei Yanuaryevich Vyshinsky, Minister of Foreign Affairs of the USSR, acting for the Presidium of the Supreme Soviet of the Union of Soviet Socialist Republics. Both plenipotentiary representatives having communicated their full powers found them in good and due form, have agreed upon the following:

Article 1

Both Contracting Parties undertake jointly to adopt all necessary measures at their disposal for the purpose of preventing the resumption of aggression and violation of peace on the part of Japan or any other state that may collaborate with Japan directly or indirectly in acts of aggression. In the event of one of the Contracting Parties being attacked by Japan or any state allied with her and thus being involved in a state of war, the other Contracting Party shall immediately render military and other assistance by all means at its disposal.

The Contracting Parties also declare their readiness to participate in a spirit of sincere co-operation in all international actions aimed at ensuring peace and security throughout the world and to contribute their full share to the earliest implementation of these tasks.

Article 2

Both Contracting Parties undertake in a spirit of mutual agreement to bring about the earliest conclusion of a peace treaty with Japan jointly with other powers which were Allies in the Second World War.

Article 3
Each Contracting Party undertakes not to conclude any alliance directed against the other Contracting Party and not to take part in any coalition or in any actions or measures directed against the other Contracting Party.

Article 4
Both Contracting Parties, in the interests of consolidating peace and universal security, will consult with each other in regard to all important international problems affecting the common interests of China and the Soviet Union.

Article 5
Each Contracting Party undertakes, in a spirit of friendship and co-operation and in conformity with the principles of equality, mutual benefit and mutual respect for the national sovereignty and territorial integrity and non-interference in the internal affairs of the other Contracting Party, to develop and consolidate economic and cultural ties between China and the Soviet Union, to render the other all possible economic assistance and to carry out necessary economic co-operation.

Article 6
The present Treaty shall come into force immediately after its ratification; the exchange of instruments of ratification shall take place in Peking.

The present Treaty shall be valid for thirty years. If neither of the Contracting Parties gives notice a year before the expiration of this term of its intention to denounce the Treaty, it shall remain in force for another five years and shall be further extended in compliance with this provision.

Done in Moscow on February 14, 1950, in two copies, each in the Chinese and the Russian languages, both texts being equally valid.

> On the authorization of the Central People's Government of the People's Republic of China
> Chou En-lai

> On the authorization of the Presidium of the Supreme Soviet of the Union of Soviet Socialist Republics
> A. Y. Vyshinsky

*

A visit to Peking by Khrushchev in September–October 1954 was followed by an agreement to supply further economic and technical assistance. In 1955 China and the Soviet Union appeared to be united in a spirit of friendly co-operation.

DOCUMENT 6. EXTRACTS FROM A REPORT ON CHINA'S FIRST FIVE YEAR PLAN TO THE NATIONAL PEOPLE'S CONGRESS, 5–6 JULY 1955, BY LI FU-CHUN, CHAIRMAN OF THE STATE PLANNING COMMISSION (*Current Background*, NO. 335, PP. 52–4)

Our country's being able so speedily to carry out the first Five Year Plan for the development of national economy is inseparable from the assistance of the Soviet Union and the people's democracies, particularly the assistance of the Soviet Union. The 156 industrial construction projects which the Soviet Union is helping our country to design constitute the nucleus of industrial construction in our first Five Year Plan.

Soviet assistance to our country's construction is all-round and systematic. On the 156 industrial projects which the Soviet Union is helping us to build, she assists us throughout the whole process from start to finish, from geological survey, selecting construction sites, collecting basic data for designing, supplying equipment, directing the work of construction, installation, and getting into production and supplying technical information on new types of products, right down to directing the work of the manufacture of the new products. Designs provided by the Soviet Union make extensive use of the most up-to-date technical achievements and all the equipment supplied to us by the Soviet Union is first rate and most advanced. In order to help us, the great Soviet working class work with the highest labor enthusiasm in an effort to produce more quickly the best possible equipment we require; and the great government of the Soviet Union also gives us first priority in the supply of the best equipment. The Soviet Government has also concluded a scientific and technical agreement with our government, through which the Soviet Union also renders great help to the economic construction of our country. The Soviet Government has also offered, on its own initiative, to give our country scientific, technical and industrial assistance in promoting research work in the peaceful use of atomic energy. The Soviet

Government has also concluded an agreement with our country on the peaceful use of atomic energy.

In the midst of her own bustling Communist construction, the Soviet Union has sent large numbers of experts to our country to help us. They supply us with advanced experience from the Socialist construction of the Soviet Union and give concrete help to us in all kinds of economic work. All the experts sent to our country from the Soviet Union possess not only profound scientific and technical knowledge and rich experience in practical work, but also a lofty spirit of internationalism and selfless working attitude. In industry, agriculture, forestry, water conservancy, geology, transport, posts and telecommunications, building construction, geology, education, public health and other departments, in scientific, technical and cultural cooperation, the Soviet experts faithfully and unreservedly contribute their experience, knowledge and skill. They regard the great cause of Socialist construction of our country as their own cause. The Communist working attitude of the Soviet experts has set an example for the people of our country. It must be said that the great achievements of our economic construction are inseparable from the help of the Soviet experts.

Tremendous efforts have been made by the Soviet Union in helping our country to train technical personnel. The Soviet Union has accepted a large number of students and trainees from our country and provided them with every convenience in their studies and practical training. This is highly important for us in mastering modern industrial technique, guaranteeing the putting into operation of our new enterprises and raising our scientific level. The Soviet experts who have come to our country have also made great contributions to the training of technical personnel of our country.

The Soviet Union has extended great financial aid to our country by granting us successive loans on the most favorable terms and selling us technical equipment and materials at low prices in trade relations. Such benefits in loans and trade also help in the speedy restoration and development of our country's economy, particularly our country's industrial construction.

It is clear from the above that Soviet assistance plays an extremely important role in enabling us to carry on our present construction work on such a large scale, at such high speed, on such a high technical level, and at the same time, avoiding many mistakes. . . .

The Chinese Government and people give heartfelt thanks for the assistance of the Soviet Union and the people's democracies, especially the great, long-term, all-round and unselfish assistance of the Soviet Union. To consolidate and develop the Socialist industrialization of our country, we should further consolidate and develop our economic alliance and friendly cooperation with the Soviet Union and the people's democracies, so as to promote a common economic upsurge of the Socialist camp and strengthen the world forces of peace and democracy.

(b) CONFRONTING THE UNITED STATES

The status of Taiwan (Formosa) has been a major factor in Sino-American hostility. The Chinese, both Communist and Nationalist, have consistently maintained that the island is an integral part of China. Their case is based on history, race and the Cairo Declaration.

The original inhabitants were of proto-Malay and Polynesian stock. Japanese merchants and fishermen, the first to establish small immigrant villages, were followed by the Spanish and the Dutch in the eighteenth century. An influx of Chinese settlers in the last years of the Ming dynasty drove the original inhabitants into the hills but after twenty years of independence the settlers had to submit to the rule of the Manchus in 1682. Thereafter for two centuries the Chinese migrants, mostly Hoklos from Fukien Province with an intermixture of Hakkas and Cantonese, lived uneasily under imperial rule, until in 1887 the island was raised from the status of a Fukien dependency to the rank of a province, only to be ceded 'in perpetuity' to Japan in 1895 as a consequence of the Sino-Japanese War. In the Cairo Declaration (1 December 1943) it was announced that Taiwan, along with Manchuria and the Pescadores should be restored to the Republic of China. This was reaffirmed at Potsdam and, at the end of the war, Nationalist troops were transported by the Americans to Taiwan to accept the surrender of the Japanese. To summarize the unhappy outcome; corrupt, brutal and rapacious rule by the newcomers culminated in protest, rebellion and massacre in 1947. On 10 December 1949, Chiang Kai-shek arrived on the island.

President Truman stated clearly that the United States would not provide military aid or advice to the Chinese forces on Taiwan.

DOCUMENT 7. EXTRACT FROM PRESIDENT TRUMAN'S STATEMENT ON THE STATUS OF FORMOSA, 5 JANUARY 1950 (*American Foreign Policy 1950–5*), DEPARTMENT OF STATE, WASHINGTON, 1957, II, PP. 2448–9).

In the joint declaration at Cairo on December 1, 1943, the President of the United States, the British Prime Minister, and the President of China stated that it was their purpose that territories Japan had stolen from China, such as Formosa, should be restored to the Republic of China. The United States was a signatory to the Potsdam declaration of July 26, 1945, which declared that the terms of the Cairo declaration should be carried out. The provisions of this declaration were accepted by Japan at the time of its surrender. In keeping with these declarations, Formosa was surrendered to Generalissimo Chiang Kai-shek, and for the past 4 years, the United States and the other Allied Powers have accepted the exercise of Chinese authority over the Island.

The United States has no predatory designs on Formosa or on any other Chinese territory. The United States has no desire to obtain special rights or privileges or to establish military bases on Formosa at this time. Nor does it have any intention of utilizing its armed forces to interfere in the present situation. The United States Government will not pursue a course which will lead to involvement in the civil conflict in China.

Similarly, the United States Government will not provide military aid or advice to Chinese forces on Formosa. In the view of the United States Government, the resources on Formosa are adequate to enable them to obtain the items which they might consider necessary for the defense of the Island. The United States Government proposes to continue under existing legislative authority the present ECA program of economic assistance.

*

The American protestations were derided in an editorial article in *People's China*.

DOCUMENT 8. 'NO SMOKE-SCREEN ROUND TAIWAN', EDITORIAL ARTICLE IN *People's China*, 1, 2, 16 JANUARY 1950, P. 4

The President of the United States broke his five-months' silence about China on January 5 by bursting out with a 'statement on Formosa (Taiwan)'. He said, among other things, that 'the United States had no desire to obtain special rights or privileges or to establish military bases on Formosa at this time. Nor does it have any intention of utilizing its armed forces to interfere in the present situation.'

This statement reminds us strongly of the Chinese fable about a country idiot who having buried 300 taels of silver beneath a wall, put up a notice saying: 'There are no 300 taels of silver under here.'

Long before the Kuomintang remnants had been kicked out from China's mainland, the American imperialists were plotting to take Taiwan away from China and transform it into an American military base. In this way, Washington hoped to rescue some part of its aggressive policies in Asia from the total débâcle confronting the imperialists.

But in recent months, the increasingly rapid advance of the People's Liberation Army has forced the American State Department to speed up its schemes. In a secret agreement with the Kuomintang clique, the American government agreed to pour further military aid into Taiwan. The United States undertook to provide US $75,000,000 worth of 'aid to China in general' for Chiang Kai-shek's counter-offensive against the Chinese mainland. In return, the American government's military commission in Taiwan received what amounts to full control over the island's military, political and economic affairs.

A batch of 32 American military 'advisors' has already arrived at Taipei, the provincial capital of Taiwan. Military supplies, including 250 American tanks, have been shipped to the southern part of the island. A 27,000-ton aircraft carrier and two destroyers have been sent to reinforce the US Navy's 7th Task Force, which is now described as a mobile force for strengthening American policy in the western Pacific. General MacArthur, the protagonist of American aggression in Asia, is reported to have recruited 4,000 Japanese aviation experts and naval specialists to help with 'the defence of Taiwan'.

According to the latest schemes, should these precautions fail to achieve their aim, the American imperialists will then try to place Taiwan under United Nations' trusteeship until the peace treaty is signed with Japan.

Apparently, the plotters have no confidence in their own last-minute plans. That is why the 'battle of Taiwan' is now raging in Washington even before the real battle to liberate the island has begun. Few American militarists deny that 'the loss of the island is merely a matter of time'. Even the US Secretary of State, Dean Acheson, has admitted that the Kuomintang remnants are most lacking in something with which the United States cannot provide them—the will to fight.

None of these intrigues, whatever the form they assume, can escape the watchful eyes of the Chinese people. The statement which Truman put out as a smokescreen could only, in fact, confirm the American imperialists' intention to annex Taiwan and it therefore aroused intense indignation throughout China.

The Chinese people, now victoriously concluding their long revolution, consider such American ambitions utterly ridiculous. Taiwan is Chinese territory. This is beyond question. Even Truman had to admit in the same statement that in joint declaration at Cairo on December 1, 1943, the United States, Great Britain and China had agreed that 'it was their purpose that the territories Japan had stolen from China such as Formosa should be restored to the Republic of China. The United States was the signatory to Potsdam Declaration of July 26, 1945, which declared that terms of Cairo Declaration should be carried out.'

The liberation of Taiwan is listed among the Chinese people's tasks for 1950, which include the liberation of the whole of China. The powerful People's Liberation Army was not deterred from its tasks of the last three years by the

US$6,000,000,000 worth of American aid to the Kuomintang reactionaries, or even by more direct American participation in China's civil war. How can the sum of US$75,000,000 and a few shiploads of military supplies halt the liberation of Taiwan? The designs of the American adventurists are bound to meet with fiasco in Taiwan just as they did on the continent.

The impending liberation of Taiwan by the PLA will no doubt serve as the final touch to the complete fiasco of American imperialism in China.

*

The problem of the defence of Taiwan was temporarily resolved for the Americans by the Korean War. Within two days of the outbreak of war Truman announced (27 June 1950) that the Seventh Fleet would insulate Taiwan, preventing both a Communist invasion and Nationalist operations against the mainland. When in September the United States began negotiations for the long delayed peace settlement with Japan, it was proposed initially that Japan should merely give up sovereignty over Taiwan and that subsequently the United States, the United Kingdom, the Soviet Union and China should decide on the permanent status of the island. If the four powers failed to reach agreement within one year, the matter was to be put before the United Nations assembly. Since the Chinese Nationalists, as well as the Communists, refused to entertain any solution which legally divorced Taiwan from the mainland, and as the United States changed its mind about submitting the question to the United Nations, the status of Taiwan was left unsettled when the peace treaty with Japan was signed in 1951. Japan simply gave up her claims and a loophole was left for escape from the intentions expressed at Cairo and Potsdam.

The Chinese were not immediately drawn into the Korean War. But when American forces, in the name of the United Nations, had pushed the North Koreans back to the 38th parallel, and were preparing to drive north to the Manchurian border, the Chinese began (October 1950) to issue public and private warnings that they would not tolerate American troops in North Korea.

DOCUMENT 9. CHOU EN-LAI IN A MIDNIGHT MEETING WITH THE INDIAN AMBASSADOR WARNS THE AMERICANS NOT TO CROSS THE 38TH PARALLEL (EXTRACT FROM K. M. PANIKKAR, *In Two Chinas, Memoirs of a Diplomat*, ALLEN & UNWIN, LONDON, 1955, PP. 109–11)

At midnight on the 2nd of October, after I had been asleep for an hour and a half, I was awakened by my steward with the news that Chen Chia-kang the Director of the Asian Affairs of the Foreign Ministry, was waiting for me in the drawing-room. I hastily put on my dressing-gown and went downstairs, not knowing what it could be which had brought so important an officer at midnight to my house. Chen was very apologetic about the lateness of the hour but added that the matter was most important and that the Prime Minister desired to see me immediately at his residence. I said I would be ready to accompany him in ten minutes and went upstairs to dress. When my wife heard that I was going out in the company of a Foreign Office official at that unusual time she was uncertain whether she was awake and witnessing my arrest and deportation or seeing a nightmare. It took me some time to persuade her that it was not usual to kidnap ambassadors and in my case she need not lose even a wink of sleep for fear that the Chinese would do any personal harm to me.

We left my house at twenty minutes past midnight. The streets were practically deserted and the clear October air in Peking added serenity to the silence of the night. Though I had guessed from the beginning that the reason for this sudden call was something connected with Korea, I was bursting with impatience to know what the matter actually was. Was it that Chou En-lai had fresh proposals that he desired to be communicated to Nehru? Was it to let me know that war had already started? Anyway I decided to wait and not to try and get an inkling from Chen. So we conversed about the magnificence of the celebrations of the previous day and the order and discipline which marked the proceedings. At 12.30 I was with Premier Chou En-lai at his official residence.

Though the occasion was the most serious I could imagine, a midnight interview on questions affecting the peace of the world, Chou En-lai was as courteous and charming as ever and did not give the least impression of worry or nervousness or indeed of being in any particular hurry. He had the usual tea served and the first two minutes were spent in normal courtesies, apology for disturbing me at an unusual hour, etc. Then he came to the point. He thanked Pandit Nehru for what he had been doing in the cause of peace, and said no country's need for peace was greater than that of China, but there were occasions when peace could only be defended by determination to resist aggression. If the Americans crossed the 38th parallel China would be forced to intervene in Korea. Otherwise he was most anxious for a peaceful settlement, and generally accepted Pandit Nehru's approach to the question. I asked him whether he had already news of the Americans having crossed the borders. He replied in the affirmative but added that he did not know where they had crossed. I asked him whether China intended to intervene, if only the South Koreans crossed the parallel. He was emphatic: 'The South Koreans did not matter but American intrusion into North Korea would encounter Chinese resistance.'

I returned home at 1.30 where my first secretary and cypher assistant were waiting. A telegram conveying the gist of the conversation with my own appreciation of the situation went the same night to New Delhi. I was fully satisfied that as Chou En-lai had claimed that the Americans had crossed the parallel, the Chinese troops which had been concentrated in Manchuria had also moved across the Yalu into North Korean territory. In the morning I contacted Hutchison, the British Minister, and told him briefly how matters stood. The Burmese Ambassador, who called later, was also kept informed and he also agreed to inform Thakin Nu immediately.

Nothing very much happened during the following two days. There was no definite information that the Americans had crossed the parallel. But the UN with historical insouciance was discussing a resolution to authorize MacArthur to cross the parallel and bring about the unification of Korea. On the 8th of October at eight o'clock in the evening I heard on the radio that the United Nations had formally approved the resolution in the full knowledge (which had been communicated to the State Department) that the Chinese would intervene in force.

*

The warnings went unheeded. On 7 October American troops crossed the 38th parallel, and before the end of the month Chinese forces were in action in Korea. The Chinese view of the events leading to their intervention was given in an article in *People's China*.

DOCUMENT 10. EXTRACTS FROM C. C. FANG, 'THE WAY OF THE US AGGRESSOR: KOREA' (*People's China*, 2, 12, 16 DECEMBER 1950, PP. 5–7)

In the UN Secretariat, there is a file marked 'Secret Documents of Syngman Rhee' that anyone can consult today. Captured in his 'presidential' palace when Rhee fled from Seoul, they provide documentary evidence that he plotted and launched the treacherous June 25th attack across the 38th Parallel under the instigation and with the active support of the US government.

It is small wonder, therefore, that since they were laid before the UN, these documents have been sedulously ignored by the imperialist press. Mostly in the form of correspondence between the head of the South Korean puppet regime and his agents in the United States . . . they prove that the plan for the armed conquest of the whole of Korea was being prepared as early as the winter of 1948.

From that time onward, as the plot took shape, the arming and training of Syngman Rhee's troops by the Americans was intensified. Preparations developed into action. From January 1949 to April 1950, the Syngman Rhee troops made 1,274 raids across the 38th Parallel. His naval vessels shelled areas north of the Parallel 42 times and his aircraft bombed targets there in 71 sorties. These provocative attacks made from South Korea by forces controlled by the US military mission were, of course, seldom mentioned in the capitalist press. Those that were reported were lightly dismissed as 'border incidents'. They were, in fact, part of the plan to whip up war hysteria in South Korea as well as armed patrols to test out the strength and dispositions of the Korean People's Army.

By September 1949, Syngman Rhee thought he had the answer to the key question of the strength of the KPA. He began to press for decisive action.

'I feel strongly,' he wrote on September 30th, 1949, to Dr Robert T. Oliver, his paid agent in the United States, 'that now is the most psychological moment when we should take an aggressive measure . . . to clean up the rest of them in Pyongyang. We will drive some of Kim Il Sung's men to the mountain region and where we will gradually starve them out. . . .'

A week later, on October 7, he assured an American *UP* correspondent that the South Korean army was in battle trim and 'could seize Pyongyang in three days'. On October 31, his Defence Minister Sin Sen Mo made a similar statement to the press. A rabid war-like atmosphere was built up in Seoul. Syngman Rhee was faced with a growing economic crisis. In South Korea, the people's discontent was rising, the guerrilla resistance movement was spreading. The puppets were only too anxious to seek a solution of their difficulties in a war adventure that would put the flourishing economy of North Korea into their hands and pour more US dollars into their depleted treasury.

US Brigadier General Roberts, who was responsible for the training of the Syngman Rhee army, was, however, not convinced. The moment might well be 'psychological' for the Rhee puppets, but the US was not yet ready for the adventure.

The tempo of the plot was, however, quickened. In early 1950, Syngman Rhee was summoned to Tokyo to confer with MacArthur, who had now emerged as the leading agent of American imperialism in Asia. In June, the chief war-makers of the Pentagon and State Department, the then Defence Secretary Johnson, Bradley, Chairman of the Joint Chiefs of Staff, and John Foster Dulles, the leading US strategist of the global 'cold war', arrived in Japan for a series of special conferences with MacArthur. Dulles went on to South Korea in June, where in a 'pep talk' to the puppet 'assembly' in Seoul, he promised 'all necessary moral and material support' to the Syngman Rhee regime in its 'fight against Communism'. This was the green light for action. Syngman Rhee bellicosely declared: 'If we cannot defend democracy in a cold war, we will win victory in a hot war.' On June 25, with US advisers directing operations, the long premeditated attack was launched against North Korea. . . .

Part of a Vaster Plan

From the very outset, it was clear that the American aggression in Korea was merely a part of a vaster plan. At the same time that Truman ordered the armed forces of the US to Korea, he ordered the US 7th Fleet 'to prevent any attack on Formosa [Taiwan]'. Despite the warning of Chou En-lai, Minister for Foreign Affairs of the People's Republic of China, that this constituted a direct armed aggression against the territory of China, for the consequences of which the US would be held answerable, Washington expanded its aggressive action by increasing the number of its military advisers, stationing the US 13th Air Force and increasing its aid to the KMT remnants on the island.

In addition to this as the United States forces in Korea advanced north again towards the Chinese border, the number of reconnaissance and bombing raids on Northeast China increased. Between August 27 and November 30, no less than 268 raids were made over the frontier areas and as far as 100 miles into the hinterland.

In the same notorious June 27 statement, Truman announced US measures to accelerate the 'furnishing of military assistance' to the reactionary French forces invading Viet-Nam and also to the Quirino regime that was vainly trying to crush the people's forces in the Philippines.

The US aggression in Korea emerged clearly as the most advanced front of the American offensive against the Asian peoples and, in particular, against the Chinese People's Republic.

As the dust left behind by Chiang Kai-Shek's routed armies settled, Acheson had evidently seen that there was no hope of an internal overthrow of the People's rule in China and that the only possibility left of stopping the rapid progress of peaceful construction in People's China was by direct armed US aggression. The courageous resistance of the Korean people to the US attack was, indeed, a battle not only for their own existence as a free and united nation, but for all Asia, against the aggressor.

Violating the UN Charter and the accepted standards of civilized conduct and international law, the US invasion of

Korea and its related aggressive acts menaced the peace of the whole world.

The Soviet Union, spokesman for the camp of peace at the United Nations, made proposals at an early stage for a peaceful settlement of the question of Korea by the withdrawal of foreign armed forces, to enable the Korean people to settle their own domestic affairs. These proposals were fully supported by China and all other peace-loving peoples. The US, however, rejected these proposals and intensified its attacks on Korea in the vain hope of getting a quick decision by force. At the same time, they tried to frighten the Chinese people by intensified bombings of the Northeast and by wild talk about the Yalu River not being the natural boundary between Korea and China. After being reduced to the Pusan beachhead, the US mustered 40,000 troops, 300 vessels and 500 aircraft from all over Asia and after landing near Inchun at great cost, made straight for the Chinese border on the Yalu.

In this situation the Chinese people showed their awareness of the true interests of their country and of world peace and security by volunteering in their thousands for service with the Korean People's Army, to preserve the Korean people's democracy and to protect their own homes.

They realized that the American invasion of Korea was merely the prelude to the invasion of China, that the reconstruction of their country could not be completed unless the flames of war started by the American imperialists in neighbouring Korea were quenched.

There can be no question of the right and justice of such aid. The Chinese people have followed the great democratic tradition of the past, of the volunteers for the Spanish Republic and of Lafayette in his fight on the side of the American people in their just War of Independence. If, at the dawn of American democracy, Canada had been attacked by a ruthless invader who repeatedly bombarded the State of Michigan and declared that the St Lawrence was not the real national boundary between Canada and the USA and had given repeated proofs of its hostility to the latter, would the democratic American people not have risen in defence of their neighbour and their own hearths and homes?

*

On 24 November 1950 General MacArthur announced the beginning of an offensive to end the war in Korea. Two days later the Chinese launched a massive counter attack which was to force the United Nations armies back over the 38th parallel. On 28 November the leader of a special CPR delegation to the United Nations addressed the Security Council. The delegation had originally been invited some weeks earlier at the behest of the Soviet Union to discuss Taiwan. In the event the Chinese spokesman also denounced US policy in Korea.

DOCUMENT 11. EXTRACTS FROM SPEECH BY WU HSIU-CHÜAN, DELEGATE OF THE PEOPLE'S REPUBLIC OF CHINA AT THE SECURITY COUNCIL, 28 NOVEMBER 1950 (UNITED NATIONS, *Security Council Official Records*, 5TH YEAR, 527 MEETING: 28 NOVEMBER 1950, NO. 69, PP. 2–25)

Mr President, members of the Security Council: on the instructions of the Central People's Government of the People's Republic of China, I am here in the name of the 475 million people of China to accuse the United States Government of the unlawful and criminal act of armed aggression against the territory of China, Taiwan—including the Penghu Islands. . . .

I would like to remind the members of the Security Council that so long as the United Nations persists in denying admittance to a permanent member of the Security Council representing 475 million people, it cannot make lawful decisions on any major issues or solve any major problems, particularly those which concern Asia. Indeed, without the participation of the lawful delegates of the People's Republic of China, representing 475 million people, the United Nations cannot in practice be worthy of its name. Without the participation of the lawful representatives of the People's Republic of China, the people of China have no reason to recognize any resolutions or decisions of the United Nations.

Therefore, in the name of the Central People's Government of the People's Republic of China, I once more demand that the United Nations expel the so-called 'delegates' of the Kuomintang reactionary remnant clique and admit the lawful delegates of the People's Republic of China. . . .

My government has protested in strong terms to the United

Nations General Assembly, resolutely opposing the inclusion of the so-called 'Question of Formosa'—concerning the status of Taiwan—in the agenda of the fifth session of the General Assembly. Whatever decision the United Nations General Assembly may take on the so-called question of the status of Taiwan, whether it be to hand over the island to the United States so that it might administer it openly under the disguise of 'trusteeship', or 'neutralization', or whether it be to procrastinate by way of 'investigation', thereby maintaining the present state of actual United States occupation, it will, in substance, be stealing China's legitimate territory and supporting United States aggression against Taiwan in opposition to the Chinese people. Any such decision would in no way shake the resolve of the Chinese people to liberate Taiwan, nor would it prevent action by the Chinese people to liberate Taiwan. . . .

Since the Chinese people won their victory on the Chinese mainland, the United States Government has still more frantically carried out a policy of rearming Japan to oppose the Chinese people and the other Asian peoples. At present, the United States Government has not only turned Japan into its main base in the Far East in preparation for aggressive war, but it has already begun to use this base as a means to launch aggressive wars against a series of Asian countries. The headquarters of the United States Government for its aggression against Korea and Taiwan is in Japan. . . .

In order to safeguard international peace and security and to uphold the sanctity of the United Nations Charter, the United Nations Security Council has the inalienable duty to apply sanctions against the United States Government for its criminal acts of armed aggression upon the territory of China, Taiwan, and its armed intervention in Korea. In the name of the Central People's Government of the People's Republic of China, I therefore propose to the United Nations Security Council:

First, that the United Nations Security Council should openly condemn, and take concrete steps to apply severe sanctions against, the United States Government for its criminal acts of armed aggression against the territory of China, Taiwan, and armed intervention in Korea.

Second, that the United Nations Security Council should immediately adopt effective measures to bring about the complete withdrawal by the United States Government of its forces of armed aggression from Taiwan, in order that peace and security in the Pacific and in Asia may be ensured.

Third, that the United Nations Security Council should immediately adopt effective measures to bring about the withdrawal from Korea of the armed forces of the United States and all other countries and to leave it to the people of North and South Korea to settle the domestic affairs of Korea themselves, so that a peaceful solution of the Korean question may be achieved.

*

After the entry of Chinese forces into the Korean War the Americans extended their restrictions on trade with China, first introduced in 1949, into a complete embargo. In December 1950 the Truman administration, in addition to stopping all imports and exports to and from China, blocked Chinese-owned assets in the US and sought to prevent the trans-shipment of US exports to China.

The United States Senate resolved on 23 January 1951 that the United Nations should declare Communist China an aggressor in Korea, which it did on 1 February, and that the Communist Chinese Government should not be admitted to the United Nations as the representative of China.

The following extract is an extreme but not unrepresentative American view of the 'threat' of Red China. MacArthur himself claims that his objectives were limited to winning the Korean War, and any measures taken against China would have stopped short of sending ground forces into continental China.

DOCUMENT 12. EXTRACT FROM SPEECH BY CONGRESSMAN DORN SUPPORTING A JOINT RESOLUTION TO AWARD THE THANKS OF CONGRESS TO GENERAL DOUGLAS MACARTHUR (MACARTHUR, *Reminiscences*, HEINEMANN, LONDON, 1964, P. 407)

If General MacArthur's recommendations had been followed during the early stages of the Korean war, the world would not be in such critical condition today. If General MacArthur had been permitted to win the Korean war conclusively, Red China would have been destroyed in a matter of months and the balance of world power would have been tipped heavily today in favor of the cause of freedom. The North Korean attack and the subsequent entrance of Red China into the war was a God-given opportunity for the United States to correct with little cost the tragic mistakes of Yalta and Potsdam. Red China's only armies were ground to pieces in North Korea. The Russians were recuperating from World War II and did not have nuclear weapons in mass production. MacArthur noted with regret and much sadness the passing of this unbelievable opportunity.

Some day we will have to fight Red China on her terms at a time of her choosing. She will have atomic power backed by the entire Eurasian land mass. This issue could have been resolved forever in our favor in 1951 had those of us in Washington had the foresight to give MacArthur the green light in Asia. This great general could have secured the peace and could have assured the ascendency of the Western democratic world. MacArthur was right and many of us here in Washington, in London, and in the United Nations were wrong.

*

The United States Central Intelligence Agency attempted to organize and support subversive activity in Northeast China (Manchuria). On the night of 29 November 1952, two Americans, Downey and Fecteau, on a mission to contact agents in Kirin Province, were shot down and captured.

DOCUMENT 13. EXTRACT FROM JUDGMENT OF MILITARY TRIBUNAL ON US SPIES IN THE DOWNEY-FECTEAU ESPIONAGE CASE, 23 NOVEMBER 1954 (SUPPLEMENT TO *People's China*, 16 DECEMBER 1954, PP. 7–8)

The nine defendants, Chang Tsai-wen, Hsu Kwang-chih, Yu Kwan-chou, Niu Sung-lin, Luan Heng-shan, Wang Wei-fan, Wang Chin-sheng, Chung Tien-hsing, Li Chun-ying were all former military officers of the Chiang Kai-shek gang. They took part in the civil war against the people and fled to Hongkong after the collapse of the Chiang Kai-shek regime. They were taken up in 1951 by the 'Free China Movement', a US espionage organization in Hongkong. Under the guise of being employed by the 'Far East Development Company' for work on Guam, they were flown in groups to espionage training centres of the US Central Intelligence Agency in Chigasaki, Kanagawa Prefecture, Japan, and on Saipan Island, for secret training. The training courses were mainly how to carry out assassination, demolition, armed riots, the collection of intelligence, secret communications, and other espionage activity in China. After training, they were selected by John Thomas Downey and another US special agent to receive training under the personal direction of Downey. They were later organized into groups and dropped in succession from US planes into Kirin Province in Northeast China to set up 'bases' there for armed agents and 'safety points' for sheltering agents, to build 'parachuting grounds' to receive air-dropped supplies and agents, to establish secret communication lines connecting the 'bases' with Shen-yang (Mukden), to collect information about the national defences of China, location of industrial areas and meteorological conditions, to rescue such intruding American airmen as were shot down and to gather lurking elements of the traitorous Chiang Kai-shek gang in order to foment armed riots. The mission of defendant Li Chun-ying after being dropped was to report on the activities of 'Team Wen' and engage in liaison work and subversive activity. These defendants were all captured on different occasions.

All the defendants in this case have after capture admitted the crimes committed by them. Their crimes are also borne out by a vast amount of captured material evidence such as weapons, ammunition, radio sets, maps, parachutes, equipment for dropping special agents, forged safe-conducts of the Chinese People's Liberation Army, certificates for wounded soldiers, passes, as well as gold, paper currency and other equipment for conducting espionage activity. In view of such conclusive evidence of their crimes, it is beyond doubt that the defendants were dropped into Chinese territory in order to conduct espionage activity, thereby seriously jeopardizing the security of China, in an attempt to carry out the plan of the American aggressors to extend their aggression against China and undermine the cause of people's democracy in China.

The defendant John Thomas Downey actively assembled and trained special agents and had them secretly dropped into Chinese territory to conduct subversive activity. He also personally violated China's territorial air to carry out criminal activity. He is the chief criminal in this case and should be punished with the full rigour of the law. The defendant Richard George Fecteau, who assisted John Thomas Downey in entering China to conduct espionage activity, should also be severely punished. The defendants Hsu Kwang-chih, Wang Wei-fan, Wang Chin-sheng, Yu Kwan-chou committed high treason against their native land by joining the US espionage organization. They were dropped into China to carry out subversive activity at the instigation of the US espionage organization. They have committed the heinous crime of endangering the security of the state, and should all be severely punished according to law. The defendants Chang Tsai-wen, Luan Heng-shan, Chung Tien-hsing, Li Chun-ying and Niu Sung-lin, have committed crimes of equal gravity, but as the defendants Chang Tsai-wen, Luan Heng-shan, Chung Tien-hsing and Li Chun-ying have shown repentance during the trial, they are therefore given lighter sentences. The defendant Niu Sung-lin has shown true repentance during the trial and will be given a mitigated sentence.

In accordance with Articles 6, 3, 7, 11, 14 and 16 of the Law of the People's Republic of China for the Punishment of Counter-Revolutionaries, judgement is hereby passed:

1 The defendant John Thomas Downey, sentenced to life imprisonment.

2 The defendant Richard George Fecteau, sentenced to 20 years' imprisonment.

3 The defendants Hsu Kwang-chih, Yu Kwan-chou, Wang Wei-fan and Wang Chin-sheng, all sentenced to death, deprived of political rights for all time.

4 The defendants Chang Tsai-wen, Luan Heng-shan, Chung Tien-hsing and Li Chun-ying, all sentenced to life imprisonment, deprived of political rights for all time.

5 The defendant Niu Sung-lin, sentenced to 15 years' imprisonment, deprived of political rights for 10 years.

6 The captured weapons, ammunition, radio sets, maps, parachutes and equipment for air-dropping are to be confiscated.

Chia Chien, Chief Judge

Chu Yao-tang, Judge

Chang Hsiang-chien, Judge

The Military Tribunal of the Supreme People's Court of the People's Republic of China.

23 November 1954

*

After the armistice in Korea (July 1953) the Republican administration in the United States became increasingly fearful of Communist advances in Indochina. Dulles doubted whether a settlement should be made with the insurgents in Indochina. On the eve of the Geneva Conference he made the following speech, which represents the American attitude to 'Red China' at that time. (For details of the Geneva settlement and subsequent developments in Indochina, see Part III.)

DOCUMENT 14. EXTRACT FROM SPEECH BY JOHN FOSTER DULLES TO THE OVERSEAS PRESS CLUB, NEW YORK CITY, 29 MARCH 1954 (*Department of State Bulletin*, XXX, 12 APRIL 1954, PP. 539–40)

If the Communist forces won uncontested control over Indochina or any substantial part thereof, they would surely resume the same pattern of aggression against other free peoples in the area.

The propagandists of Red China and Russia make it apparent that the purpose is to dominate all of Southeast Asia. . . .

The United States has shown in many ways its sympathy for the gallant struggle being waged in Indochina by French forces and those of the Associated States. Congress has enabled us to provide material aid to the established governments and their peoples. Also, our diplomacy has sought to deter Communist China from open aggression in that area.

President Eisenhower, in his address of April 16, 1953, explained that a Korean armistice would be a fraud if it merely released aggressive armies for attack elsewhere. I said last September that if Red China sent its own army into Indochina, that would result in grave consequences which might not be confined to Indochina.

Recent statements have been designed to impress upon potential aggressors that aggression might lead to action at places and by means of free-world choosing, so that aggression would cost more than it could gain.

The Chinese Communists have, in fact, avoided the direct use of their own Red armies in open aggression against Indochina. They have, however, largely stepped up their support of the aggression in that area. Indeed, they promote that aggression by all means short of open invasion.

Under all the circumstances it seems desirable to clarify further the United States position.

Under the conditions of today, the imposition on Southeast Asia of the political system of Communist Russia and its Chinese Communist ally, by whatever means, must be a great threat to the whole community. The United States feels that that possibility should not be passively accepted but should be met by united action. This might involve serious risks. But these risks are far less than those that will face us a few years from now if we dare not be resolute today.

The free nations want peace. However, peace is not had merely by wanting it. Peace has to be worked for and planned for. Sometimes it is necessary to take risks to win peace just as it is necessary in war to take risks to win victory. The chances for peace are usually bettered by letting a potential aggressor know in advance where his aggression could lead him.

I hope that these statements which I make here tonight will serve the cause of peace. . . .

*

The Geneva agreements were concluded on 21 July 1954 (see Document 36). Almost immediately afterwards Peking began to mount a campaign against American support for Taiwan. Certainly American aid for the Nationalists had increased substantially since the 'unleashing of Chiang Kai-shek' in February 1953. Fears of an American-backed attack by the Nationalists may explain the Chinese decision to bombard Quemoy on 3 September 1954. The Nationalists retaliated with air attacks against the Chinese mainland. On 2 December the United States signed a Mutual Defence Treaty with the regime on Taiwan.

DOCUMENT 15. EXTRACTS FROM 'CHINA WILL LIBERATE TAIWAN', EDITORIAL ARTICLE *People's Daily*, 5 DECEMBER 1954 (SUPPLEMENT TO *People's China*, 24, 16 DECEMBER 1954, PP. 6–8)

The Chinese people will offer the most vehement opposition to the latest step taken by the United States aggressors in preparation for world war—the open occupation of Chinese territory, Taiwan.

They will not forget the date—December 2, 1954—on which this criminal act was committed by the signing of the so-called 'mutual security treaty' with the traitor Chiang Kai-shek. They will not permit Taiwan to remain in the grip of the United States. . . .

Dulles' statement that the US–Chiang Kai-shek treaty is 'purely defensive' is a lie. Its Articles 2 and 5 make it clear that the US will even gamble on war to intervene in China's internal affairs and prevent the Chinese people from liberating Taiwan and the Penghu Islands. This treaty is an open encouragement to Chiang Kai-shek to invade the mainland and provoke a large-scale war. Article 6 states that the scope of armed action as defined in Articles 2 and 5 'will be applicable to such other territories as may be determined by mutual agreement'.

During the past few days, American and British reactionary propagandists have been busy whitewashing the American aggressors and deceiving the public. They even suggested that the treaty was aimed at preserving peace. The very wording of Article 6 gives the lie to this.

Dulles himself has admitted: 'The pact provides for US base rights in Formosa (Taiwan),' and that the US 'must be at liberty to mobilize its forces to retaliate. . . .' He added: 'This treaty will forge another link in the system of collective security established by the various collective defence treaties already concluded between the US and other countries in the Pacific area' and that 'together these arrangements provide the central framework for the defence by the free peoples of the Western Pacific against Communist aggression.' . . .

Judging from the provisions of this treaty and from Dulles' statement, the US attempts to link up this treaty with the Southeast Asia aggressive bloc, the projected 'Northeast Asia Alliance' and other military treaties, are all meant to extend its aggression against China and Asia, to drag those who follow at the heels of the US into military adventures leading to war. Nothing could be clearer than the fact that the US-Chiang Kai-shek treaty is an alliance for aggressive war.

Dulles declared that if the United States launches an attack on the Chinese People's Republic, it 'technically does not constitute war' as 'a state of war only exists between two governments that recognize each other'. This is a trick to give the American aggressors a get-out, whenever they unleash aggressive war against China. . . .

Faced with a situation in which the American aggressive clique has embarked on a policy of war provocation, the British Government has supported American action. On the one hand it has recognized the Government of the People's Republic of China as a lawful government of China, but on the other it has gone so far as to support US action of occupying China's territory at Taiwan, thereby agreeing that renegades and traitors to China can continue to hold Taiwan. This is not only morally indefensible, but runs counter to all principles of international relations.

On December 1, a spokesman of the British Foreign Office made a statement on the conclusion of this US-Chiang war treaty. He said that the British Government had for a long time been 'generally informed' of the negotiations on this treaty and was 'in contact all the time with the US Government about the general situation in the Far East'. The US further stated that it had informed Britain of the text of the treaty. This shows that it was concluded not only with British concurrence but that the British Government also had a finger in the pie.

The British spokesman also stated that there was a question of 'the future status' of Taiwan and that status 'would have to be acceptable to the parties immediately concerned who must be consulted'. It need hardly be said that this obviously refers to proposals for the so-called 'neutralization of Taiwan' or an 'independent state of Taiwan'. But the status of Taiwan was fixed long ago. Taiwan was, is and will be Chinese territory. The question now is to end US armed occupation of Taiwan, oppose US interference in China's internal affairs and have the US forces withdrawn. The Chinese people will not tolerate the occupation of Taiwan in whatever shape or form. Let that be clear.

*

Air and sea actions continued in the Taiwan Strait during the first months of 1955. In February the Nationalists were evacuated from the most vulnerable of the off-shore islands, the Tachens, by the American fleet. In return the Nationalists expected the Americans to guarantee the defence of the other off-shore islands Quemoy and Matsu. The actual American commitment was ambiguous. The Formosa Resolution passed by both Houses of Congress late in January authorized the President to defend the islands only if he judged that an attack on them was an attack on Taiwan itself.

It should be noted that in both the United States and Britain there was anxiety to leave open the question of the future status of Taiwan. In passing the Mutual Defence Treaty the Senate had secured an understanding from Dulles 'that by this treaty the United States does not recognize the sovereignty of the Republic of China over Formosa even though the treaty expressly lists the island as its territory'. In the House of Commons Churchill stated on 1 February 1955 that the Cairo Declaration and the Japanese Peace Treaty did not make Formosa legally a part of China.

In April at the Bandung Conference (see Document 47) Chou En-lai offered to negotiate with the United States on the relaxation of tension in the Taiwan area, and held out the possibility of direct negotiation with the Chiang Kai-shek government. Subsequently he made a report in Peking to the annual session of the 1,200 strong National People's Congress.

DOCUMENT 16. EXTRACT FROM SPEECH BY CHOU EN-LAI TO FIRST NATIONAL PEOPLE'S CONGRESS, 30 JULY 1955 (*Current Background*, 342, 3 AUGUST 1955, PP. 5–8)

After the Korean armistice and the restoration of peace in Indo-China, the situation in the Taiwan area has become the most tense in the Far East. It must be pointed out that this tension has been caused by the United States' occupation of China's territory Taiwan and its interference with the liberation of China's coastal islands. This is an international issue between China and the United States. The exercise by the Chinese people of their sovereign rights in liberating Taiwan is a matter of China's internal affairs. These two questions cannot be mixed up. During the Asian-African Conference, the Chinese Government already proposed that China and the United States should sit down and enter into negotiations to discuss the question of easing and eliminating the tension in the Taiwan area. There is no war between China and the United States; the peoples of China and the United States are friendly toward each other; the Chinese people want no war with the United States, so the question of cease-fire between China and the United States does not arise. After the Asian-African Conference, the Chinese Government has further stated that there are two possible ways for the Chinese people to liberate Taiwan, namely, by war or by peaceful means. Conditions permitting, the Chinese people are ready to seek the liberation of Taiwan by peaceful means. In the course of the liberation by the Chinese people of the mainland and the coastal islands, there was no lack of precedents for peaceful liberation. Provided that the United States does not interfere with China's internal affairs, the possibility of peaceful liberation of Taiwan will continue to increase. If possible, the Chinese Government is willing to enter into negotiations with the responsible local authorities of Taiwan to map out concrete steps for Taiwan's peaceful liberation. It should be made clearly [sic] that these would be negotiations between the Central Government and local authorities. The Chinese people are firmly opposed to any ideas or plots of the so-called 'two Chinas'. . . .

On August 1st, China and the United States will start talks in Geneva at the ambassadorial level. The purpose of these talks will be to aid in settling the matter of the repatriation of civilians of both sides, and to facilitate further discussions and settlement of certain other practical matters now at issue between both sides.

In the past year, Sino-American talks at the consular level have been going on in Geneva, during which data concerning civilians of each country in the other were exchanged. So far as our side is concerned, we supplied promptly to the United States concrete data concerning American civilians in China. We are of the opinion that provided both sides are sincerely desirous of negotiation and conciliation, it should be possible in the forthcoming talks at the ambassadorial level to reach, first of all, a reasonable settlement of the question of the return of civilians to their respective countries. The number of American civilians in China is small, and their question can be easily settled. There are a great many overseas Chinese in the United States, among whom students alone number several thousands. Most of them have relatives on the Chinese mainland. The situation of the Chinese students is particularly inconsistent with humanitarian principles as they are obstructed from returning home while their relatives have no way to aid them financially. We are of the opinion that since there are no diplomatic relations between China and the United States at the present time, each of them can entrust to a third country the task of looking after the affairs of its civilians in the other country, and primarily the affairs concerning the return of these civilians to their own country.

As stated in the press announcement agreed upon between both sides, the forthcoming Sino-American talks at the ambassadorial level should also 'facilitate further discussions and settlement of certain other practical matters now at issue between both sides', so as to contribute to the relaxation of the tension between China and the United States. Mr Dulles, quoting the words of President Eisenhower, said at a press conference on July 26th, 1955, that the United States would follow the principle of working cooperatively with all peoples in the ambassadorial level talks in Geneva. If these words signify that the United States is prepared to cooperate with China, the Sino-American talks at the ambassadorial level should be able to make preparations for negotiations between China and the United States for relaxing and eliminating the tension in the Taiwan Area.

The Chinese people are also concerned about the extremely unjust policy of blockade and embargo which obstructs trade between countries. It should be possible to remove such barriers so that peaceful trade between all countries will not be hindered.

The Chinese people would like to see the United States with-draw its armed forces from Taiwan and the Taiwan Straits, leaving the Chinese territorial air free from further intrusions and China free from the threat of demonstrative war man-oeuvres, so as to implement the stipulation in the United Nations Charter that 'all members shall refrain in their inter-national relations from the threat or use of force against the territorial integrity or political independence of any state, or any other manner inconsistent with the purposes of the United Nations', and to vindicate Mr Dulles' statement at the press conference on July 26th, 1955 that: 'The United States believes that whatever may be the differences which now divide countries, these differences should not be settled by recourse to force where this would be apt to provoke international war.' ...

The Chinese people hope that the countries of Asia and the Pacific Region, including the United States, will sign a pact of collective peace to replace the antagonistic military blocs now existing in this part of the world, so that the collective peace first advocated by the Indian Government may be realized.

We recognize that for the above wishes to be fulfilled, it is necessary first of all that China and the United States should display sincerity in negotiations, that the two sides establish contacts to increase mutual understanding and trust. Only by efforts of both sides and reciprocal demonstration of good will, can the tension in the Taiwan area be relaxed and ultimately eliminated.

The Chinese Government and people will continue to strive indefatigably, as they did in the past, for a universal and lasting peace. However, if anybody should take our efforts as a sign of weakness or imagine that pressure or threats will have effect on us, he will not only meet with the opposition of the people of the world, but quickly find out that his calculations are totally wrong.

*

The Sino-American ambassadorial talks began hopefully with an agreement on the exchange of civilians on 10 September 1955. The talks continued with virtually no further agreement and in a peculiarly constrained manner as the following extract shows. Nevertheless the talks have provided the only direct official contact between the United States and China prior to 1971 and so may have helped both sides to signal intentions and to ease tension at times of crisis.

DOCUMENT 17. EXTRACT FROM K. J. YOUNG, *Negotiating with the Chinese Communists. The United States Experience 1953-1967*, MCGRAW-HILL, NEW YORK, 1968, PP. 7-9

The Talks opened in Geneva in August 1955 and were conducted there until December 1957 when Ambassador Johnson was transferred to Thailand. Seventy-three numbered Talks took place in Geneva, which gave them the name 'Geneva Talks.' The Ambassadors met in a conference room provided by the Secretary-General of the United Nations at the Palais des Nations where the United Nations has its headquarters in Europe. Both governments shared the rent: $1.15 per month. The two parties, or sides, as they customarily call themselves, sat opposite each other at an oval table with a map of the world carved in inlaid Swedish wood between them. Each Ambassador brought three or four of his own aides, but no one else attended. They conducted the Talks in a correct and proper diplomatic manner, with the amenities and civilities being recognized even though the presentation was often vigorous and the official language usually firm and sometimes harsh. Ritualistic repetition and ambassadorial stamina soon came to characterize the Talks at Geneva. After the fifty-third meeting in 1956, *The New York Times* correspondent in Geneva remarked, 'For sheer endurance there has been no United States diplomatic performance comparable to Mr Johnson's since Benjamin Franklin's efforts to get financial help from the French monarchy for the American Revolution.'

After Ambassador Johnson's departure and the lapse of some nine months, the location of the Talks shifted in the fall of 1958 to Warsaw, Poland, where a new American Ambassador was taking up his duties and where Ambassador Wang Ping-nan was already in residence. One reason for choosing Warsaw was to reduce the burden on the Ambassadors of leaving their posts and traveling often to another country. In Warsaw they resumed the regular sessions. The Polish government provided the eighteenth-century Myslewicki Palace where the Talks have since been held. Fifty-eight were held in Warsaw during 1958–1966, and they came to be referred to as the 'Warsaw Talks.'

According to press accounts, the Talks have now reached a well-understood and mutually-accepted style and method of operation. The two Ambassadors with their three or four aides arrive separately at the Palace. They enter the conference room by different doors on either side of green-covered tables which are placed parallel to each other with a space between them. Usually the Peking delegation is already at the table when the Americans enter. After the Americans have come to their chairs, each side nods slightly to the other and all sit down. There is a 'ritual' of procedure. Each side takes turns, automatically opening every other meeting so there is never any question of deciding—or arguing—as to who speaks first; the side which does not make the closing statement of the day then proposes the adjournment of that session and the date for the next meeting. The Ambassadors cannot leave the table until that date has been agreed to. The whole exchange is oral; only sound waves cross the space between the Ambassadors. They avoid any official physical contact, apparently to symbolize the immense divide and total separation between the two governments and peoples. The Ambassadors apparently do not hand documents across the tables to each other. The representatives nod to one another, but they do not mix much. Fortunately, however, the diplomatic aides of both sides in each embassy now frequently consult each other by phone—in Chinese, not English—regarding difficulties in translation and various procedural matters. Similarly, copies of papers and documents are handed back and forth in this informal contact.

To judge from journalists' accounts, the secret proceedings follow a pattern of alternating oral statements. The format imitates the particular style developed at Panmunjom, which set a somewhat new and peculiar pattern in diplomatic practice. The Ambassador opening the meeting customarily starts with a standard introduction in somewhat the following terms: 'I am deeply disappointed to note that your side has continued since our last meeting to pursue the same unreasonable policies and that, in fact, your aggressive policy has not changed in any respect.' This opening statement then proceeds to expound whatever subject that side prefers to begin with, such as the renunciation of force or bilateral contacts in the case of the Americans, or the withdrawal from Taiwan or Vietnam in the case of the Chinese Communists. There are usually few interruptions for questions or comments from across the table. When the opening side has concluded its opening statement, the other Ambassador takes his turn to make his first statement which leads off with a variation of the following: 'I am saddened to have to note that your side has completely misconstrued our policy and purpose. Everything that we do is strictly defensive and made necessary only by the aggressive policy of your side.'

The opening statements are always read from a prepared text—a position paper—with immediate sentence-by-sentence translation into Chinese or English by an interpreter for the speaking side. This is a slow, tedious process but it permits each side to make a reasonably accurate and complete stenographic record of that statement as well as to prepare for the rebuttal. After the first side has finished its initial statement, the other side either responds directly on that subject by reading from an already-prepared rebuttal or presents a prepared statement concerning some other matter. Since this initial round covers fairly predictable items, both sides come with written statements prepared for a long list of grievances. It apparently is just a question of taking the appropriate paper out of the briefcase to read into the record. This opening round usually takes about an hour.

Then the second phase of several alternating statements and rebuttals follow, again based on previously prepared positions. When both sides have finished that process, one or the other may then make extemporaneous remarks on what has occurred. This exchange is somewhat more spontaneous than the formal 'readings', but it is not a dialogue or exploration. These oral replies are denials, rebuttals, accusations, explanations, and repetitions. This volley goes back and forth until neither Ambassador has anything more to add. There comes a pause; one Ambassador then proceeds to announce that he has nothing more to say; the other responds with the same words; a date is mutually agreed upon for the next session; all present pick up their papers, stand, nod, and leave separately. . . .

*

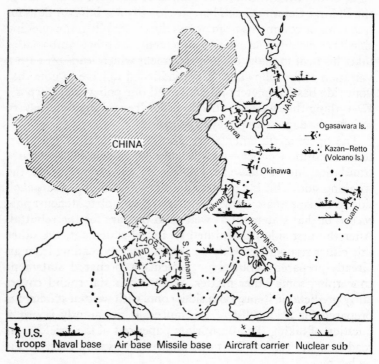

In spite of the contact provided by the ambassadorial talks the United States and China continued to be separated by fear and suspicion. The advent of Democratic administrations under Kennedy and Johnson brought no major change in the China policy which had been established by John Foster Dulles in the fifties. The fears implicit in the 'domino' theory, i.e. that if one state in Southeast Asia fell to the Communists the neighbouring states would topple, inspired and justified the massive flow of America aid and the build-up of American forces around China.

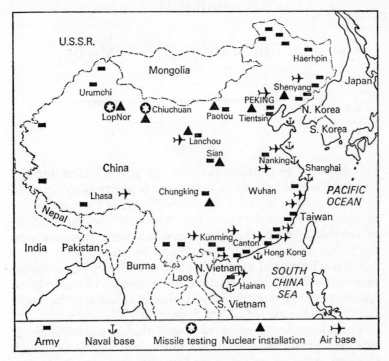

U.S.S.R.

Mongolia

Haerhpin

Urumchi

Shenyang

Japan

PEKING

N. Korea

LopNor Chiuchuan Paotou Tientsin

S. Korea

Lanchou

Sian

Nanking

China

Shanghai

Lhasa

Chungking

Wuhan

PACIFIC
OCEAN

Nepal

Taiwan

India Pakistan

Kunming Canton

Hong Kong

Burma

N. Vietnam

SOUTH
CHINA
SEA

Laos

Hainan

S. Vietnam

■	⚓	✪	▲	✈
Army	Naval base	Missile testing	Nuclear installation	Air base

MAP 2 AMERICAN VIEW OF CHINESE FORCES (FROM *Newsweek*, 17 MARCH, 1966, © RAND MCNALLY & CO., ROBERT RITTER

To many Americans Chinese military preparations seemed to foreshadow the extension of Chinese power in Asia. American journals published maps depicting the deployment of China's armed forces. A few thoughtful commentators noted that the disposition of those forces seemed primarily defensive but most saw them as a threat not only to Taiwan but to America's other allies in Asia.

The escalation of the Indochinese conflicts (see Part III) had brought Sino-American hostility to a high pitch by the mid-sixties.

PART II

The Sino-Soviet Rift 1956–65

Looking back at relations between the Soviet Union and the Chinese Communists since 1921 there is plenty of evidence of lack of common interests. In perspective it is the Sino-Soviet alliance in the period 1950 to 1957 which requires explanation, rather than the rift which became increasingly apparent after 1957. But to pose either question in isolation would be inadequate. Factors of geography, power and ideology combine to give Soviet-Chinese relations their special characteristics. Moreover the relationship must always be seen in its world context and in terms of United States policy.

There is evidence, as we have seen, that in the mid-fifties it was the United States led by the intransigent Mr Dulles which chose to maintain an inflexible Cold War position in the Far East, and American pressure undoubtedly helped to hold the Communist partners together. At Liberation China was inevitably dependent on co-operation with the Soviet Union but as the new nation began to cope with its domestic difficulties it was bound to gain confidence in international relations. Never a Soviet satellite, China was unlikely to remain long as the junior partner. Stalin had foreseen this. After his death in 1953 his successors, anxious at first to placate China, tided over the potential differences and created a short-lived era of goodwill. Khrushchev visited Peking in September and October 1954. The ensuing agreement provided that Port Arthur and Dairen were to be returned to China by the following May, the USSR gave up its share in the joint-stock companies formed in 1950, and further economic and technical assistance was promised.

Thus in the mid-fifties there was every sign of harmony in the Sino-Soviet alliance.

This harmony was reflected in the fact that the Five Year Plan initiated in 1953 was based on the Soviet development model and gave priority to heavy industry. The plan was to be achieved with the aid of loans and technical assistance from the Soviet Union and by transferring some of the profits from agriculture. A moderate and phased programme of collectivization was begun in 1954; but, following an exceptionally good harvest in 1955, Mao gave the signal for more rapid collectivization. To reconcile the intellectuals and technicians, so important to the development programme, with the party cadres Chou En-lai proposed in January 1956 that more of them should be admitted as party members.

The first disagreement between the Chinese and Soviet Parties arose, according to the Chinese, when Khrushchev repudiated Stalin at the Twentieth Congress of the CPSU in February 1956 (see Document 18). The destruction of the Stalin myth was for the Chinese a potentially dangerous and divisive step. For Khrushchev it was a ploy to justify his policies and promote himself. To Mao it was unnecessarily undermining the Marx-Lenin-Stalin ideological historiography, and moreover it had been done without consultation. Indirectly it might be seen as threatening his position at home. The cult of Chairman Mao was far from the heights it was to reach in the Cultural Revolution, but for those in China who resented Mao's pre-eminence there was, in the toppling of Stalin, food for thought.

To the Chinese leadership the Hungarian crisis of October–November 1956 appeared as a disturbing example of the consequences of de-Stalinization. When addressing the comrades in Eastern Europe they urged solidarity under Soviet leadership. At home, possibly to provide a safety valve against similar outbursts of discontent, Mao renewed his appeal, originally issued in May 1956, to 'let a hundred flowers bloom, a hundred schools of thought contend'. The intellectuals who spoke out soon found their freedom curtailed in a new anti-rightist movement. Whether this was the work of Mao's opponents in the Central Committee, whether Mao was all along playing cat and mouse in order to trap the dissident intellectuals into revealing themselves, or whether the movement simply threatened to get out of hand is still open to debate and research. If the fiasco of the 'hundred flowers movement' is interpreted as a personal set-back for Mao, it was in contrast to Khrushchev's triumph (in June 1957) over an anti-Party group led by Malenkov and Molotov. Mao's desire to assert himself both in the international Communist movement and against critics at home may help to explain his provocative speech at Moscow in November 1957. Addressing the meeting of Communist and Workers' Parties, Mao declared that the East (meaning the Communist world led by the Soviet Union) should use its recently demonstrated capability in sputniks and rocketry to embark on a more active confrontation with the United States (Document 19).

Mao's views on the possible outcome of a nuclear war, expressed in this speech, must have caused disquiet to his Russian hosts. According to later Chinese accounts, an agreement had been signed only a month before guaranteeing Soviet assistance to China in building its own nuclear weapons. This agreement was abrogated two years later on 20 June 1959. The Soviets, increasingly confident in their own nuclear strength, were preparing to seek a *modus vivendi* with the United States and may well have doubted whether the prospects for world peace would be enhanced if the Chinese had their own nuclear weapons.

Meanwhile economic difficulties in China, for example the disastrous harvest of 1956, highlighted both the inadequacies of Soviet aid and the inappropriateness of the Soviet development model. It was such considerations which impelled Mao formally to inaugurate the 'Great Leap Forward' on 1 February 1958. Using her own resources with the maximum mobilization of human effort China would, in fifteen years, surpass Great Britain in industrial development. For Mao the 'Great Leap' was an answer to the critics and the doubters, a response to the disappointing achievements of the Five Year Plan. The achievement of 'socialism' was to be speeded up; rural China was to be organized into self-reliant Commune units. Living and working together the peasants would be forged into a truly revolutionary corps, while at the same time industry would be diversified. Such was to be the actual and symbolic reality of the 'backyard furnaces'.

China's vigorously socialist measures in 1958 were in effect a challenge to the policies and outlook of the Soviet allies. In the same year the alliance was put to the test by the Chinese decision to bombard Quemoy, beginning on 23 August. Increasingly war-like statements were issued by Peking and Washington while Moscow reported the crisis quietly. Khrushchev's expressions of support, issued after the crisis had passed its peak, earned a letter of thanks from Chairman Mao, but the Chinese had noted Soviet hesitancy. It was clear that Soviet advances in nuclear technology had not tilted the balance of power sufficiently to force a settlement of the off-shore islands question. In any case the Soviet leaders were bent on achieving a *détente* with the United States.

Soviet indifference to China's problems was further demonstrated the following year during the Tibetan disturbances which led to the flight of the Dalai Lama to India. Indian sympathy for the rebels in exile and subsequent border clashes between Chinese and Indian troops caused resentment in China which was compounded by Khrushchev's refusal to place all the blame on the Indians. A Tass statement of 9 September 1959 on the border dispute was published in spite of Peking's formal request that it be withheld. Subsequently both the Chinese and the Soviets have stated that open discord between them began with the publication of this statement. But perhaps even more disturbing was the Soviet initiative for summit talks which led to Khrushchev's meeting with President Eisenhower in September 1959. On his way back from America Khrushchev visited Peking. At a banquet in his honour he attacked those who wanted to 'Test by force the stability of the capitalist system', and he asserted 'The forces of peace are now strong as never before. There are quite realistic possibilities of barring the way to war.' The Chinese were far from reconciled to this view, and continued to insist on the need for vigilance in dealing with the imperialists.

1960–65: THE BREACH WIDENS IRREVOCABLY

In April 1960 the Chinese Party began a large-scale propaganda attack on the policies and by implication the authority of the Soviet Communist Party. The Chinese argued that the line of peaceful co-existence was undermining the forces of revolution throughout the world. Paradoxically it was the Soviet Union's failure to give moral support in China's disputes with India and Indonesia which gave offence. In neither case was the position of local Communists at stake; indeed in Indonesia China was protesting against government measures against Chinese traders. The fact was that China regarded Asian states as primarily within her sphere of influence, and resented Soviet attempts to woo neutralist governments. Khrushchev's tour of South and Southeast Asia at the beginning of 1960 added to the Chinese resentment.

Chinese pressure may have had something to do with the breakdown of the Paris summit conference (May 1960), although the U2 incident was the foremost cause. It has since been disclosed that four days before the Paris meeting Mao had been invited to come to Moscow and had refused. It was decided that an attempt should be made to thrash out differences at a meeting in Bucharest (June 1960) which would be attended by delegates from all over the Communist world. Khrushchev used this occasion to rally opinion against the Chinese. Then in July the Soviets suddenly decided to withdraw all Soviet experts from China within one month. When the conference of Communist parties met at Moscow in November, the outcome was an ambiguous document (Document 20), an ingenious blend of Soviet and Chinese views.

By 1960 the problems of the Chinese economy, due in part to natural calamities and in part to the over-enthusiasm of the Great Leap Forward, made it clear that there must be some modification of policy. For agriculture this meant decentralization within the Communes. The winter of 1960–1 was particularly bitter, exacerbated by the Soviet unwillingness to help. But efficient rationing and grain purchases from abroad, notably Canada, averted famine.

In April 1961 Soviet technicians and Soviet aid were withdrawn from Albania as a punishment for supporting the Chinese at Bucharest and Moscow. The Chinese sent aid and technicians, aware that every attack on Albania was also a blow aimed at themselves. The polemics continued. It was the North Vietnamese party which took the initiative in January 1962, calling for a world Communist conference to settle the quarrel. Superficially both Moscow and Peking appeared to heed this plea and during the spring of 1962 the public recriminations were toned down in an effort to convince the West that harmony had been restored. In the event this appearance of unity was short-lived.

A further problem for the Chinese leadership was the emigration in April 1962 of a large number, certainly tens of thousands, of Chinese people. The movement may have been prompted by both economic and political difficulties. Some moved from Kwantung to Hong Kong, while others crossing the border of Sinkiang into the Soviet Union caused additional contention with Moscow. The Soviets accused Peking of creating unrest on both sides of the border and refused to repatriate the emigrés. At about the same time it became known that renewed military preparations were being made on Taiwan, the situation in Laos was causing concern and the border dispute with India was coming to a head.

In the Sino-Indian border war which erupted in October 1962, the Soviet Union remained neutral while supplying fighter aircraft to India. Temporarily Moscow appeared to be trying to placate Peking, when, on 13 and 14 October, Khrushchev suggested to the Chinese ambassador that the past should be forgotten in order to 'start our relations with a clear page'. This was followed by an editorial article in *Pravda* (25 October) sympathizing with the Chinese in their dispute with India. This posture, unique and short-lived as it was, may be explained by the imminence of the Cuban crisis which became public on 22 October. Khrushchev may have been trying to buy Chinese support. In the event Khrushchev's capitulation over Cuba was seen by Mao as proof that the Soviet Union under such leadership was not fit to head the Communist bloc. By now the antagonism was barely concealed, and in January 1963 *Pravda* was for the first time openly attacking the Chinese leaders, instead of referring to them obliquely as 'dogmatists', 'leftists' or indirectly by attributing their sins to the Albanians. The signing of the Test Ban Treaty in July 1963 appeared to confirm the extent of the breach between Peking and Moscow (Document 22). From about this time there was a change in Chinese strategy. They began to emphasize the revolutionary struggle of the oppressed peoples (see Document 23 and Document 48).

Moreover instead of pressing for unity within the Communist bloc they began to promote themselves as bearers of the true faith, and tried to win other parties to their side. The result was initially a division along geographical lines. The Asian parties except India joined with Peking, while most of the others, except Albania, joined Moscow.

In 1963-4 the Sino-Soviet boundary became a matter of open dispute. Negotiations on this issue during 1964 appear to have broken down by September. Meanwhile Soviet forces in the Far East carried out extensive manoeuvres based on the assumption of an invasion by a Chinese army from Manchuria. In October, when the Chinese were on the point of testing their first atomic bomb, Khrushchev was ousted from power (Document 25). His fall made little difference to Sino-Soviet relations. With barely a pause the polemics continued. Increasing American pressure in Indochina in 1965 far from uniting the Communist world added a source of contention (Documents 28 and 29). Peking's campaign to win support in the Third World was a main issue in 1965, while the internal conflict in China, in which Mao's opponents were coming under attack for their relatively pro-Soviet outlook, caused concern in Moscow. With the unfolding of the Cultural Revolution a new virulence was injected into Sino-Soviet relations, and the Chinese polemics took on an enhanced ideological hue, although they were intended primarily as a warning to revisionists inside China.

(a) ORIGINS

DOCUMENT 18. EXTRACTS FROM 'THE ORIGIN AND DEVELOPMENT OF THE DIFFERENCES BETWEEN THE LEADERSHIP OF THE CPSU AND OURSELVES . . .' *People's Daily*, 6 SEPTEMBER 1963 (FOREIGN LANGUAGES PRESS, PEKING, 1963)

There is a saying, 'It takes more than one cold day for the river to freeze three feet deep.' The present differences in the international communist movement did not, of course, begin just today.

The Open Letter of the Central Committee of the CPSU spreads the notion that the differences in the international communist movement were started by the three articles which we published in April 1960 under the title of 'Long Live Leninism!' This is a big lie.

What is the truth?

The truth is that the whole series of differences of principle in the international communist movement began more than seven years ago.

To be specific, it began with the 20th Congress of the CPSU in 1956.

The 20th Congress of the CPSU was the first step along the road of revisionism taken by the leadership of the CPSU. From the 20th Congress to the present, the revisionist line of the leadership of the CPSU has gone through the process of emergence, formation, growth and systematization. And by a gradual process, too, people have come to understand more and more deeply the revisionist line of the CPSU leadership.

From the very outset we held that a number of views advanced at the 20th Congress concerning the contemporary international struggle and the international communist movement were wrong, were violations of Marxism-Leninism. In particular, the complete negation of Stalin on the pretext of 'combating the personality cult' and the thesis of peaceful transition to socialism by 'the parliamentary road' are gross errors of principle.

The criticism of Stalin at the 20th Congress of the CPSU was wrong both in principle and in method.

It was necessary to criticize Stalin's mistakes. But in his secret report to the 20th Congress, Comrade Khrushchov completely negated Stalin, and in doing so defamed the dictatorship of the proletariat, defamed the socialist system, the great CPSU, the great Soviet Union and the international communist movement. Far from using a revolutionary proletarian party's method of criticism and self-criticism for the purpose of making an earnest and serious analysis and summation of the historical experience of the dictatorship of the proletariat, he treated Stalin as an enemy and shifted the blame for all mistakes on to Stalin alone. . . .

Stalin's life was that of a great Marxist-Leninist, a great proletarian revolutionary. For thirty years after Lenin's death, Stalin was the foremost leader of the CPSU and the Soviet Government, as well as the recognized leader of the international communist movement and the standard-bearer of the world revolution. During his lifetime, Stalin made some serious mistakes, but compared to his great and meritorious deeds his mistakes are only secondary....

In completely negating Stalin at the 20th Congress of the CPSU, Krushchov in effect negated the dictatorship of the proletariat and the fundamental theories of Marxism-Leninism which Stalin defended and developed. It was at that Congress that Khruschov, in his summary report, began the repudiation of Marxism-Leninism on a number of questions of principle.

In his report to the 20th Congress, under the pretext that 'radical changes' had taken place in the world situation, Khrushchov put forward the thesis of 'peaceful transition'. He said that the road of the October Revolution was 'the only correct road in those historical conditions', but that as the situation had changed, it had become possible to effect the transition from capitalism to socialism 'through the parliamentary road'. In essence, this erroneous thesis is a clear revision of the Marxist-Leninist teachings on the state and revolution and a clear denial of the universal significance of the road of the October Revolution.

In his report, under the same pretext that 'radical changes' had taken place in the world situation, Khrushchov also questioned the continued validity of Lenin's teachings on imperialism and on war and peace, and in fact tampered with Lenin's teachings.

Khrushchov pictured the US Government and its head as people resisting the forces of war, and not as representatives of the imperialist forces of war. He said, '. . . the advocates of settling outstanding issues by means of war still hold strong positions there [in the United States], and . . . they continue to exert big pressure on the President and the Administration.' He went on to say that the imperialists were beginning to admit that the positions-of-strength policy had failed and that 'symptoms of a certain sobering up are appearing' among them. It was as much as saying that it was possible for the US Government and its head not to represent the interests of the US monopoly capital and for them to abandon their policies of war and aggression and that they had become forces defending peace.

Khrushchov declared: 'We want to be friends with the United States and to co-operate with it for peace and international security and also in the economic and cultural spheres.' This wrong view later developed into the line of 'Soviet-US co-operation for the settlement of world problems'.

Distorting Lenin's correct principle of peaceful coexistence between countries with different social systems, Khrushchov declared that peaceful coexistence was the 'general line of the foreign policy' of the USSR. This amounted to excluding from the general line of foreign policy of the socialist countries their mutual assistance and co-operation as well as assistance by them to the revolutionary struggles of the oppressed peoples and nations, or to subordinating all this to the policy of so-called 'peaceful coexistence'.

The questions raised by the leadership of the CPSU at the 20th Congress, and especially the question of Stalin and of 'peaceful transition', are by no means simply internal affairs of the CPSU; they are vital issues of common interest for all fraternal Parties. Without any prior consultation with the fraternal Parties, the leadership of the CPSU drew arbitrary conclusions; it forced the fraternal Parties to accept a *fait accompli* and, on the pretext of 'combating the personality cult', crudely interfered in the internal affairs of fraternal Parties and countries and subverted their leaderships, thus pushing its policy of sectarianism and splittism in the international communist movement.

Subsequent developments show with increasing clarity that the revision and betrayal of Marxism-Leninism and proletarian internationalism by the leaders of the CPSU have grown out of the above errors. . . .

*

The meeting of representatives of Communist and workers' parties in Moscow in November 1957 was held in two parts, firstly a meeting of representatives of twelve socialist countries, which produced the Moscow Declaration; secondly a meeting of the representatives of 64 parties which adopted the Moscow Peace Manifesto.

Mao himself called for the recognition of the leadership of the

Soviet Union (appealing in particular to Gomulka of Poland who preferred to emphasize the equality of the states in the socialist bloc), in order to present a strong and united front to the United States. The Declaration upheld the real possibility of *détente* in the Cold War while recognizing that wars in the cause of anti-imperialism and socialism might be necessary. The text was a skilful blending of the Chinese and Soviet positions.

Following the unanimously agreed Declaration, Mao's 'East Wind' speech—delivered to the full session of party representatives—must have emphasized China's distinctive views, and was in contrast to the pacific tone of the Moscow Peace Manifesto adopted at the same session. The following version of Mao's speech, which was not published at the time, is from a much later article in the Chinese press. The statesman referred to is undoubtedly Nehru.

DOCUMENT 19. MAO TSE-TUNG ON THE PREVAILING EAST WIND AND THE POSSIBLE OUTCOME OF A NUCLEAR WAR, SPEECH OF 18 NOVEMBER 1957 (*Peking Review*, 6 SEPTEMBER 1963, P. 10)

Comrade Mao Tse-tung said:

'It is my opinion that the international situation has now reached a new turning point. There are two winds in the world to-day, the East wind and the West wind. There is a Chinese saying, "Either the East wind prevails over the West wind or the West wind prevails over the East wind." It is characteristic of the situation today, I believe, that the East wind is prevailing over the West wind. That is to say, the forces of socialism are overwhelmingly superior to the forces of imperialism.'

Proceeding from that estimation, Comrade Mao Tse-tung pointed to the steadily growing possibility of preventing imperialism from launching a new world war.

Comrade Mao Tse-tung then added,

'At present another situation has to be taken into account, namely, that the war maniacs may drop atomic and hydrogen bombs everywhere. They drop them and we act after their fashion; thus there will be chaos and lives will be lost. The question has to be considered for the worst. The political Bureau of our Party has held several sessions to discuss this question. If fighting breaks out now, China has got only hand-

74

grenades and not atomic bombs—which the Soviet Union has though. Let us imagine, how many people will die if war should break out? Out of the world's population of 2,700 million, one third—or, if more, half—may be lost. It is they and not we who want to fight; when a fight starts, atomic and hydrogen bombs may be dropped. I debated this question with a foreign states-man. He believed that if an atomic war was fought, the whole of mankind would be annihilated. I said that if the worst came to the worst and half of mankind died, the other half would remain while imperialism would be razed to the ground and the whole world would become socialist; in a number of years there would be 2,700 million people again and definitely more. We Chinese have not yet completed our construction and we desire peace. However, if imperialism insists on fighting a war we will have no alternative but to make up our minds and fight to the finish before going ahead with our construction. If every day you are afraid of war and war eventually comes, what will you do then? First I have said that the East wind prevails over the West wind and that war will not break out, and now I have added these explanations about the situation in case war should break out. In this way both possibilities have been taken into account.'

*

Against the background of increasing dissension between the Soviet and Chinese parties during 1960 the Chinese mounted their attack on Khrushchev's policies at the meeting of 81 Communist parties in Moscow in November 1960. The very fact that the conference had to be held was a success for Peking and showed that the Communist party of China could not be easily silenced. The conference issued a Statement which represented a compromise between the Chinese and the Soviet views.

DOCUMENT 20. EXTRACTS FROM THE STATEMENT OF EIGHTY-ONE COMMUNIST PARTIES MEETING IN MOSCOW, NOVEMBER 1960

The problem of war and peace is the most burning problem of our time.

War is a constant companion of capitalism. The system of

exploitation of man by man and the system of extermination of man by man are two aspects of the capitalist system. Imperialism has already inflicted two devastating world wars on mankind and now threatens to plunge it into an even more terrible catastrophe. Monstrous means of mass annihilation and destruction have been developed which, if used in a new war, can cause unheard-of destruction to entire countries and reduce key centres of world industry and culture to ruins. Such a war would bring death and suffering to hundreds of millions of people, among them people in countries not involved in it. Imperialism spells grave danger to the whole of mankind. . . .

The development of international relations in our day is determined by the struggle of the two social systems—the struggle of the forces of socialism, peace and democracy against the forces of imperialism, reaction and aggression—a struggle in which the superiority of the forces of socialism, peace and democracy is becoming increasingly obvious.

For the first time in history, war is opposed by great and organized forces: the mighty Soviet Union, which now leads the world in the decisive branches of science and technology; the entire socialist camp, which has placed its great material and political might at the service of peace; a growing number of peace-loving countries of Asia, Africa and Latin America, which have a vital interest in preserving peace; the international working class and its organizations, above all the Communist Parties; the national-liberation movement of the peoples of the colonies and dependent countries; the world peace movement; and the neutral countries which want no share in the imperialist policy of war and advocate peaceful coexistence. The policy of peaceful coexistence is also favoured by a definite section of the bourgeoisie of the developed capitalist countries, which takes a sober view of the relationship of forces and of the dire consequences of a modern war. The broadest possible united front of peace supporters, fighters against the imperialist policy of aggression and war inspired by US imperialism, is essential to preserve world peace. Concerted and vigorous actions of all the forces of peace can safeguard the peace and prevent a new war. . . .

The foreign policy of the socialist countries rests on the firm foundation of the Leninist principle of peaceful coexistence and economic competition between the socialist and capitalist countries. In conditions of peace, the socialist system increasingly reveals its advantages over the capitalist system in all fields of economy, culture, science and technology. The near future will bring the forces of peace and socialism new successes. The USSR will become the leading industrial power of the world. China will become a mighty industrial state. The socialist system will be turning out more than half the world industrial product. The peace zone will expand. The working-class movement in the capitalist countries and the national-liberation movement in the colonies and dependencies will achieve new victories. The disintegration of the colonial system will become completed. The superiority of the forces of socialism and peace will be absolute. *In these conditions a real possibility will have arisen to exclude world war from the life of society even before socialism achieves complete victory on earth, with capitalism still existing in a part of the world.* The victory of socialism all over the world will completely remove the social and national causes of wars.

The Communists of all the world uphold peaceful coexistence unanimously and consistently, and battle resolutely for the prevention of war. The Communists must work untiringly among the masses to prevent underestimation of the possibility of averting a world war, underestimation of the possibility of peaceful coexistence and, at the same time, underestimation of the danger of war. . . .

The policy of peaceful coexistence meets the basic interests of all peoples, launching vigorous action against the enemies of peace. Peaceful coexistence of states does not imply renunciation of the class struggle as the revisionists claim. The coexistence of states with different social systems is a form of class struggle between socialism and capitalism. In conditions of peaceful coexistence favourable opportunities are provided for the development of the class struggle in the capitalist countries and the national-liberation movement of the peoples of the colonial and dependent countries. In their turn, the successes of the revolutionary class and national-liberation struggle promote peaceful coexistence. The Communists consider it their duty to fortify the faith of the people in the possibility of furthering peaceful coexistence, their determination to prevent world war. They will do their utmost for the people to weaken imperialism and limit its sphere of action by an active struggle for peace, democracy and national liberation.

Peaceful coexistence of countries with different social systems does not mean conciliation of the socialist and bourgeois ideologies. On the contrary, it implies intensification of the struggle of the working class, of all the Communist Parties, for the triumph of socialist ideas. But ideological and political disputes between states must not be settled through war. . . .

National-liberation revolutions have triumphed in vast areas of the world. About forty new sovereign states have arisen in Asia and Africa in the fifteen post-war years. The victory of the Cuban revolution has powerfully stimulated the struggle of the Latin-American peoples for complete national independence. A new historical period has set in in the life of mankind: the peoples of Asia, Africa and Latin America that have won their freedom have begun to take an active part in world politics.

The complete collapse of colonialism is imminent. The breakdown of the system of colonial slavery under the impact of the national-liberation movement is a development ranking second in historic importance only to the formation of the world socialist system.

The Great October Socialist Revolution aroused the East and drew the colonial peoples into the common current of the world-wide revolutionary movement. This development was greatly facilitated by the Soviet Union's victory in the Second World War, the establishment of people's democracy in a number of European and Asian countries, the triumph of the socialist revolution in China, and the formation of the world socialist system. The forces of world socialism contributed decisively to the struggle of the colonial and dependent peoples for liberation from imperialist oppression. The socialist system has become a reliable shield for the independent national development of the peoples who have won freedom. The national-liberation movement receives powerful support from the international working-class movement. . . .

The choice of social system is the inalienable right of the people of each country. Socialist revolution cannot be imported, nor imposed from without. It is a result of the internal development of the country concerned, of the utmost sharpening of social contradictions in it. *The Communist Parties, which guide themselves by the Marxist-Leninist doctrine, have always been against the export of revolution. At the same time they fight resolutely against imperialist export of counter-revolution. They consider it their internationalist duty to call on the peoples of all countries to unite, to rally all their internal forces, to act vigorously and, relying on the might of the world socialist system, to prevent or firmly resist imperialist interference in the affairs of any people who have risen in revolution. . . .*

In the event of the exploiting classes resorting to violence against the people, the possibility of non-peaceful transition to socialism should be borne in mind. Leninism teaches, and experience confirms, that the ruling classes never relinquish power voluntarily. In this case the degree of bitterness and the forms of the class struggle will depend not so much on the proletariat as on the resistance put up by the reactionary circles to the will of the overwhelming majority of the people, on these circles using force at one or other stage of the struggle for socialism.

The actual possibility of the one or the other way of transition to socialism in each individual country depends on the concrete historical conditions. . . .

The Communist and Workers' Parties unanimously declare that the Communist Party of the Soviet Union has been, and remains, the universally recognized vanguard of the world Communist movement, being the most experienced and steeled contingent of the international Communist movement. The experience which the CPSU has gained in the struggle for the victory of the working class, in socialist construction and in the full-scale construction of communism, is of fundamental significance for the whole of the world Communist movement. The example of the CPSU and its fraternal solidarity inspire all the Communist Parties in their struggle for peace and socialism, and represent the revolutionary principles of proletarian internationalism applied in practice. The historic decisions of the 20th Congress of the CPSU are not only of great importance for the CPSU and communist construction in the USSR, but have initiated a new stage in the world Communist movement, and have promoted its development on the basis of Marxism-Leninism.

All Communist and Workers' Parties contribute to the development of the great theory of Marxism-Leninism. Mutual assistance and support in relations between all the fraternal Marxist-Leninist Parties embody the revolutionary principles of proletarian internationalism applied in practice.

*

(b) OPEN CONFLICT

The Chinese considered that the Soviet Union's attitude at the time of the Sino-Indian conflict in 1962 (see Part III) was biased against them.

DOCUMENT 21. EXTRACT FROM 'THE TRUTH ABOUT HOW THE LEADERS OF THE CPSU HAVE ALLIED THEMSELVES WITH INDIA AGAINST CHINA', *People's Daily*, 2 NOVEMBER, 1963 (*Peking Review*, 6, 45, 8 NOVEMBER 1963, PP. 18–27)

On October 8, 1962, a Chinese leader told the Soviet Ambassador that China had information that India was about to launch a massive attack along the Sino-Indian border and that should India attack we would resolutely defend ourselves. He also pointed out that the fact that Soviet-made helicopters and transport planes were being used by India for airdropping and transporting military supplies in the Sino-Indian border areas was making a bad impression on our frontier guards and that we deemed it our internationalist duty to inform the Soviet side of the situation.

On October 13 and 14, 1962, Khrushchov told the Chinese Ambassador the following: Their information on Indian preparations to attack China was similar to China's. If they were in China's position, they would have taken the same measures. A neutral attitude on the Sino-Indian boundary question was impossible. If anyone attacked China and they said they were neutral, it would be an act of betrayal.

On October 20, 1962, the Indian reactionaries launched a massive attack on China. On October 25, *Pravda* carried an editorial pointing out that the notorious McMahon Line was imposed on the Chinese and Indian peoples and had never been recognized by China. It said that the three proposals put forward by the Chinese Government in its statement of

October 24 were constructive and constituted an acceptable basis for opening negotiations and settling the dispute between China and India peacefully.

On December 12, 1962, forgetting everything he had said less than two months earlier, Khrushchov reverted to his original tune and made the following insinuations at a session of the Supreme Soviet of the USSR: The areas disputed by China and India were sparsely populated and of little value to human life. The Soviet Union could not possibly entertain the thought that India wanted to start a war with China. The Soviet Union adhered to Lenin's views on boundary disputes. Her experience over 45 years proved that there was no boundary dispute which could not be solved without resorting to arms. Of course, it was good that China had unilaterally ordered a ceasefire and withdrawn its troops; but would it not have been better if the Chinese troops had not advanced from their original positions?

By publishing the article of the *Pravda* Editorial Board on September 19, 1963, the Soviet leaders discarded all camouflage and openly sided with the US imperialists in supporting the Indian reactionaries against socialist China.

It is clear from the above facts that China has done her utmost to eliminate the Sino-Soviet differences on the Sino-Indian boundary question. But the leaders of the CPSU have persisted in their attitude of great-power chauvinism, acted arrogantly and turned a deaf ear to China's opinions. They brought the Sino-Soviet differences into the open in order to create the so-called Camp David spirit and make a ceremonial gift to the US imperialists. During the Caribbean crisis, they spoke a few seemingly fair words out of considerations of expediency. But when the crisis was over they went back on their words. They have sided with the Indian reactionaries against China all the time. As facts show, the stand taken by the leaders of the CPSU is a complete betrayal of proletarian internationalism.

*

Mao, in a conversation with the American correspondent Anna Louise Strong in 1946, said that the atom bomb was a paper tiger which the US reactionaries use to scare people. He believed that men and not weapons, however terrible they might be, would decide the future. It could be argued, as Mao did at Moscow (Document 19) that in the event of a nuclear war the effect on China would be relatively less disastrous than on certain other countries. Nevertheless the leaders of the People's Republic had reason to ponder seriously on the effects of nuclear war. On several occasions they were reminded of America's power to subject them to nuclear punishment. In February 1953, in an attempt to break the deadlock in the Korean peace talks, the new Eisenhower administration threatened to extend the war to the mainland of China and to use nuclear weapons. In March 1955, during the Taiwan Strait crisis, Dulles stated that 'open armed aggression' by China would be met with tactical nuclear weapons. At one stage of the 1958 Quemoy crisis the United States was, according to Eisenhower's memoirs, prepared to use nuclear weapons to defend Quemoy. It is not surprising that the Chinese attached great importance to the nuclear striking power of their Soviet ally.

At first the Chinese appeared to consider the possibility of forgoing their own nuclear programme in return for increased Soviet aid. By 1958, less certain of the reliability of their ally, the Chinese began to press the development of their own atom bomb with all speed. In June 1958 Mao said that he considered it possible for China to make her own nuclear weapons within ten years. The Chinese claimed later (15 August 1963) that in October 1957 the Soviets agreed to provide them with 'a sample of an atomic bomb and technical data concerning its manufacture', only to cancel the agreement in June 1959.

In 1962-3 the negotiations for a partial test-ban treaty by the United States, Britain and the Soviet Union brought protests from the Chinese government that this was a betrayal of the cause of socialism 'aimed at depriving the Chinese people of their right to take steps to resist the nuclear threats of US imperialism . . .'. When the treaty was signed in July 1963, the Chinese were quick to make their views known.

DOCUMENT 22. EXTRACTS FROM CHINESE GOVERNMENT STATEMENT ON TEST BAN TREATY, 31 JULY 1963 (*Peking Review*, 6, 31, 2 AUGUST 1963, PP. 7–8)

A treaty on the partial halting of nuclear tests was initialled by the representatives of the United States, Britain and the Soviet Union in Moscow on July 25.

This is a treaty signed by three nuclear powers. By this treaty they attempt to consolidate their nuclear monopoly and bind the hands of all the peace-loving countries subjected to the nuclear threat.

This treaty signed in Moscow is a big fraud to fool the people of the world. It runs diametrically counter to the wishes of the peace-loving people of the world. . . .

Clearly, this treaty has no restraining effect on the US policies of nuclear war preparation and nuclear blackmail. It in no way hinders the United States from proliferating nuclear weapons, expanding nuclear armament or making nuclear threats. The central purpose of this treaty is, through a partial ban on nuclear tests, to prevent all the threatened peace-loving countries, including China, from increasing their defence capability, so that the United States may be more unbridled in threatening and blackmailing these countries. . . .

The treaty just signed is a reproduction of the draft treaty on a partial nuclear test ban put forward by the United States and Britain at the meeting of the Disarmament Commission in Geneva on August 27, 1962. On August 29, 1962, the Head of the Soviet Delegation, Kuznetsov, pointed out that the obvious aim of the United States and Britain in putting forward that draft was to provide the Western powers with one-sided military advantage to the detriment of the interests of the Soviet Union and other Socialist countries. He pointed out that the United States had been using underground tests to improve its nuclear weapons for many years already, and that should underground nuclear tests be legalized with a simultaneous prohibition of such tests in the atmosphere, this would mean that the United States could continue improving its nuclear weapons and increase their yield and effectivity. The Head of the Soviet Government Khrushchev also pointed out on September 9, 1961, that 'the programme of developing new types of nuclear weapons which has been drawn up in the United States now requires precisely underground tests', and that 'an agreement to cease only one type of testing, in the atmosphere, would be a poor service to peace; it would deceive the peoples.'

But now the Soviet Government has made a 180-degree about-face, discarded the correct stand they once persisted in and accepted this reproduction of the US-British draft treaty, willingly allowing US imperialism to gain military superiority. Thus the interests of the Soviet people have been sold out, the interests of the people of the countries in the Socialist camp, including the people of China, have been sold out, and the interests of all peace-loving people of the world have been sold out. . . .

Why should the Soviet leaders so anxiously need such a treaty? Is this a proof of what they call victory for the policy of peaceful co-existence? No! This is by no means a victory for the policy of peaceful co-existence. It is a capitulation to US imperialism.

The US imperialists and their partners are with one voice advertising everywhere that the signing of a treaty on the partial halting of nuclear tests by them is the first step towards the complete prohibition of nuclear weapons. This is deceitful talk. The United States has already stockpiled large quantities of nuclear weapons, which are scattered in various parts of the world and seriously threaten the security of all peoples. If the United States really will take the first step towards the prohibition of nuclear weapons, why does it not remove its nuclear threat to other countries? Why does it not undertake to refrain from using nuclear weapons against non-nuclear countries and to respect the desire of the people of the world to establish nuclear weapon-free zones? And why does it not undertake in all circumstances to refrain from handing over to its allies its nuclear weapons and the data for their manufacture? On what grounds can the United States and its partners maintain that the United States may use nuclear threat and blackmail against others and pursue policies of aggression and war, while others may not take measures to resist such threat and blackmail and defend their own independence and freedom? To give the aggressors the right to kill while denying the victims of aggression the right to self-defence—is this not like the Chinese saying: 'The magistrate may burn down houses but the ordinary people cannot even light their lamps'? ...

The Chinese Government holds that the prohibition of nuclear weapons and the prevention of nuclear war are major questions affecting the destiny of the world, which should be discussed and decided on jointly by all the countries of the world, big and small. Manipulation of the destiny of more than one hundred non-nuclear countries by a few nuclear powers will not be tolerated.

The Chinese Government holds that on such important issues as the prohibition of nuclear weapons and the prevention of nuclear war, it is impermissible to adopt the method of deluding the people of the world. It should be affirmed unequivocally that nuclear weapons must be completely banned and thoroughly destroyed and that practical and effective measures must be taken so as to realize step by step the complete prohibition and thorough destruction of nuclear weapons, prevent nuclear war and safeguard world peace.

For these reasons, the Government of the People's Republic of China hereby proposes the following:

(1) All countries in the world, both nuclear and non-nuclear, solemnly declare that they will prohibit and destroy nuclear weapons completely, thoroughly, totally and resolutely. Concretely speaking, they will not use nuclear weapons, nor export, nor manufacture, nor test, nor stockpile them; and they will destroy all the existing establishments for the research, testing and manufacture of nuclear weapons in the world.

(2) In order to fulfil the above undertakings step by step, the following measures shall be adopted first:

(a) Dismantle all military bases, including nuclear bases, on foreign soil, and withdraw from abroad all nuclear weapons and their means of delivery.

(b) Establish a nuclear weapon-free zone of the Asian and Pacific region, including the United States, the Soviet Union, China and Japan; a nuclear weapon-free zone of Central Europe; a nuclear weapon-free zone of Africa; and a nuclear weapon-free zone of Latin America. The countries possessing nuclear weapons shall undertake due obligations with regard to each of the nuclear weapon-free zones.

(c) Refrain from exporting and importing in any form nuclear weapons and technical data for their manufacture.

(d) Cease all nuclear tests, including underground nuclear tests.

(3) A conference of the government heads of all the countries of the world shall be convened to discuss the question of the complete prohibition and thorough destruction of nuclear weapons and the question of taking the above-mentioned four measures in order to realize step by step the complete prohibition and thorough destruction of nuclear weapons.

The Chinese Government and people are deeply convinced that nuclear weapons can be prohibited, nuclear war can be prevented and world peace can be preserved. We call upon the countries in the Socialist camp and all the peace-loving countries and people of the world to unite and fight unswervingly to the end for the complete, thorough, total and resolute prohibition and destruction of nuclear weapons and for the defence of world peace.

*

By 1963 China was openly proclaiming a different line from that of the Soviet Union on the question of revolutionary struggles against imperialism. The attack on 'certain persons' (Khrushchev and the Soviet leaders) must undoubtedly be viewed in the light of the Sino-Soviet dispute and of Peking's claim to be leading the cause of the 'oppressed' peoples of the world (Document 48), but it may also reflect the particular ideological concerns of Mao and his followers in China on matters on which the Chinese leadership was not entirely of one mind.

DOCUMENT 23. EXTRACTS FROM 'CCP'S PROPOSAL CONCERNING THE GENERAL LINE OF THE INTERNATIONAL COMMUNIST MOVEMENT', 14 JUNE 1963 (*Peking Review*, 6, 25, 21 JUNE 1963, PP. 6–22)

Certain persons have one-sidedly exaggerated the role of peaceful competition between socialist and imperialist countries in their attempt to substitute peaceful competition for the revolutionary struggles of the oppressed peoples and nations. According to their preaching, it would seem that imperialism will automatically collapse in the course of this peaceful competition and that the only thing the oppressed peoples and nations have to do is to wait quietly for the advent of this day. What does this have in common with Marxist-Leninist views?

Moreover, certain persons have concocted the strange tale that China and some other socialist countries want 'to unleash wars' and to spread socialism by 'wars between states'. As the Statement of 1960 points out, such tales are nothing but imperialist and reactionary slanders. To put it bluntly, the purpose of those who repeat these slanders is to hide the fact that they are opposed to revolutions by the oppressed peoples and nations of the world and opposed to others supporting such revolutions. . . .

As Marxist-Leninists see it, war is the continuation of politics by other means, and every war is inseparable from the political system and the political struggles which give rise to it. If one departs from this scientific Marxist-Leninist proposition which has been confirmed by the entire history of class struggle, one will never be able to understand either the question of war or the question of peace.

There are different types of peace and different types of war. Marxist-Leninists must be clear about what type of peace or what type of war is in question. Lumping just wars and unjust wars together and opposing all of them undiscriminatingly is a bourgeois pacifist and not a Marxist-Leninist approach.

Certain persons say that revolutions are entirely possible without war. Now which type of war are they referring to—is it a war of national liberation or a revolutionary civil war, or is it a world war?

If they are referring to a war of national liberation or a revolutionary civil war, then this formulation is, in effect, opposed to revolutionary wars and to revolution.

If they are referring to a world war, then they are shooting at a non-existent target. Although Marxist-Leninists have pointed out, on the basis of the history of the two world wars, that world wars inevitably lead to revolution, no Marxist-Leninist ever has held or ever will hold that revolution must be made through world war. . . .

Lenin's principle of peaceful co-existence is very clear and readily comprehensible by ordinary people. Peaceful co-existence designates a relationship between countries with different social systems, and must not be interpreted as one pleases. It should never be extended to apply to the relations between oppressed and oppressor nations, between oppressed and oppressor countries or between oppressed and oppressor classes, and never be described as the main content of the transition from capitalism to socialism, still less should it be asserted that peaceful co-existence is mankind's road to socialism. The reason is that it is one thing to practise peaceful co-existence between countries with different social systems. It is absolutely impermissible and impossible for countries practising peaceful co-existence to touch even a hair of each other's social system. The class struggle, the struggle for national liberation and the transition from capitalism to socialism in various countries are quite another thing. They are all bitter, life-and-death revolutionary struggles which aim at changing the social system. Peaceful co-existence cannot replace the revolutionary struggles of the people. The transition from capitalism to socialism in any country can only be brought about through the proletarian revolution and the dictatorship of the proletariat in that country.

In the application of the policy of peaceful co-existence, struggles between the socialist and imperialist countries are unavoidable in the political, economic and ideological spheres, and it is absolutely impossible to have 'all-round-co-operation'.

It is necessary for the socialist countries to engage in negotiations of one kind or another with the imperialist countries. It is possible to reach certain agreements through negotiation by relying on the correct policies of the socialist countries and on the pressure of the people of all countries. But necessary compromises between socialist countries and the imperialist countries do not require the oppressed peoples and nations to follow suit and compromise with imperialism and its lackeys. No one should ever demand in the name of peaceful co-existence that the oppressed peoples and nations should give up their revolutionary struggles. . . .

In our view, the general line of the foreign policy of the socialist countries should have the following content: to develop relations of friendship, mutual assistance and co-operation among the countries in the socialist camp in accordance with the principle of proletarian internationalism; to strive for peaceful co-existence on the basis of the Five Principles with countries having different social systems and oppose the imperialist policies of aggression and war; and to support and assist the revolutionary struggles of all the oppressed peoples and nations. These three aspects are interrelated and indivisible, and not a single one can be omitted.

*

Chinese views on revolutionary wars and China's stand on nuclear weapons were both attacked in an article by I. I. Yermashev, which appeared in the restricted-circulation Soviet General Staff journal.

DOCUMENT 24. EXTRACTS FROM 'THE PEKING VERSION OF "TOTAL STRATEGY"' *Voennaya mysl'* (MILITARY THOUGHT), NO. 10, OCTOBER 1963 (R. L. GARTOFF, (ED) *Sino-Soviet Military Relations*, PRAEGER, NEW YORK, 1966, APPENDIX D)

Mao Tse-tung blandly declared that, in case of world nuclear war, in his opinion half the population of our planet, or perhaps more than half, would perish. What does that mean, half? That is one and a third to one and a half billion people! And what conclusion did the leader of the CCP draw from his calculations? Did he express alarm over the fact that the imperialists are preparing for mankind a bloody war of unprecedented scale? No! On the contrary, he distinctly left one to understand that he considered such a 'development' completely acceptable for socialism. He set forth his point of view with an equanimity to the fate of *over a billion people*, mainly workers, impermissible for a Communist, and still more for a leader of the party. In his speech he said: '. . . If half of mankind is destroyed, then half will remain, while imperialism will be completely destroyed and there will be only socialism in the whole world, and in half a century or a century the population will again grow even more than that half.'

Mao Tse-tung in essence called for a world nuclear war, presuming that it would have its 'favorable' side: the hydrogen bomb in 'one blow' would decide the main contradiction of our epoch—the contradiction between the world system of socialism and the system of capitalism. And that thought is in fact propagated by the Chinese leaders and the Chinese press today too, advancing it at the same time in crying contradiction with their own evaluation, since despite elementary logic they contend that the might of nuclear weapons is, as it were, exaggerated. Thus, on the one hand the thermonuclear weapon would cause at least half the population of the world to perish, while on the other hand it is a 'paper tiger'. It's not worth searching for logic in the Chinese 'theoreticians'; they just haven't got it. . . .

But why is the top leadership of the CCP so rabid to tear off after the nuclear weapon? After all, not a single socialist state except China considers it necessary to have its 'own' nuclear weapons, considering entirely correctly that the power of the Soviet nuclear forces reliably protects the entire socialist camp from attack. The leaders of the CCP do not believe in fraternal friendship with the other socialist countries and do not value this friendship, orienting themselves only on 'their own strength'. They consider that world thermonuclear war is inevitable and, attempting to hurry it along, they evidently suppose that the Chinese people will have the best chance since they are the most populous people on the earth. In case of the destruction of the majority of the peoples of the world [*sic*] and their states, their culture (and this, in the language of the Peking political hysterics, is called 'the fall of imperialism') there would remain, in their opinion, the epoch of world domination by people of the yellow race. The Peking leaders have already come to terms with the idea of dividing people by race, by the color of their skin rather than by class, social characteristics. Thus they have entered the path leading into the swamp of racism, with all of the consequences that flow from that. The Peking version of 'total strategy' is the fruit of the reactionary utopia of the leaders of the CCP, who have broken with Marxism-Leninism.

When one acquaints himself closely with the theories of the Peking leaders and their practical activity in the international arena, it becomes clear that they put in first place not the interests of the peoples struggling for peace, socialism, and national liberation, but their own great power aims. When they call on the peoples not to consider the concrete situation, not to consider the potentiality and consequences of thermonuclear war, the true aims of the Chinese leaders stand all the further away from the interests of the struggle for the development of the international Communist movement, for the victory of socialism in all countries of the globe.

*

Even without Soviet help the Chinese were making remarkable progress in developing their own nuclear weapons. The Chinese exploded their first atomic bomb on 16 October 1964—the day after Khrushchev was ousted from power. It has been suggested that Khrushchev had toyed with the idea of using missiles to destroy China's nuclear installations. Whatever truth, if any, there may be in such conjectures, it is likely that Khrushchev's China policy was a major factor in his downfall.

DOCUMENT 25. THE CHINESE NUCLEAR TEST AND THE FALL OF KHRUSHCHEV (H. C. HINTON, *Communist China in World Politics*, MACMILLAN, LONDON, 1966, PP. 478–83)

For the events that were to happen later, at least a plausible explanation is that Khrushchev decided about this time, probably in July [1964], to knock out the CPR's nuclear weapons installations with a missile strike, probably with nonnuclear warheads. This would be done after the first Chinese nuclear test, so as to have as much justification as possible. It has been reported by a reputable source that Governor Harriman had suggested some such procedure to Khrushchev at the time of the test ban negotiations. Certainly this way of dealing with the problem, which has been described by an American journalist as no more difficult than performing a tonsillectomy, would have been much more effective than another method that Khrushchev was reported to have considered, that of destroying the installations by means of a raid by dissident Kazakhs. If Khrushchev in fact formulated such a plan, it is easy to understand the thinking that lay behind a subsequent charge made by Jacques Grippa, a Belgian Communist very close to the CPC, that Khrushchev had made a 'threat of military aggression against the CPR.'

As will be indicated later, there is reason to think that some of Khrushchev's colleagues were aware of his plan, objected to it as an example of 'harebrained scheming,' and conveyed a warning to the CPR. The latter had very few ways of deterring Khrushchev, apart from the obvious but unacceptable option of abandoning any idea of holding a nuclear test. The most obvious form of deterrence was a threat to invade Outer Mongolia, the only one of the Asian Communist countries the dominant faction of whose leadership had consistently supported the Soviet Union in its quarrel with the CPR. The loss of Outer Mongolia, with which the Soviet Union had had an alliance since 1936, would deprive the Soviet Union of much of the credibility of its claim to speak as an Asian power.

Relations between the CPR and Outer Mongolia . . . had been deteriorating since early 1963. In the spring of 1964, Outer Mongolia ordered the remaining Chinese technicians out. Soon afterward the CPR imposed a boycott on trade with Outer Mongolia, and by September it was being reported from Yugoslav sources that the CPR was concentrating troops along the Sino-Mongolian border. Outer Mongolian sources denied rather unconvincingly that they had any information on such troop concentrations.

Yumzhaagin Tsedenbal, the Outer Mongolian leader, who had been a frequent visitor to the Soviet Union for several years past, especially during the summer campaigning season, continued this practice in 1964. . . .

Tsedenbal talked with Mikoyan in Moscow on July 21. On August 23, Tsedenbal held a 'friendly and cordial conversation' with Khrushchev in the Crimea. This was the twenty-fifth anniversary of the Hitler-Stalin pact, which Stalin had concluded partly in order to free his hands in the west for the time being and turn his full attention to the Japanese invasion of Outer Mongolia that was then in progress. The analogy with the present is obvious: Tsedenbal probably urged Khrushchev either to put his European concerns on ice for the time being and come to the defense of Outer Mongolia as Stalin had or, better still, to drop his 'harebrained scheming' and thereby relieve the Chinese pressure on Outer Mongolia. A few days later, while Khrushchev was in Czechoslovakia, Tsedenbal visited Moscow again and held talks with other Soviet leaders.

A week after the Soviet Union published its attack on Mao's statement to the Japanese Socialists, Outer Mongolia did the same. The Mongolian statement accused the CPR of trying to annex Outer Mongolia and praised the Soviet Union as 'our true, unselfish friend and reliable protector.' ...

Secretary Rusk's announcement of September 29, which was evidently based on American satellite reconnaissance, that the CPR would soon conduct its first nuclear test, perhaps on October 1, probably brought the tension in Moscow to a peak. But no test occurred on October 1, or for about two weeks thereafter. If Khrushchev was planning to destroy the CPR's atomic installations after the first test, and if the CPR was aware of that fact, it obviously would not have tested while Khrushchev was still in power. On October 2, it was announced in Moscow that a new economic plan had just been decided on in accordance with Khrushchev's preference for stressing investment in agriculture and consumer good, not defense. Evidently Khrushchev believed that with his existing strategic forces he could manage the Chinese nuclear problem, and if necessary the Sino-Soviet border dispute as well, without disrupting his economic planning by large new investments in conventional military forces, such as his ground generals were probably urging him to make in view of the deteriorating state of Sino-Soviet relations. ...

It is abundantly evident that if Khrushchev was in fact planning to destroy the Chinese nuclear installations, and if the Chinese were threatening to retaliate by invading Outer Mongolia, some at least of those of Khrushchev's colleagues who were aware of the situation must have considered this to be a classic example of 'harebrained scheming.' The 'unity' of the 'socialist camp' would be shattered beyond repair. If they protested, as they probably did, it is clear that their protests were to no avail. The only solution as with Stalin in February, 1953, was to remove the dangerous leader with the minimum necessary use of force.

The first overt indication that important changes in the Soviet hierarchy might be in the making came on July 18, three days after Mao's interview with the Japanese Socialists, when Leonid Brezhnev gave up his time-consuming figurehead position as Chairman of the Praesidium of the Supreme Soviet, probably in order to devote all his time to work within the Praesidium and Secretariat of the CPSU.

On September 30, the eve of the CPR's National Day, Khrushchev left for another vacation in the Crimea. In paying this insult to the CPR he evidently felt sure that his plans were in order, and he can have had no serious suspicion that anything was afoot against him in Moscow.

On October 7, East Germany celebrated the fifteenth anniversary of the inauguration of its Communist regime. The chief Soviet delegate was Brezhnev; the chief Chinese delegate was Ulanfu, a Mongol and the CPR's leading specialist in the affairs of both Inner and Outer Mongolia. The chief Outer Mongolian delegate was of course Tsedenbal who had stopped in Moscow on his way to East Berlin. After the celebration Tsedenbal had discussions with Ulbricht and rather ostentatiously decorated a Soviet tank unit stationed in East Germany, to the accompaniment of loud talk about the Soviet Union as the protector of Outer Mongolia. It was probably at about this time that the news of the plot to overthrow Khrushchev was disseminated among the handful of Communist leaders including Tsedenbal who needed to know.

Khrushchev was evidently ousted from the Praesidium and Secretariat, in his absence, on the night of October 12, and from the Central Committee, by a rump meeting of that body, on October 15. His removal as Chairman of the Council of the Ministers (i.e. Premier) was evidently also arranged on October 15. Those who engineered his ouster were probably aware that October 12 was the tenth anniversary of an agreement by which Khrushchev had promised to give the CPR scientific and technological aid with a supposedly peaceful nuclear program, and that October 15 was the seventh anniversary of his agreement to give the CPR at least token aid with the construction of nuclear weapons, as well as the first anniversary of the coming into force of the test ban treaty. The irony of Khrushchev's relationship to the CPR's nuclear weapons program was that he had given it valuable, probably indispensable, aid, but he had soon regretted having done so and had pushed his efforts to undo his own mistake, as he now considered it, to the brink of war. This was certainly an example of 'harebrained scheming.'

Once Khrushchev's fall had been accomplished and announced, it was safe for the CPR to conduct its nuclear test. This it did, secure in the knowledge that there would be no tonsillectomy, on October 16.

*

The fall of Khrushchev was followed by a temporary lull in the dispute. Chou En-lai led a Chinese delegation to Moscow for the anniversary of the 1917 October Revolution, 7 November 1964. It is believed that the Soviets raised the possibility of increasing aid to China and also to North Korea and North Vietnam. In return for Soviet aid the Chinese were expected to co-operate at least to the extent of ceasing public polemics against Khrushchev's successors. It is possible that some of the Chinese leaders favoured the acceptance of the Soviet proposals, but it is certain that Mao himself objected to them probably for domestic as well as external reasons. An editorial in *Red Flag* reviewed Soviet policy under Khrushchev and indicated that it was up to the new Soviet leaders to decide whether they would take a new path.

DOCUMENT 26. EXTRACT FROM 'WHY KHRUSHCHEV FELL', EDITORIAL ARTICLE, *Red Flag*, 21 NOVEMBER 1964 (*Peking Review* 7, 48, 28 NOVEMBER 1964, PP. 6–9)

Khrushchev has fallen.

This arch-schemer who usurped the leadership of the Soviet Party and state, this Number One representative of modern revisionism, has finally been driven off the stage of history.

This is a very good thing and is advantageous to the revolutionary cause of the people of the world.

The collapse of Khrushchev is a great victory for the Marxist-Leninists of the world in their persistent struggle against revisionism. It marks the bankruptcy, the fiasco, of modern revisionism.

How was it that Khrushchev fell? Why couldn't he muddle on any longer? . . .

People may list hundreds or even thousands of charges against Khrushchev to account for his collapse. But the most important one of all is that he has vainly tried to obstruct the advance of history, flying in the face of the law of historical development as discovered by Marxism-Leninism and of the revolutionary will of the people of the Soviet Union and the whole world. Any obstacle on the people's road of advance must be removed. The people were sure to reject Khrushchev, whether he and his kind liked it or not. Khrushchev's downfall is the inevitable result of the anti-revisionist struggle waged staunchly by the people of the Soviet Union and revolutionary people throughout the world.

Ours is an epoch in which world capitalism and imperialism are moving down to their doom and socialism and communism are marching towards victory. . . . This historical trend is an objective law which operates independently of man's will, and it is irresistible. But Khrushchev, this buffoon on the contemporary political stage, chose to go against this trend in the vain hope of turning the wheel of history back on to the old capitalist road and of thus prolonging the life of the moribund exploiting classes and their moribund system of exploitation. . . .

In the last eleven years, exploiting the prestige of the Communist Party of the Soviet Union and of the first socialist country that had been built up under the leadership of Lenin and Stalin, Khrushchev committed all the bad things he possibly could in contravention of the genuine will of the Soviet people. These bad things may be summed up as follows:

1 On the pretext of 'combating the personality cult' and using the most scurrilous language, he railed at Stalin, the leader of the Communist Party of the Soviet Union and the Soviet people. In opposing Stalin, he opposed Marxism-Leninism. He tried at one stroke to write off all the great achievements of the Soviet people in the entire period under Stalin's leadership in order to defame the dictatorship of the proletariat, the socialist system, the great Soviet Communist Party, the great Soviet Union and the international communist movement. In so doing, Khrushchev provided the imperialists and the reactionaries of all countries with the dirtiest of weapons for their anti-Soviet and anti-Communist activities.

2 In open violation of the Declaration of 1957 and the Statement of 1960, he sought 'all-round co-operation' with US imperialism and fallaciously maintained that the heads of the

Soviet Union and the United States would 'decide the fate of humanity,' constantly praising the chieftains of US imperialism as 'having a sincere desire for peace.' Pursuing an adventurist policy at one moment, he transported guided missiles to Cuba, and pursuing a capitulationist policy at another, he docilely withdrew the missiles and bombers from Cuba on the order of the US pirates. He accepted inspection by the US fleet and even tried to sell out Cuba's sovereignty by agreeing, behind the Cuban Government's back, to the 'inspection' of Cuba by the United Nations, which is under US control. In so doing, Khrushchev brought a humiliating disgrace upon the great Soviet people unheard of in the forty years and more since the October Revolution.

3 To cater to the US imperialist policy of nuclear blackmail and prevent socialist China from building up her own nuclear strength for self-defence, he did not hesitate to damage the defence capabilities of the Soviet Union itself and concluded the so-called partial nuclear test ban treaty in collusion with the two imperialist powers of the United States and Britain. Facts have shown that this treaty is a pure swindle. In signing this treaty Khrushchev perversely tried to sell out the interests of the Soviet people, the people of all the socialist countries and all the peace-loving people of the world.

4 In the name of 'peaceful transition' he tried by every means to obstruct the revolutionary movements of the people in the capitalist countries, demanding that they take the so-called legal, parliamentary road. This erroneous line paralyses the revolutionary will of the proletariat and disarms the revolutionary people ideologically, causing serious setbacks to the cause of revolution in certain countries. It has made the Communist Parties in a number of capitalist countries lifeless social-democratic parties of a new type and caused them to degenerate into servile tools of the bourgeoisie.

5 Under the signboard of 'peaceful coexistence' he did his utmost to oppose and sabotage the national-liberation movement and went so far as to work hand in glove with US imperialism in suppressing the revolutionary struggles of the oppressed nations. He instructed the Soviet delegate at the United Nations to vote for the dispatch of forces of aggression to the Congo, which helped the US imperialists to suppress

the Congolese people, and he used Soviet transport facilities to move these so-called United Nations troops to the Congo. He actually opposed the revolutionary struggles of the Algerian people, describing the Algerian national-liberation struggle as an 'internal affair' of France. He had the audacity to 'stand aloof' over the events in the Gulf of Bac Bo [Tonkin Gulf] engineered by US imperialism against Viet Nam and cudgelled his brains for ways to help the US provocateurs get out of their predicament and to whitewash the criminal aggression of the US pirates.

6 In brazen violation of the Statement of 1960, he spared no effort to reverse its verdict on the renegade Tito clique, describing Tito who had degenerated into a lackey of US imperialism as a 'Marxist-Leninist' and Yugoslavia which had degenerated into a capitalist country as a 'socialist country.' Time and again he declared that he and the Tito clique had 'the same ideology' and were 'guided by the same theory' and expressed his desire to learn modestly from this renegade who had betrayed the interests of the Yugoslav people and sabotaged the international communist movement.

7 He regarded Albania, a fraternal socialist country, as his sworn enemy, devising every possible means to injure and undermine it, and only wishing he could devour it in one gulp. He brazenly broke off all economic and diplomatic relations with Albania, arbitrarily deprived it of its legitimate rights as a member state in the Warsaw Treaty Organization and in the Council of Mutual Economic Assistance, and publicly called for the overthrow of its Party and state leadership.

8 He nourished an inveterate hatred for the Communist Party of China which upholds Marxism-Leninism and a revolutionary line, because the Chinese Communist Party was a great obstacle to his effort to press on with revisionism and capitulationism. He spread innumerable rumours and slanders against the Chinese Communist Party and Comrade Mao Tsetung and resorted to every kind of baseness in his futile attempt to subvert socialist China. He perfidiously tore up several hundred agreements and contracts and arbitrarily withdrew more than one thousand Soviet experts working in China. He engineered border disputes between China and the Soviet Union and even conducted large-scale subversive activities in

Sinkiang. He backed the reactionaries of India in their armed attacks on socialist China and, together with the United States, incited and helped them to perpetrate armed provocations against China by giving them military aid. . . .

Khrushchev has fallen and the revisionist line he enthusiastically pursued is discredited, but Marxism-Leninism will continue to overcome the revisionist trend and forge ahead, and the revolutionary movement of the people of all countries will continue to sweep away the obstacles in its path and surge forward.

Nevertheless, the course of history will continue to be tortuous. Although Khrushchev has fallen his supporters—the US imperialists, the reactionaries and the modern revisionists —will not resign themselves to this failure. These hobgoblins are continuing to pray for Khrushchev and are trying to 'resurrect' him with their incantations, vociferously proclaiming his 'contributions' and 'meritorious deeds' in the hope that events will develop along the lines prescribed by Khrushchev, so that 'Khrushchevism without Khrushchev' may prevail. It can be asserted categorically that theirs is a blind alley.

Different ideological trends and their representatives invariably strive to take the stage and perform. It is entirely up to them to decide which direction they will take. But there is one point on which we have not the slightest doubt. History will develop in accordance with the laws discovered by Marxism-Leninism; it will march forward along the road of the October Revolution. Beyond all doubt, the great Communist Party of the Soviet Union and the great Soviet people, with their revolutionary traditions, are fully capable of making new contributions in safeguarding the great socialist achievements, the lofty prestige of the first socialist power founded by Lenin, the purity of Marxism-Leninism and the victorious advance of the revolutionary cause of the proletariat.

Let the international communist movement unite on the basis of Marxism-Leninism and proletarian internationalism!

*

A proposal by the Soviet Central Committee led to a meeting of the drafting committee of twenty-six communist parties in

Moscow in March 1965 with the object of preparing for a full assembly of the communist parties. The meeting was poorly attended and was not a success. The Chinese, who had refused to attend, described the meeting as 'a gloomy and forlorn affair'. The meeting produced a statement on Vietnam calling for 'united action' to support the Vietnamese people. In rejecting this appeal the Chinese argued that the policies of the new Soviet leaders were as revisionist as those of Khrushchev, and that Soviet revisionism was the ally of US imperialism.

DOCUMENT 27. EXTRACT FROM 'REFUTATION OF THE NEW LEADERS OF THE CPSU ON "UNITED ACTION" ', EDITORIAL ARTICLE, *People's Daily*, 11 NOVEMBER 1965 (*Peking Review*, 8, 46, 12 NOVEMBER 1965, PP. 10-21)

Persevere in the Struggle Against Khrushchev Revisionism

A fierce struggle is going on between the revolutionary people of the world on the one hand and the imperialists headed by the United States and their lackeys on the other. The characteristic of the present world situation is that with the daily deepening of the international class struggle, a process of great upheaval, great division and great reorganization is taking place. The revolutionary movement of the people of the world is surging vigorously forward. Imperialism and all other decadent reactionary forces are putting up a wild death-bed fight. Drastic divisions and realignments of political forces are taking place on a world scale. . . .

As the struggle against the United States reaches a crucial phase, US imperialism needs the services of Khrushchev revisionism all the more acutely. Hence it is inevitable that the struggle against Khrushchev revisionism must sharpen.

In the course of combating Khrushchev revisionism, there is bound to be a certain unevenness in the degree of people's understanding of the struggle. This kind of phenomenon becomes particularly conspicuous when the struggle becomes sharp. That is both natural and inevitable. Lenin said that when astonishingly abrupt changes took place, people 'who were suddenly confronted with extremely important problems could not long remain on this level. They could not continue without a respite, without a return to elementary questions, without a new training which would help them "digest" lessons of unparalleled richness and make it possible for incomparably wider masses again to march forward, but now far more firmly more consciously, more confidently and more steadfastly.' Just such a situation exists at present.

As the struggle against Khrushchev revisionism becomes sharper and deeper, a new process of division will inevitably occur in the revolutionary ranks, and some people will inevitably drop out. But at the same time hundreds of millions of revolutionary people will stream in. . . .

In the final analysis, in all parts of the world including the Soviet Union, the masses of the people, who constitute the overwhelming majority of the population, and the overwhelming majority of Communists and cadres want revolution and are upholding or will uphold Marxism-Leninism. They are steadily awakening and joining the ranks of the struggle against imperialism and revisionism. It is certain that over 90 per cent of the world's population will become more closely united in the fight against imperialism, reaction and modern revisionism. . . .

Unless the new leaders of the CPSU stop practising Khrushchevism without Khrushchev, admit and correct their mistakes and genuinely return to the revolutionary path of Marxism-Leninism it is absolutely out of the question to expect the Marxist-Leninists to abandon the struggle against Khrushchev revisionism.

With power and to spare, we must not cease the pursuit
Or halt in mid-course for the sake of idle laurels.

This couplet summarizes an extremely important historical lesson. The Marxist-Leninists and all the other revolutionary people of the world must continue their victorious pursuit and carry the struggle against Khrushchev revisionism through to the end!

*

At the time of the Tonkin Gulf incident (Bac Bo Gulf) the Soviet Union had supported the American proposal, turned down by North Vietnam, that the matter should be referred to the UN Security Council. The Soviet attitude had brought criticism from China. After Khrushchev's fall, the Soviet Union, partly in reaction to the mounting American assault on Vietnam, and hoping to improve its own relationship with Hanoi (and possibly North Korea) published a strong pledge of support for North Vietnam, and invited the National Liberation Front of South Vietnam to establish a permanent mission in Moscow. In April the Soviet Union proposed a summit meeting with North Vietnamese and Chinese leaders to discuss joint co-operation. This proposal, accepted by Hanoi, was rejected by the Chinese. There was unseemly bickering over the arrangements for the transport of Soviet supplies to North Vietnam via China, and both sides accused the other of failing to support the just struggle of the Vietnamese people.

The fact was that Vietnam, as before and since, was the uncomfortable focal point of the power politics of three great states. The Chinese were bound morally by their own revolutionary precedent to support the Vietnamese, even though their own interests demanded no more than a peaceful zone on their southern flank. The Soviets, mindful of their own interests in reaching a *modus vivendi* with the United States in Europe and elsewhere, were nevertheless impelled both to stand up to the American challenge in Vietnam and to maintain their credibility as a leading supporter of just communist struggles. Both Soviets and Chinese would probably have preferred to disengage from Vietnam.

DOCUMENT 28. 'SOVIET LEADERS' ULTERIOR MOTIVE IN "AIDING" VIETNAM', EXTRACT FROM 'VICE-PREMIER CHEN YI'S ANSWERS TO QUESTIONS PUT BY TAKANO YOSHIHISA, PEKING CORRESPONDENT OF THE JAPANESE PAPER *Akahata*', 30 DECEMBER 1965 ('VICE-PREMIER CHEN YI ANSWERS QUESTIONS PUT BY CORRESPONDENTS', FOREIGN LANGUAGES PRESS, PEKING, 1966, PP. 34–5)

Question: The people of China and the whole world have given material and moral support to the Vietnamese people in their struggle. In this connection, in the spring of 1965 the rumour was spread through the medium of the Western press that China was holding up the transport of Soviet aid material to Viet Nam. This rumour has recently cropped up again. Would you please tell me the facts of the matter?

Answer: China has abided by agreement and punctually transported the military material for Viet Nam which the Soviet Union asked us to help transport. And this has always been done free of any charge. Such is the truth of the matter. It is an absolutely deliberate slander to say that China has held up the transport of Soviet military material for Viet Nam.

The Soviet Union is the largest European socialist country. If it really wanted to help the Vietnamese people, if it really wanted to support and help their struggle against US aggression and for national salvation in an effective and all-round way, it could have taken all kinds of measures in many fields to immobilize forces of the United States and constantly exposed the US plots of peace talks. But the Soviet leaders have not done so; on the contrary, they have in fact been giving the United States every facility, so that it can concentrate its forces against Viet Nam and continuously spread smokescreen of peace talks to becloud world opinion. In these circumstances, who can believe that the Soviet leaders are giving genuine support to Viet Nam?

The Soviet leaders are evading the major issue when they deliberately reduce the important political question of supporting the Vietnamese people's struggle against US aggression and for national salvation to a matter of 'transit of aid material for Viet Nam', to say nothing of their complete lack of justification on the latter question. The Soviet leaders harp on the fact that the Soviet Union has no common borders with Viet Nam, as if all aid material for Viet Nam has of necessity to go through China. This is not true. There are sea routes between the Soviet Union and Viet Nam. Why can't Soviet military material for Viet Nam be shipped by sea as is that of other countries? But the Soviet Union dare not take the sea routes. It has asked us to transport all of its military material for Viet Nam. We know very well what are the things we have helped it to transport. Both in quantity and quality, they are far from commensurate with the strength of the Soviet Union. But the Soviet leaders are boasting about this meagre aid and have constantly and everywhere spread the rumour that China is obstructing the transit of Soviet aid material for Viet Nam. Naturally, this cannot but strengthen people's conviction that their so-called aid to Viet Nam is given with ulterior motives. In reality, the Soviet leaders have not been sincerely helping the Vietnamese people to carry their struggle against US aggression and for national salvation through to the end, but want to make use of their so-called aid to control the Vietnamese situation and bring the Viet Nam question into the orbit of US-Soviet collaboration. Otherwise, why should they have been continuously and groundlessly slandering the Chinese people, who are giving full support to the struggle of the Vietnamese people?

*

A Soviet view of Chinese policy in Southeast Asia was published in 1969. For the 'theory of people's war' see Document 53 in Part IV.

DOCUMENT 29. EXTRACT FROM LIPARIT KYUZAJHYAN, *The Chinese Crisis: Causes and Character*, NOVOSTI PRESS AGENCY PUBLISHING HOUSE, MOSCOW, 1969, PP. 96–8

The point of departure in the Peking drive on Asia, Africa and Latin America was quite simple—the thesis of 'the decisive role of the world village' in the world revolutionary process. . . .

If the 'theory of the people's war' is cleared of the verbal camouflage, it discloses an attempt to use the forces of the national-liberation movement as an instrument in creating seats of tension in different parts of the world, such as would provoke an armed conflict with American imperialism. The Chinese leaders believed that in such a situation they would be able to lead the anti-American struggle and play for influence in the modern world, while actually remaining uninvolved. This gambling policy combined with open anti-Sovietism is intended to win an exceptional place for China in the world and influence world politics even before China's military and economic potential reaches a high level. The Maoists' chauvinism is most vividly displayed in their approach to the Vietnam issue. They need a lengthy war in Vietnam for the implementation of their plans in the international arena. On the one hand, they renounce unity of action with the socialist countries and persistently worsen their relations with the Soviet Union. On the other hand, they are doing everything in their power to prevent a political solution of the Vietnamese problem in the interests of the Vietnamese people, and for the sake of world peace. When the Vietnamese leaders outlined (at the beginning of 1967) the terms for the opening of negotiations with the United States on political adjustment, Peking did not support that move and, moreover, hinted that it would oppose it.

In the final analysis Mao Tse-tung's stand on Vietnam is objectively identical with the stand of the American political and military leaders who insist that the war must go on at any cost.

At the same time it is remarkable that Peking makes use of various occasions to remind Washington of the 'inadvisability' of a direct Sino-American conflict over Vietnam. And it finds understanding there.

In an interview to Edgar Snow, the American publicist, at the beginning of 1965, Mao Tse-tung himself hinted rather obviously that China was not going to fight outside her boundaries. In 1967 high-ranking officials impressed the same point time and again, varying one and the same idea: do not touch us and we will not touch you. This position was approved in Washington. In 1966 McNamara said that the United States would spare no effort publicly and confidentially to inform the Chinese leadership of the limited nature of US objects in Vietnam, which presented no danger to the Chinese People's Republic.

If all the components of Chinese policy on Vietnam are combined, the inevitable conclusion will be that the Mao group are objectively encouraging escalation of the war in Southeast Asia.

The Mao group's degradation has ended, as it was bound to, in cynical deals, adventurism and betrayal of the interests of a neighbouring socialist country for the sake of their selfish interests.

PART III

China and its Asian Neighbours

After more than a hundred years of 'unequal treaties' and imperialist exploitation, the CPR has been understandably sensitive both with regard to its territorial boundaries and to the presence of potentially hostile regimes in neighbouring states. We have seen (Part I), that the Americans have acted on the assumption that China is an expansionist power which can only be restrained by powerful defensive alliances, notably SEATO (September 1954), the US-Japanese Security Treaty (September 1951), the US-South Korean Alliance (October 1953) and the defensive alliance with Taiwan (December 1954).

With the widening of the Sino-Soviet rift, China's border with the USSR has become a matter of bitter dispute, although in the case of the much publicized Chenpao Island in the Ussuri River, the area in question is a few acres, frequently flooded and normally uninhabited. On occasion the Chinese have accused the Soviets of widely expansionist designs (e.g. Document 39) and have also criticized the inclusion of Outer Mongolia in the Soviet defensive system.

Possibly the most important and certainly the most dramatic boundary dispute has been with India. The area in question has been substantial and of undoubted strategic importance. Nevertheless the territorial question alone does not explain the transition from friendly relations in the mid-fifties to open warfare in 1962. In the Chinese view India's regime had become ideologically distasteful and a potential rival for influence in the Third World. Moreover, in 1962 China's leaders were about to launch a major domestic campaign, the Socialist Education Movement, dissident tribesmen were crossing the border from Sinkiang to Soviet Central Asia, and the Taiwan regime was making belligerent gestures which heralded a possible attack on the mainland. Such was the background to the detailed events of border confrontation and the Chinese decision to inflict a sharp humiliating military defeat.

THE HIMALAYAN FRONTIER

India, which recognized the People's Republic in January 1950, was the second neutral independent Asian state (after Burma) to do so. At first good relations were inhibited by the 'liberation' of Tibet. As early as October 1949 it was announced that Tibet, which had long been virtually independent as a Buddhist state, would be liberated and in October 1950 the task was begun. The Indian government protested against the Chinese use of force, while the Chinese repudiated the charge and, in the spring of 1951, when Tibet was effectively incorporated into China, promised autonomy to the Tibetans. Although Tibet appealed to the United Nations, it gained no support. The Nationalists were as adamant as the Communists in upholding Chinese sovereignty over Tibet and both the United States and Great Britain had in the past admitted the legality of the Chinese claim. Peking propaganda, which initially denounced Nehru as the lackey of Western imperialism, was gradually modified following India's sympathetic efforts to mediate in Korea, and as part of a new policy of peaceful co-existence with non-aligned states. In April 1954 India recognized the Chinese position in Tibet, giving up its residual rights from British days in return for the pledge of friendship dramatically publicized in the *Panch Shila*, the Five Principles (see Part IV, Document 45). Clarification of the Sino-Indian border was postponed.

By 1958 settlement of the border question became urgent with the growth of unrest in Tibet. Beginning in 1955 with the revolt of the Khamba tribesmen in Eastern Tibet, insurrection spread to Tibet proper and the Chinese took military counter action. About that time the Indians learnt of the existence of a military road built by the Chinese across the Aksai Chin Plateau, in territory claimed by India. This route linking Sinkiang with Tibet was of particular importance when the Khambas threatened communications in the East. In the correspondence between China and India, Chou En-lai suggested that for the time being the *de facto* occupation by the Chinese of the Aksai Chin area should be accepted in return for Chinese *de facto* acceptance of the Indian position in the North-east Frontier Agency region (see Document 32). This sugges-tion, understandable in the light of the fighting in Tibet, was officially ignored in New Delhi. The Dalai Lama had asked for asylum during a visit to India (November 1956 to March 1957) and had been persuaded with difficulty to return to Tibet. In February 1959, having secured his position as religious leader by passing the final examinations required by lamaism, he was scheduled to pay a visit to Peking. Instead, following a demon-stration in Lhasa, which was quelled by Chinese troops, he fled with a bodyguard of Khambas. Crossing the border into India on 31 March he requested asylum, which was granted. There was considerable sympathy for the Dalai Lama in India, but the Indian government did not accord him the status of a head of government in exile and did not support his appeals to the United Nations. Meanwhile the Chinese had to deal with insurgents who had escaped from Tibet into India and Nepal, acquired arms and reappeared in Tibet. To close the frontier Chinese troops moved forward, Indian troops also advanced, in places to the limits of India's interpretation of the Mac-Mahon Line, and there were a number of armed clashes in the late summer of 1959.

One result of the conflict was to bring India and the Soviet Union closer together. The Chinese view that a frontier fixed by imperialism was invalid had disturbing implications for the Sino-Soviet boundary, itself a product of Tsarist imperialism. The Soviets agreed to give India a substantial development credit (30 July 1959) and began to speak out in favour of the Indian side in the dispute.

With the lesser states on its borders the People's Republic concluded satisfactory border agreements, delimiting the frontiers with some mutual exchange of territory. Agreement was reached with Burma (January 1960), Nepal (March 1960), Pakistan (March 1963), the People's Republic of Mongolia (December 1962), and Afghanistan (November 1963). In the case of Pakistan the agreement was provisional pending a settlement of the Indo-Pakistan dispute over Kashmir. In the case of Burma (Document 33) and Afghanistan, China also concluded Treaties of Friendship and Mutual Non-Aggression which contained the provision that neither party should join any military alliance directed against the other. This has been interpreted by some authorities (e.g. W. C. Johnstone, *Burma's Foreign Policy: A Study in Neutralism,* Harvard University Press, 1963) as restricting the scope of independent policy for the Burmans and the Afghans and opening the way for Chinese penetration and influence. It has been suggested that the relationship created by such treaties is analogous to the old 'tributary' status. But China may have had nothing more sinister in mind than insuring that Burma and Afghanistan would not join pro-Western military alliances.

It may be noted that Nepal did not sign a Mutual Non-Aggression Pact. The border was mutually agreed, and a compromise arrived at on the question of the summit of Everest (adorned at one time with a bust of Mao wrapped in a Chinese flag). When the King of Nepal, Mahendra, assumed personal rule he was able to rely on Chinese support against a guerrilla movement backed by the Indians.

Meanwhile negotiations on the Sino-Indian boundary continued after 1959. In 1960 Chou En-lai repeated more explicitly his suggestion that China give up its claims to the NEFA in return for concessions in Ladakh. However, because of the dispute with Pakistan over Kashmir and popular pressure at home, the Indian government refused to acquiesce in the Chinese occupation of the Aksai Chin plateau. With arms and equipment purchased in the Soviet Union and the United States, India moved its military outposts forward. China, no doubt worried by the unrest of dissident Kazakhs in Sinkiang, warned Nehru to 'rein in on the brink of the precipice'. Khrushchev, preoccupied with his Cuban policy, added his pleas for Indian conciliation. Apparently undeterred by these warnings Nehru declared in mid-October that Indian troops would soon succeed in driving the Chinese out of all territory claimed by India. At this point China launched a carefully controlled offensive in two stages, culminating on November 21 with the announcement of a unilateral cease-fire which established the line as it had been in November 1959.

The Premier of Ceylon attempted to mediate by organizing the Colombo Conference of six Afro-Asian nations (Burma,

Cambodia, Ceylon, Ghana, Indonesia, and the UAR) in December 1962. Mrs Bandaranaike visited Peking and New Delhi; India accepted the Colombo proposals with clarifications. The clarifications were not acceptable to China. The USSR entered the dispute with a statement which refrained from blaming the Chinese for aggression, but placed on China the onus for not accepting the Colombo proposals, without however mentioning the 'clarifications'.

The Sino-Indian border has continued to exercise diplomats since 1962. Document 34 illustrates the Chinese case. If China hoped by its military action in 1962 to force India to the conference table it has singularly failed. India has stubbornly refused to negotiate a settlement of the *de facto* boundary since the war.

When in 1969 the Indian Prime Minister, Mrs Indira Gandhi, suggested that the time had come to improve relations with China, she was criticized in Parliament. Public opinion in India will not readily admit that India was not an innocent victim of Chinese aggression in 1962.

INDOCHINA

It is significant that the 'unequal' treaties which have been cited by the Chinese (see Document 31) do not include the Sino-French agreements detaching Vietnam from Chinese suzerainty. China does not appear to have disputed the frontiers between China and Vietnam and Laos, which were demarcated at the end of the nineteenth century, nor do Chinese maps of the borders differ from others. It may be that the critical situation in Indochina and the fact that China enjoys relatively good relations with North Vietnam have helped to preclude any possible controversy.

To the Chinese Indochina was an area in which broad considerations of peace and security should take precedence over local struggles for liberation. In the mid-fifties the Americans, obsessed with the 'domino' theory and their vision of impending Red Chinese aggression (Document 14), viewed any settlement which left the nationalists in control of substantial parts of Indochina with concern. The Chinese position was crucial in persuading the Vietminh to accept the partition of

Vietnam and the promise of free elections preceding unification.

Seven years later the Chinese and the Americans were again to meet in an International Conference at Geneva in order to settle the problem of Laos arising from the failure of the 1954 agreement. The promised elections in Vietnam had been forestalled, largely by the Americans, who gave increasing support to the Diem regime in South Vietnam. In Laos, too, the United States worked to secure a base against 'Communist aggression'. The neutralist Prime Minister, Prince Souvanna Phouma, faithful to the terms agreed at Geneva, arranged in 1956–7 to integrate the territory of the pro-Hanoi Pathet Lao into his regime, with the result that, following an election in 1958, the Pathet Lao gained a number of seats in the National Assembly. The United States, dismayed by this outcome, forced Souvanna Phouma to resign in favour of the strongly anti-Communist Phoui Sananikone, who in turn was overthrown by a patriotic paratroop captain in 1960. Souvanna Phouma was brought back to power temporarily, only to be driven into the hills by an American backed right-wing group. At this point the Soviet Union began to airlift military supplies into the Laos highlands, via China and North Vietnam. On 6 January 1961 in the course of a speech reporting on the Moscow Conference, Khrushchev promised support for 'wars of national liberation'. The Kennedy administration, inaugurated in January 1961, recognized the implications of the Soviet airlift not only for Laos but also for the supply lines of the insurgents in South Vietnam. It was agreed to hold a major international conference at Geneva to settle the Laotian crisis. Intermittent meetings from May 1961 to July 1962 led to an agreement, incidentally the first to be signed by both a Chinese Foreign Secretary and a US Secretary of State. The Chinese had pressed for the complete abolition of SEATO, but settled for an agreement on neutrality for Laos with Prince Souvanna Phouma as premier, two vice-premiers, one pro-communist, one anti-communist, and a revived international control commission. The Pathet Lao remained in the highland areas, but both Peking and Hanoi have shown greater interest in using the area as a supply route to South Vietnam than in supporting any forward moves in Laos itself.

OUTER MONGOLIA

Outer Mongolia, at one time within the Chinese empire (see map, Document 30), has leaned heavily to the Soviet side in the Sino-Soviet dispute. Independent (since 1924) but under Soviet protection, the status of the Mongolian People's Republic was confirmed at the time of the Sino-Soviet alliance. Until 1962 Chinese maps showed the border with the MPR as undemarcated. No doubt anxious to bring pressure to bear on India and the Soviet Union by settling border disputes with other countries, China began negotiations in the autumn of 1962 leading to a border treaty on 26 December 1962. There are signs that the Mongolians were not entirely satisfied with the agreement. There was a three months' delay over ratification, the treaty was given much more publicity in China than in Mongolia, and the Mongolian Foreign Minister was relieved of his duties two days after the exchange of ratification.

The Sino-Soviet border became a matter of hot dispute in 1963–4 and a breakdown in negotiations on this question may explain Mao's outspoken comment on Soviet expansionism, and possibly his gratuitous references to Mongolia (Document 39), which were in contrast to a statement on the Mongolian boundary by the Chinese Foreign Minister in 1965 (Document 40).

JAPAN

The relations of the People's Republic with Japan have been overshadowed by memories of the Japanese invasion and occupation. Chinese fears of revived Japanese militarism were reinforced by the post-war American policy of rehabilitating Japan as a bulwark of American power. In the early 1950s the Americans insisted as a condition for ending the US occupation of Japan that the Japanese government should recognize the KMT regime. Japan already saddled with American military bases was thereby forced into diplomatic relations with Taiwan.

Chinese propaganda attacks on the US-Japanese alliance made a clear distinction between the government and the people of Japan (Document 41). There was considerable anti-American feeling in Japan and a popular outcry at the time of the signing of a new Treaty of Mutual Co-operation and Security with the US in 1960 helped to bring about the resignation of Prime Minister Kishi (July 1960). His successor Ikeda, although not immediately welcomed by the People's Republic, sought to make Japan's foreign policy more independent of the United States, stressing autonomy within the alliance. For the Chinese there were advantages, at a time when the breach with the Soviet Union was widening, in expanding Sino-Japanese trade. Negotiations in 1962 led to the first long-term trade agreement (1963–7) between the two countries.

Ikeda was replaced in November 1964 by Sato who proved less acceptable to the Chinese. In June 1965 a treaty signed by Japan and the Republic of Korea (South Korea) after years of negotiation led to renewed propaganda attacks from Peking. China reminded Tokyo that trade and politics were inseparable and hinted that if Japan would loosen its ties with the United States, it would be rewarded by an increase in trade with China. However, the Sato government compounded its sins in the spring of 1966 by negotiating for increased trade with the Soviet Union.

During the Cultural Revolution Peking's attacks on the Sato government mounted. When the trade agreement expired in 1967, the Chinese only agreed to a renewal after prolonged and, for the Japanese, humiliating negotiations. Subsequently the Sino-US *détente* destroyed the foundations of Sato's policy. His replacement in 1972 by Tanaka was followed by a rapid settlement of differences between China and Japan (see Part VI, Document 69).

(a) CHINA'S BORDERS

In 1960 an Indian student brought home from China a Chinese textbook, published in 1954, which included a map showing Chinese territories 'lost' to the imperialist powers in the period 1840–1919. The Chinese have explained that this map was not official. It probably represents an historian's view of the past rather than a modern assertion of China's unredeemed territory and should not be taken too seriously.

DOCUMENT 30. MAP OF 'THE OLD DEMOCRATIC REVOLUTIONARY ERA (1840–1919)—CHINESE TERRITORIES TAKEN BY IMPERIALISM' ADAPTED FROM ORIGINAL MAP IN LIU PEI-HAU, ED., *A Short History of Modern China*, PEKING, 1954 (KEY NUMBERS AND TRANSLATION FROM D. J. DOOLIN, *Territorial Claims in the Sino-Soviet Conflict*, STANFORD UNIVERSITY, 1965)

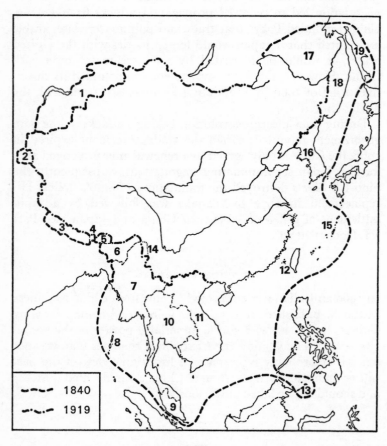

Shortly after the Cuban crisis the Chinese exchanged verbal blows with the Communist Party of the USA. The American comrades had objected to the Chinese criticism of the Khrushchev–Kennedy agreement and suggested that the Chinese were not following the adventurous policy that they advocated for the Soviets. An Editorial in the *People's Daily* commenting comprehensively on the 'incorrect' views of the American party, included a significant statement of China's policy on the question of boundary revision. It should be noted that the Treaties of Aigun, Peking and Ili, listed among the 'unequal treaties', had been concluded with Tsarist Russia.

*

Key to map opposite

1 The Great Northwest: seized by Imperial Russia under the Treaty of Chuguchak, 1864. (Parts of present Soviet Kazakhstan, Kirghizstan, and Tadzhikstan.)
2 Pamirs: secretly divided between England and Russia in 1896.
3 Nepal: went to England after 'independence' in 1898.
4 Sikkim: occupied by England in 1889.
5 Bhutan: went to England after 'independence' in 1865.
6 Assam: given to England by Burma in 1826.
7 Burma: became part of the British Empire in 1886.
8 Andaman Archipelago: went to England.
9 Malaya: occupied by England in 1895.
10 Thailand: declared 'independent' under joint Anglo-French control in 1904.
11 Annam: occupied by France in 1885.
12 Taiwan and P'eng-hu Archipelago (Pescadores): relinquished to Japan per the Treaty of Shimonoseki, 1895.
13 Sulu Archipelago: went to England.
14 Region where the British crossed the border and committed aggression.
15 Ryukyu Archipelago: occupied by Japan in 1879.
16 Korea: 'independent' in 1895—annexed by Japan in 1910.
17 The Great Northeast: seized by Imperial Russia under the Treaty of Aigun, 1858.
18 The Great Northeast: seized by Imperial Russia under the Treaty of Peking, 1860.
19 Sakhalin: divided between Russia and Japan.

*

DOCUMENT 31. A STATEMENT ON BORDER POLICY, EXTRACT FROM 'A COMMENT ON THE STATEMENT OF THE COMMUNIST PARTY OF THE USA', EDITORIAL IN *People's Daily*, 8 MARCH 1963 (*Peking Review*, 15 MARCH 1963, 6, 10 & 11, P. 61)

In the hundred years or so prior to the victory of the Chinese revolution, the imperialist and colonial powers—the United States, Britain, France, Tsarist Russia, Germany, Japan, Italy, Austria, Belgium, the Netherlands, Spain and Portugal—carried out unbridled aggression against China. They compelled the governments of old China to sign a large number of unequal treaties—the Treaty of Nanking of 1842, the Treaty of Aigun of 1858, the Treaty of Tientsin of 1858, the Treaty of Peking of 1860, the Treaty of Ili of 1881, the Protocol of Lisbon of 1887, the Treaty of Shimonoseki of 1895, the Convention for the Extension of Hongkong of 1898, the International Protocol of 1901, etc. By virtue of these unequal treaties, they annexed Chinese territory in the north, south, east and west and held leased territories on the seaboard and in the hinterland of China. Some seized Taiwan and the Penghu Islands, others occupied Hongkong and forcibly leased Kowloon, still others put Macao under perpetual occupation, etc., etc.

At the time the People's Republic of China was inaugurated, our government declared that it would examine the treaties concluded by previous Chinese governments with foreign governments, treaties that had been left over by history, and would recognize, abrogate, revise or renegotiate them according to their respective contents. In this respect, our policy towards the socialist countries is fundamentally different from our policy towards the imperialist countries. When we deal with various imperialist countries, we take differing circumstances into consideration and make distinctions in our policy. As a matter of fact, many of these treaties concluded in the past either have lost their validity, or have been abrogated or have been replaced by new ones. With regard to the outstanding issues, which are a legacy from the past, we have always held that, when conditions are ripe, they should be settled peacefully through negotiations and that, pending a settlement, the *status quo* should be maintained. Within this category are the questions of Hongkong, Kowloon and Macao and the questions of all those boundaries which have not been formally delimited by the parties concerned in each case. As for Taiwan and the Penghu Islands, they were restored to China in 1945, and the question now is the US imperialist invasion and occupation of them and US imperialist interference in China's internal affairs. We Chinese people are determined to exercise our sovereign right to liberate our own territory of Taiwan; at the same time, through the ambassadorial talks between China and the United States in Warsaw we are striving to solve the question of effecting the withdrawal of US armed forces from Taiwan and the Taiwan Straits. Our position as described above accords not only with the interests of the Chinese people but also with the interests of the people of the socialist camp and the people of the whole world.

*

(b) THE HIMALAYAN FRONTIER

DOCUMENT 32. EXTRACTS FROM CORRESPONDENCE BETWEEN INDIA AND CHINA CONCERNING THE BORDER, 1958–9. *Notes, Memoranda and Letters exchanged between the Governments of India and China* (*White Paper No. 1*), INDIAN MINISTRY OF EXTERNAL AFFAIRS, NEW DELHI, 1959, PP. 48–54

Letter from the Prime Minister of India to the Prime Minister of China

NEW DELHI,
December 14, 1958.

HIS EXCELLENCY,
MR CHOU EN-LAI,
Prime Minister of the People's Republic of China,
Peking.

MY DEAR PRIME MINISTER,

I am writing to you after a long time. We have watched with great interest and admiration the progress made by the People's Government of China in recent years. In particular, we have been deeply interested in the remarkable advance in the yield of rice per hectare as well as in the total yield, as also in the great increase in production of pig iron and steel.

2 As we are faced with somewhat similar problems in our country in regard to rice production and steel manufacture, we would naturally like to benefit by the example of what China has done. For this purpose we decided to send two delegations to China, one consisting of farmers and agricultural specialists and the other of experts in iron and steel. Your Government was good enough to agree to this. It was pointed out however that the next season for rice sowing and cultivation would be in March-April next. We hope to send our farmers and agricultural experts then, if it suits the convenience of your Government. But we shall be sending our iron and steel experts to China fairly soon. I hope that they will learn much from the methods being now employed in China and we could then profit by their experience.

3 My purpose in troubling you with this letter, however, relates to another matter. This is in regard to the border between India and China. You will remember that when the Sino-Indian Agreement in regard to the Tibet region of China was concluded, various outstanding problems, including some relating to our border trade, were considered. A number of mountain passes were mentioned which should be used for purposes of travel between the two countries. No border questions were raised at that time and we were under the impression that there were no border disputes between our respective countries. In fact we thought that the Sino-Indian Agreement, which was happily concluded in 1954, had settled all outstanding problems between our countries.

4 Somewhat later, my attention was drawn to some maps published in China. The maps I saw were not very accurate maps, but nevertheless the frontier as roughly drawn in these maps did not correspond with the actual frontier. In fact it ran right across the territory of India in several places. I was surprised to see this, as I had not been aware at any time previously that there was any frontier dispute between our two countries. No mention of this had been made in the course of the Sino-Indian talks which resulted in the Agreement of 1954.

5 Subsequently, in October 1954, I had the privilege of

visiting your great country and the happiness to meet you and other leaders of the Chinese People's Republic. We had long talks and it was a pleasure to me to find that we had a great deal in common in our approach and that there was no dispute or problem affecting our relations. In the course of our talks I briefly mentioned to you that I had seen some maps recently published in China which gave a wrong borderline between the two countries. I presumed that this was by some error and told you at the time that so far as India was concerned we were not much worried about the matter because our boundaries were quite clear and were not a matter of argument. You were good enough to reply to me that these maps were really reproductions of old pre-liberation maps and that you had had no time to revise them. In view of the many and heavy pre-occupations of your Government, I could understand that this revision had not taken place till then. I expressed the hope that the border line would be corrected before long.

6 Towards the end of 1956, you did us the honour of paying a visit to India and we had the pleasure of having you in our midst for many days. Part of this time you spent in visiting various parts of India. I had occasion to be with you both in Delhi and during some of your visits, notably to our great river valley project at Bhakra-Nangal. We had long talks and discussed many international issues which were then agitating people's minds and I was happy to know what your views were about them. In the course of these talks you referred to the Sino-Burmese border. You told me about the talks you had with U Nu at Peking and your desire to settle this problem with the Burmese Government. I had received the same information from U Nu who had told me of your wish to settle this problem to the satisfaction of both countries. It was in this connection that you mentioned to me the Sino-Indian border, and more especially the so-called MacMahon Line. This MacMahon Line covered a part of the Sino-Burmese border and a large part of the Chinese border with India. I remember your telling me that you did not approve of this border being called the MacMahon Line and I replied that I did not like that name either. But for facility of reference we referred to it as such.

7 You told me then that you had accepted this MacMahon Line border with Burma and, whatever might have happened

long ago, in view of the friendly relations which existed between China and India, you proposed to recognize this border with India also. You added that you would like to consult the authorities of the Tibetan region of China and you proposed to do so.

8 Immediately after our talk, I had written a minute so that we might have a record of this talk for our personal and confidential use. I am giving below a quotation from this minute:

'Premier Chou referred to the MacMahon Line and again said that he had never heard of this before though of course the then Chinese Government had dealt with this matter and not accepted that line. He had gone into this matter in connection with the border dispute with Burma. Although he thought that this line, established by British Imperialists, was not fair, nevertheless, because it was an accomplished fact and because of the friendly relations which existed between China and the countries concerned, namely, India and Burma, the Chinese Government were of the opinion that they should give recognition to this MacMahon Line. They had, however, not consulted the Tibetan authorities about it yet. They proposed to do so.'

9 I remember discussing this matter with you at some considerable length. You were good enough to make this point quite clear. I then mentioned that there were no disputes between us about our frontier, but there were certain very minor border problems which were pending settlement. We decided that these petty issues should be settled amicably by representatives of the two Governments meeting together on the basis of established practice and custom as well as water sheds. There was long delay in this meeting taking place, but ultimately a representative of the Chinese Government came to Delhi and discussed one of these petty issues for some time. Unfortunately no settlement about this matter was arrived at then and it was decided to continue the talks later. I was sorry that these talks had not resulted in a satisfactory agreement so far. The issue is a minor one and I wanted to remove by friendly settlement all matters that affected our two Governments and countries. I had thought then of writing to you on this subject, but I decided not to trouble you over such a petty matter.

10 A few months ago, our attention was drawn to a map

of China published in the magazine 'China Pictorial', which indicated the border with India. This map was also not very clearly defined. But even the rough border line appeared to us to be wrongly placed. This borderline went right across Indian territory. A large part of our North-East Frontier Agency as well as some other parts which are and have long been well recognized as parts of India and been administered by India in the same way as other parts of our country, were shown to be part of Chinese territory. A considerable region of our neighbour country, Bhutan, in the north-east was also shown as being on the Chinese side. A part of the North-East Frontier Agency which was clearly on the Indian side of what has been known as the MacMahon Line, was shown in this map as part of Chinese territory.

11 The magazine containing this map was widely distributed and questions were asked in our Parliament about this. I gave answers to the effect that these maps were merely reproductions of old ones and did not represent the actual facts of the situation.

12 We drew your Government's attention to this map some time ago this year. In a memorandum in reply to us, it has been stated by your Government that in the maps currently published in China, the boundary line between China and neighbouring countries including India, is drawn on the basis of maps published before the liberation. It has further been stated that the Chinese Government has not yet undertaken a survey of the Chinese boundary nor consulted with the countries concerned, and that it will not make changes in the boundary on its own.

13 I was puzzled by this reply because I thought that there was no major boundary dispute between China and India. There never has been such a dispute so far as we are concerned and in my talks with you in 1954 and subsequently, I had stated this. I could understand four years ago that the Chinese Government, being busy with major matters of national reconstruction, could not find time to revise old maps. But you will appreciate that nine years after the Chinese People's Republic came into power, the continued issue of these incorrect maps is embarrassing to us as to others. There can be no question of these large parts of India being anything but India and there is no dispute about them. I do not know what kind of surveys

can affect these well-known and fixed boundaries. I am sure that you will appreciate our difficulties in this matter.

14 I am venturing to write to you on this subject as I feel that any possibility of grave misunderstanding between our countries should be removed as soon as possible. I am anxious, as I am sure you are, that the firm basis of our friendship should not only be maintained but should be strengthened.

May I send you my warm regards and every good wish for the New Year.

Yours sincerely,

(Sd.) JAWAHARLAL NEHRU

Letter from the Prime Minister of China to the Prime Minister of India

PEKING,
January 23, 1959.

DEAR MR PRIME MINISTER,

I have received your letter dated December 14, 1958, forwarded by Mr Ambassador Parthasarthi.

Thank you for the credit you gave the achievements of our country in economic construction. It is true that, through the joint efforts of the entire Chinese people, our country made in industrial and agricultural production in 1958 an advance which we describe as a 'great leap forward'. However, as we started from a very poor economic foundation, our present level of development in production is still very low. It will take us a number of years more of hard work in order to bring about a relatively big change in the economic picture of our country.

Our government heartily welcomes the sending by the Indian Government of two delegations to study our agriculture and iron and steel industry respectively. And as I understand, another delegation has already arrived in China to study our water conservancy and irrigation work. We welcome them to our country and will be glad to provide them with every possible convenience. We also hope to learn from them Indian experience in the respective fields. The exchange of such specialized delegations and the interflow of experience will undoubtedly be helpful to the economic construction of our countries. We too have always taken a great interest in the progress of India's second five-year plan, and wish it success.

We note with pleasure that, in the past year, friendly co-operation between China and India has undergone further development. I would like to take this opportunity, on behalf of the Chinese Government, to express thanks to the Indian Government for its efforts at the 13th session of the United Nations General Assembly for restoring to China its rightful place in the United Nations. We are also grateful to the Indian Government for its support to our country on the question of Taiwan and the coastal islands.

In your letter you have taken much space to discuss the question of Sino-Indian boundary and thus enabled us to understand better the Indian Government's stand on the question. I would also like now to set forth the views and stand of the Chinese Government. First of all, I wish to point out that the Sino-Indian boundary has never been formally de-limitated. Historically no treaty or agreement on the Sino-Indian boundary has ever been concluded between the Chinese central government and the Indian Government. So far as the actual situation is concerned, there are certain differences between the two sides over the border question. In the past few years, questions as to which side certain areas on the Sino-Indian border belong were on more than one occasion taken up between the Chinese and the Indian sides through diplomatic channels. The latest case concerns an area in the southern part of China's Sinkiang Uighur Autonomous Region, which has always been under Chinese jurisdiction. Patrol duties have continually been carried out in that area by the border guards of the Chinese Government. And the Sinkiang-Tibet highway built by our country in 1956 runs through that area. Yet recently the Indian Government claimed that that area was Indian territory. All this shows that border disputes do exist between China and India.

It was true that the border question was not raised in 1954 when negotiations were being held between the Chinese and Indian sides for the Agreement on Trade and Intercourse between the Tibet Region of China and India. This was because conditions were not yet ripe for its settlement and the Chinese side, on its part, had had no time to study the question. The Chinese Government has always held that the existence of the border question absolutely should not affect the development of Sino-Indian friendly relations. We believe that, following proper preparations, this question which has been carried over from the past can certainly be settled reasonably on the basis of the Five Principles of peaceful co-existence through friendly talks. To this end, the Chinese Government has now proceeded to take certain steps in making preparations.

An important question concerning the Sino-Indian boundary is the question of the so-called MacMahon Line. I discussed this with Your Excellency as well as with Prime Minister U Nu. I would now like to explain again the Chinese Government's attitude. As you are aware, the 'MacMahon Line' was a product of the British policy of aggression against the Tibet Region of China and aroused the great indignation of the Chinese people. Juridically, too, it cannot be considered legal. I have told you that it has never been recognized by the Chinese central government. Although related documents were signed by a representative of the local authorities of the Tibet Region of China, the Tibet local authorities were in fact dissatisfied with this unilaterally drawn line. And I have also told you formally about their dissatisfaction. On the other hand, one cannot, of course, fail to take cognizance of the great and encouraging changes: India and Burma, which are concerned in this line, have attained independence successively and become states friendly with China. In view of the various complex factors mentioned above, the Chinese Government, on the one hand, finds it necessary to take a more or less realistic attitude towards the MacMahon Line and, on the other hand, cannot but act with prudence and needs time to deal with this matter. All this I have mentioned to you on more than one occasion. However, we believe that, on account of the friendly relations between China and India, a friendly settlement can eventually be found for this section of the boundary line.

Precisely because the boundary between the two countries is not yet formally delimitated and some differences exist, it is unavoidable that there should be discrepancies between the boundary lines drawn on the respective maps of the two sides. On the maps currently published in our country, the Chinese boundaries are drawn in the way consistently followed in Chinese maps for the past several decades, if not longer. We do not hold that every portion of this boundary line is drawn on sufficient grounds. But it would be inappropriate for us to make changes without having made surveys and without having consulted the countries concerned. Furthermore, there would be difficulties in making such changes, because they would give rise to confusion among our people and bring censure on our government. As a matter of fact, our people have also expressed surprise at the way the Sino-Indian boundary, particularly its western section, is drawn on maps published in India. They have asked our government to take up this matter with the Indian Government. Yet we have not done so, but have explained to them the actual situation of the Sino-Indian boundary. With the settlement of the boundary question— which, as our government has repeatedly pointed out, requires surveys and mutual consultations—the problem of drawing the boundary on the maps will also be solved.

In recent years, there occurred between China and India some minor border incidents which are probably difficult to avoid pending the formal delimitation of the boundary. In order to avoid such incidents so far as possible before the boundary is formally delimitated, our government would like to propose to the Indian Government that, as a provisional measure, the two sides temporarily maintain the *status quo*, that is to say, each side keep for the time being to the border areas at present under its jurisdiction and not go beyond them. For the differences between the two sides, naturally, a solution may be sought through consultations like those held on the Wu-Je (Hoti) question. As to the negotiations regarding Wu-Je, we also regret very much that no agreement has yet been reached, as we formally thought a solution would not be difficult to achieve through negotiations and on-the-spot investigations. We still believe that this small question can be settled satisfactorily through the continued efforts of our two sides. The Chinese Government hopes that the above proposal about temporary maintenance of the present state of the boundary between the two sides will be approved of by the Indian Government.

I need not reiterate how highly the Chinese Government and people value Sino-Indian friendship. We will never allow any difference between our two countries to affect this friendship, and we believe that India shares the same views. I hope that this letter will help you get a better understanding of our government's stand on the Sino-Indian boundary question.

With sincere regards,

CHOU EN-LAI

DOCUMENT 33. TREATY OF FRIENDSHIP AND MUTUAL NON-AGGRESSION BETWEEN THE PEOPLE'S REPUBLIC OF CHINA AND THE UNION OF BURMA, 28 JANUARY 1960

The Government of the People's Republic of China and the Government of the Union of Burma,

Desiring to maintain everlasting peace and cordial friendship between the People's Republic of China and the Union of Burma, convinced that the strengthening of good neighbourly relations and friendly co-operation between People's Republic of China and the Union of Burma is in accordance with the vital interests of both countries.

Have decided for this purpose to conclude the present Treaty in accordance with the Five Principles of Peaceful Co-existence jointly initiated by the two countries, and have agreed as follows:

Article I

The Contracting Parties recognize and respect the independence sovereign rights and territorial integrity of each other.

Article II

There shall be everlasting peace and cordial friendship between the Contracting Parties who undertake to settle all disputes between them by means of peaceful negotiation without resorting to force.

Article III

Each Contracting Party undertakes not to carry out acts of aggression against the other and not to take part in any military alliance directed against the other Contracting Party.

Article IV

The Contracting Parties declare that they will develop and strengthen the economic and cultural ties between the two States in a spirit of friendship and co-operation, in accordance with the principles of equality and mutual benefit and of mutual non-interference in each other's internal affairs.

Article V

Any difference or dispute arising out of the interpretation or application of the present Treaty or one or more of its Articles shall be settled by negotiations through the ordinary diplomatic channels.

Article VI

1 The present Treaty is subject to ratification and the instruments of ratification will be exchanged in Rangoon as soon as possible.

2 The present Treaty will come into force immediately on the exchange of the instruments of ratification and will remain in force for a period of ten years.

3 Unless either of the Contracting Parties gives to the other notice in writing to terminate it at least one year before the expiration of this period, it will remain in force without any specified time limit, subject to the right of either of the Contracting Parties to terminate it by giving to the other in writing a year's notice of its intention to do so.

In witness whereof the Premier of the State Council of the People's Republic of China and the Prime Minister of the Union of Burma have signed the present Treaty.

Done in duplicate in Peking on the twenty-eighth day of January 1960, in the Chinese and English languages, both texts being equally authentic.

For the Government of the	For the Government of
People's Republic of China:	the Union of Burma:
(Signed) CHOU EN-LAI	(Signed) NE WIN

DOCUMENT 34. 'A BRIEF ACCOUNT ON THE SINO-INDIAN BOUNDARY QUESTION', VICE-PREMIER CHEN YI'S TELEVISION INTERVIEW WITH MR KARLSSON, CORRESPONDENT OF THE SWEDISH BROADCASTING CORPORATION, 17 FEBRUARY 1963 (*The Sino-Indian Boundary Question*, II, FOREIGN LANGUAGES PRESS, PEKING, 1965, PP. 1–12)

Question 1 The Sino-Indian boundary dispute is an old question. Why, in your opinion, did it develop into a military conflict during the last months of 1962?

Answer All along the Chinese Government has sought a friendly settlement of the Sino-Indian boundary question through peaceful negotiations. China has shown the greatest forbearance and restraint in dealing with this dispute. India has refused to negotiate. Moreover, she stepped up her armed encroachment of Chinese territory, and ultimately went so far as to launch massive armed attacks along the border. The course of events was rather complicated, and I will try to explain it as briefly as possible.

India already occupied, around 1950, more than 90,000 square kilometres of Chinese territory in the eastern sector of the Sino-Indian boundary, south of the illegal McMahon Line. The occupied area was three times the size of Belgium. The Chinese Government did not accept this encroachment, but in order to seek a peaceful settlement of the question, it restrained its frontier guards from crossing the illegal McMahon Line.

Then in 1959, India laid claim groundlessly to over 30,000 more square kilometres of Chinese territory in the western sector of the Sino-Indian boundary. Moreover, India provoked sanguinary conflicts on two occasions during that year, first in the eastern and then in the western sector of the boundary. As a result, tension rose daily along the border.

Question 2 Why didn't the Sino-Indian boundary dispute develop into a large-scale armed conflict in 1959?

Answer The Chinese Government took every possible measure to prevent it. At that time, that is on November 7, 1959, we proposed that the armed forces of China and India should each withdraw 20 kilometres along the entire boundary and stop their patrol activities, so as to avoid conflicts. We also proposed to the Indian Government that negotiations should be held to seek a peaceful settlement of the boundary question.

The Indian Government did not agree that the armed forces of both countries should withdraw 20 kilometres. Then China stopped its patrol activities unilaterally in the area 20 kilometres on its side of the border. Shortly afterwards, in April 1960, Premier Chou En-lai and I went to New Delhi for talks with Prime Minister Nehru of India. If the Indian side had shared our desire for a settlement of the boundary question through negotiations based on mutual understanding and mutual accommodations, the question would have been smoothly settled then and there, or even if it were not settled, it would not have developed into a large-scale military conflict. But our talks with Prime Minister Nehru proved fruitless. The Indian Government even refused to come to a temporary agreement for maintaining the *status quo* along the border.

Then, in the latter half of 1961 and particularly in the first half of 1962, India took advantage of China's unilateral cessation of patrol activities to change the *status quo* along the boundary by armed force. She set up 43 aggressive strongpoints on Chinese territory in the western sector of the Sino-Indian boundary and encroached upon China's Che Dong area north of the illegal McMahon Line in the eastern sector.

If you leaf through the Indian newspapers of May and June 1962, you will see how the Indian Government was recklessly pursuing a policy of aggression and provocation.

Nevertheless, we did not strike back. We limited ourselves to lodging protests with the Indian Government and demanding the withdrawal of Indian troops. We continued to work for a settlement of the boundary question through negotiations. The Chinese Government proposed negotiations on three occasions between July and October, 1962. But unfortunately, our proposals were rejected by the Indian Government every time. Having made all kinds of war preparations in the meantime, Indian troops finally launched on October 20, 1962, massive attacks on the Chinese frontier guards. Thus, China struck back in self-defence only when she was pressed beyond the limits of forbearance and left with no room for retreat.

Question 3 You said that Indian troops launched massive attacks on the Chinese frontier guards. Could you please tell me why India should do so at that time?

Answer In the first place, I think that the Indian Government drew the wrong conclusions from China's repeated forbearance and imagined that China would not strike back. Then, too, the Indian Government wrongly thought that China was faced with rather difficult economic conditions at home and was quite isolated internationally. Hence it attempted to use armed force to make China submit.

Question 4 The Indians say that China could not have fought on such a large scale without having made systematic preparations. What is your opinion about this?

Answer China was prepared, because the Indian Government long ago publicly announced its intention to launch armed attacks. On three occasions between July and October 1962, the Indian Government rejected China's proposals for negotiations, and persisted in maintaining that it was legitimate to carry out armed aggression against China. All this was bound to put China on guard. On the 5th of October 1962, the Defence Ministry of India announced the establishment of a new army corps under the Eastern Command for the sole purpose of dealing with China, and appointed Lt Gen. B. M. Kaul commander. On October 12, Prime Minister Nehru declared personally that he had issued instructions to clear out the Chinese frontier guards from what he termed invaded areas, which were in reality Chinese territory. On October 14, the then Indian Minister of Defence, Krishna Menon, called for a fight to the last man and the last gun against China. In these circumstances, how could China as a sovereign state fail to make the necessary preparations?

The large-scale armed conflict on the Sino-Indian border was provoked solely by India. The Chinese frontier guards were absolutely compelled to strike back in self-defence. It is a clumsy distortion of the facts to slander China as an aggressor simply because the Chinese frontier guards made great advances when they struck back in self-defence.

Question 5 Does China consider the boundary question so important that despite the principle of peaceful coexistence, there might be a military solution if negotiations should fail?

Answer China and India together initiated the famous Five Principles of Peaceful Coexistence. China has always adhered to these principles in her relations with India. China stands for a friendly settlement of her boundary question with India through negotiations based on the Five Principles of Peaceful Coexistence. Pending a settlement, she stands for maintaining the *status quo* on the boundary and avoiding armed conflicts. The facts have demonstrated during the past years that it was not China which acted counter to the principles of peaceful coexistence and which attempted a military solution of the boundary question. China decided to effect a cease-fire and to withdraw on her own initiative even though she had made great gains during the self-defensive counter-blow which she was forced to strike. If we believe in a military solution, is it conceivable that we would withdraw the Chinese frontier guards from large tracts of territory which was south of the illegal McMahon Line and which belonged to China in the first place?

Question 6 How does China regard the Indian reaction to the Chinese proposals for ceasefire and negotiations?

Answer Frankly speaking, we are disappointed.

The Chinese side took many steps to facilitate an amicable settlement of the boundary question through negotiations. On October 24, the Chinese Government put forward three proposals for peace, namely, to stop the border conflict, to reopen peaceful negotiations and to settle the Sino-Indian boundary question. Moreover, on November 21, the Chinese Government announced a ceasefire and withdrawal on its own initiative, and proposed that officials of the two sides hold meetings immediately. China released more than 600 sick and wounded Indian military personnel. China also returned to the Indian side large stores of military equipment which had been captured in the fighting. This was something unprecedented. The Chinese frontier guards in compliance with the Statement of the Chinese Government, are about to complete their withdrawal all along the line to positions 20 kilometres behind the line of actual control as it existed on November 7, 1959. It must be evident to every unbiased person that all these actions taken by China created the necessary conditions for direct negotiations between China and India.

But what has India done in the meantime? Instead of responding positively to the ceasefire and withdrawal, undertaken on China's own initiative, the Indian side has from time to time been carrying out provocations. A *de facto* ceasefire has come into being on the border, thanks to the efforts of the Chinese side. Yet, the Indian Government has adopted measures to create an artificial war atmosphere. During the last two or three months, the Indian Government has been constantly whipping up hysteria against China and goading the Indian people on for what it calls a prolonged 'war effort'. Tearing up unilaterally the agreement for the mutual establishment of Consulates-General, the Indian Government closed down its consulates in China and compelled China to close down her consulates in India. The Indian Government groundlessly arrested and detained more than 2,000 Chinese nationals in India, putting them in concentration camps. It even went so far as to censor and detail all mail and telegrams, both private and official, between China and India. Everyone knows that these are measures taken only when a formal state of war has been declared between two countries. These acts of India have placed more and more difficulties in the way of a peaceful settlement of the Sino-Indian boundary question. . . .

Question 11 What are the prospects for direct negotiations between China and India in the near future?

Answer It is our hope that the Indian Government will not persist in its unreasonable insistence that the Colombo proposals and the clarifications be accepted *in toto* before preliminary talks can begin and that they will thus make it possible for Chinese and Indian officials to meet immediately. But, frankly speaking, I am not at all sure this will happen. You know that the Chinese Government has been consistently seeking direct negotiations between China and India. But if it can't be done, the Chinese Government is willing to wait patiently. . . .

Question 13 How does China regard her long-term relations with India?

Answer Historically, the Chinese and Indian peoples have always lived together in friendship. There is no fundamental conflict of interest between the two countries. Both China and India are great countries of Asia. We both face urgent tasks of reconstruction to transform the backward state of our economy. We both shoulder heavy responsibilities for consolidating Asian-African solidarity, safeguarding world peace and opposing imperialism. Despite the incessant anti-China clamour of the Indian Government, China has never considered India as her enemy. You, Mr Correspondent, have visited quite a few places in China. Did you hear any war propaganda directed against India? Did you see any preparation for war against India? I don't believe you did, because it is a fact that nothing of the sort exists here in our country. The Chinese people are friends of the Indian people. The tense relations between China and India were artificially created by the Indian Government alone. This is a very unfortunate situation. But, we do not believe that this state of affairs which run counter to the desires of the Chinese and Indian people can endure for long. The dark clouds which hang now over China and India are bound to disappear. In the long view, the border dispute is only a brief episode in the history of Sino-Indian friendship.

*

The following extract gives the Chinese view on the return of captured arms, a gesture which the Indians found humiliating.

DOCUMENT 35. EXTRACT FROM 'NEW DELHI RETURNS EVIL FOR GOOD!' (*Peking Review*, 6, 4, 25 JANUARY 1963, PP. 10–11)

According to a report of the Indian Information Service, a spokesman of the Indian Ministry of External Affairs stated on January 8, 1963, that India had received from the Chinese side some Indian army equipment previously captured by the Chinese frontier guards, which were all 'heavily damaged,' and that the Chinese side had returned this equipment for 'propaganda purposes.' Following the statement made by the spokesman of the Indian Ministry of External Affairs, Indian newspapers have one after another cast aspersion on the Chinese Government, alleging that the Chinese Government has 'launched a propaganda campaign' on the handing over of equipment, that the handing over is a 'treacherous manoeuvre,' and so on and so forth.

The Chinese Government did not make public, nor intended to make public, the return of captured weapons, ammunition and other military supplies to the Indian side by the Chinese frontier guards. Unexpectedly, this measure on the part of China has been distorted and slandered by the Indian side, so the Chinese Government cannot but make public the related facts.

After the ceasefire by the Chinese frontier guards on China's own initiative and during their withdrawal, the Chinese Government, in order to further demonstrate its sincerity for a peaceful settlement of the Sino-Indian boundary question and to create an atmosphere of conciliation between the two countries, instructed the Chinese frontier guards to collect the weapons, ammunition and other military supplies of the Indian troops which they had captured during their counter-attacks in self-defence and return them to the Indian side.

In resolutely carrying out the instructions of the Chinese Government, the Chinese frontier guards first left the collected captured supplies with the local headmen in Limeking, Sati and Mechukha on December 6, 8 and 11 respectively, requesting them to hand the same over to the Indian side speedily. The Chinese frontier guards also left with the headmen letters addressed to the Indian side and detailed lists of the returned supplies. Afterwards, on December 19, the Chinese frontier guards further handed over the collected captured supplies in Dirang Dzong and Walong to civil officials sent by the Indian side to receive them. After the checking and handing over, representatives of both sides signed the lists of returned supplies. Dangerous articles among the returned supplies were specially marked by the Chinese frontier guards so that the Indian side might take safety precautions while taking them over. Among the supplies returned to the Indian side were weapons, ammunition, aircraft, tanks, vehicles, various military equipment and material, clothing and bedding, etc.

(c) INDOCHINA

The part played by Chou En-lai at Geneva in 1954 in persuading the Democratic Republic of Vietnam to accept less than it hoped for and was entitled to expect on the basis of its military position is explained in the following account.

DOCUMENT 36. THE ROLE OF CHOU EN-LAI AT THE GENEVA CONFERENCE. EXTRACT FROM H. C. HINTON, *Communist China in World Politics*, MACMILLAN, LONDON, 1966, PP. 252–4

The last and crucial phase of the Geneva Conference, which began in mid-July, was marked by extremely hard bargaining between France and the DRV, the reluctance of the United States to associate itself with the settlement, and the CPR's determination that the United States should do so.

Mendès-France made skillful use of French control of the Red River delta and of threats to continue the war as a means of getting concessions from the DRV. All the negotiators were acutely aware of his self-imposed deadline, and no one seems to have been willing to take the risks and uncertainties that his resignation would entail. The DRV was presumably anxious to inherit Hanoi intact, as the CPR had inherited Peking, and therefore not to have to besiege it. The DRV probably also remembered that the CPR had fought for Peking's port, Tientsin, with serious damage to the city, and was anxious that the same thing should not happen to Haiphong. As against the 18th parallel, which Mendès-France had been demanding as the dividing line in Vietnam, the DRV had been insisting on the 13th or 14th parallel, which as a matter of fact would have corresponded fairly closely with the actual military situation. Now the DRV with Molotov's support suddenly proposed the 16th parallel, which had been the demarcation line in 1945 between the Chinese Nationalist and British occupation zones. This would still have given the DRV a common frontier with Cambodia and control over the naval base at Tourane (Danang) and a major highway leading westward from Vietnam into central Laos, both of which lie between the 16th and 17th parallels. On another vital issue, that of a time limit for general elections in Vietnam, Mendès-France was agreeing to them within eighteen months; the DRV was demanding them within six months. The deadlock was broken at the last minute by Molotov, who was obviously very tired and anxious for a settlement. He proposed the 17th parallel, thus leaving Tourane and the highway to Laos outside the DRV's control, and elections within two years. The DRV was very unhappy but could only acquiesce.

For his part, Chou En-lai appeared to be less concerned with these details than with excluding any American military presence from Indochina and ensuring that the three non-Communist Indochinese states did not join or affiliate themselves in any way with SEATO. The United States was agreeable to this, but it rejected a last-minute demand by Chou En-lai that it sign the Geneva agreements. Rather than risk the failure of the conference, Chou then accepted a unilateral declaration by the United States that it would not 'disturb' the agreements. Ho Chi Minh, for his part, indicated that his victory had been merely postponed by announcing that he expected 'the unification of the nation by means of general elections.'

The DRV had already abandoned its claim that its Cambodian puppet, the Khmer Issarak, be granted legality and territorial bases. As Mendès-France's deadline approached, however, the DRV was insisting by way of compensation on an autonomous government controlled by the Pathet Lao in the Laotian border provinces of Sam Neua and Phong Saly. On July 18, Mendès-France argued Chou En-lai into abandoning the DRV's claim which therefore had to be dropped. Pham Van Dong is reported to have been infuriated at Chou.

Under the Geneva agreements, none of the Indochina countries was to join any military alliances. Neither Vietnamese regime was allowed to receive outside military aid, except on a replacement basis. Laos was allowed to retain a small French military mission. The DRV was to withdraw its forces in Vietnam south of the 17th parallel, from Laos and from Cambodia. These military arrangements were to be supervised by three ICC's, each with India as Chairman and Poland and Canada as the other members. Vietnam was partitioned, in fact although not in name at the 17th parallel, but it was generally expected that the general elections scheduled for July, 1956, would give the entire country to the Communists. Cambodia, which had seen little fighting and bargained energetically at Geneva, secured the withdrawal of all Communist forces from its territory. In Laos, the forces of the Pathet Lao, a Communist front organization controlled by the DRV, were to concentrate in the two border provinces at Sam Neua and Phong Saly, and general elections were to be held in 1955 to integrate these two provinces into the political life of the country as a whole.

The CPR had attained at Geneva what seems to have been its main security objective at the time, the exclusion of American bases and alliance systems from Indochina. Presumably it was worried by some vague remarks by Secretary Dulles about a possible 'three-pronged attack' on the CPR based on Korea, the Taiwan Strait, and Indochina.

The CPR had enormously enhanced its international prestige, especially with the neutrals, by its role in the Geneva Conference which had been more important than that of any other participant except perhaps Britain. This was of course the first international conference that it had attended, and the impression that it made was enhanced by the glamor of the unknown. The handsome and urbane Chou En-lai was given a more enthusiastic reception by the press and the public than was any other delegate when he arrived at Geneva. There is no doubt that he performed very ably and effectively at the conference. On the other hand, the CPR made no measurable progress at Geneva toward its basic objectives with respect to Korea, Taiwan, and the United Nations, unless one assumes that the partial withdrawal of American and Chinese forces from Korea in the autumn of 1954 was the result of an un-announced arrangement concluded at or shortly after the Geneva Conference. Since the CPR did not have American recognition or a seat on the United Nations Security Council, there was no assurance that it would be invited to future con-ferences, in spite of its insistence that it should have a say in the settlement of all major international questions.

Nevertheless, the CPR had reason to feel satisfied on balance with the results of the Geneva Conference, and for this satisfac-tion a feeling of irritation and frustration on the part of the DRV was not too high a price to pay. The DRV could be squared with economic and military aid, and although its position had been seriously truncated at Geneva it still seemed strong with respect to its most important objective, South Vietnam—because of the guarantee of elections within two years—if less so with respect to Laos and much less so with respect to Cambodia.

*

The records of the Laos conference have not yet been published. The following extracts written by the head of the Indian delegation to the Laos Conference illustrate the Chinese style in negotiation.

DOCUMENT 37. EXTRACTS FROM ARTHUR LALL, *How Communist China Negotiates*, COLUMBIA UNIVERSITY PRESS, NEW YORK, 1968, PP. 1–5

The Nature of the Chinese Presence in Negotiation

The most recent of the rare manifestations of the nature of the presence of the People's Republic of China at multigovernmental negotiations with non-Communist states occurred at the Fourteen-Nation International Conference on the Settlement of the Laotian Question, which was held at Geneva from May 16, 1961, through July 23, 1962.

The delegations to the conference assembled in the spacious high-ceilinged council chamber of the Palais des Nations, the European headquarters of the United Nations. This distinguished conference room is dominated by the massive figures and forms of the murals and ceiling paintings of José Maria Sert, and this dominance is heightened by the somber glows of the browns, grays, silvers, and golds which the artist favored for such works. But when the Laos Conference met, the room's normal accent was challenged by the intrusion of a yet more serious and massive presence: the delegation of the Peking government, numbering some fifty men and women, all dressed in drab olive khaki uniforms buttoned up to the neck. This single delegation not only filled the quota of a half dozen chairs reserved for it, as for each of the other thirteen delegations, but occupied almost a full quarter of the tiered seats in the galleries along the four walls of the room. If all the fourteen countries invited to the conference had come with delegations as large as that from Peking, no room at the Palais des Nations would have been large enough for the meetings. As it was, the Chinese delegation was by far the biggest in the room. The average delegation mustered a half dozen persons, and only three delegations other than the Chinese—those of the United States, the Soviet Union, and the United Kingdom—went barely into double figures. The personnel of all the thirteen delegations other than the Chinese filled just half the seats in the room.

Consequently, the uniformed block of Chinese delegates was overwhelmingly the dominant presence at the conference. . . .

The lesson of numbers in human confrontations has been thoroughly grasped by the modern Chinese leaders. It is a weapon that is ready at hand, and its use has been extended to the negotiating table. The presence of about fifty Chinese in the room at the Laos Conference was a factor to which the other delegations had to adjust themselves, and it cannot be said that this was a factor completely without psychological effect.

It is, of course, not the case that the large size of the Chinese delegation was to be explained only by the impression of power the Peking government sought to make at Geneva. Part of the explanation was the nature of the composition of the delegation: it included, for example, representatives of Chinese publicity media.

Two other factors probably also have a direct bearing on the size of the Chinese presence at such conferences. One is that the Chinese government undoubtedly takes advantage of such rare opportunities as the Laos Conference to give its personnel some experience of observing and dealing with the officials of Western and other states. The second relevant factor could be the pre-vailing insistence of the Chinese Communists, as a tactic of dealing with issues, on intensive discussion by groups of party members before views are formulated for presentation to those who take decisions. From his early days as a leader Mao has stressed the importance of this procedure. In December 1929 he wrote a comprehensive resolution for adoption at a conference on the Communist Party organization in the army, in which he stated:

Party organisations at all levels should not make decisions without due deliberation. . . . The rank-and-file Party members must discuss in detail directives from the higher bodies in order to understand their significance thoroughly and decide on the methods to carry them out.

It was not only during meeting breaks at Geneva that groups in the Chinese delegation, heads bent closely together, would be engaged in earnest discussion; whenever I took a draft proposal to the Chinese delegation at their own quarters it would be passed from hand to hand among a group of four or five senior members of the delegation who would rapidly discuss it among themselves before their spokesman (or -men) commented. Deputy Foreign Minister, Chang Han-fu, who was the working head of the delegation, would be the first to read the proposal. His face would show no reaction. Since there was no sign of a negative response, at my first meeting of this kind I thought that my proposal—into which much thought had gone both in regard to content and wording—was acceptable or, at any rate, was being sympathetically received. I was mistaken. Chang Han-fu raised a few points after discussing my proposal with his colleagues. Then he said something to the interpreter, who took over and, in rapidly delivered Harvard English, stated a long list of objections, some of them quite fundamental. I argued in favor of my draft. Ch'iao Kuan-hua, now a Deputy Minister, answered, 'Mr Lall, I know you mean well. You think you can persuade the Americans to accept your proposal. We know them better than you. We dealt with them for a long time after the War. They went back on all the promises they made to us through General Marshall. They won't accept your proposals.'

'But you don't accept them either!'

Chang Han-fu broke in: 'We've not said we don't accept them. We've told you that many improvements could be made. Why should we accept them in their present form when, as you can see now, they can be improved? Don't you think our suggestions are good? Then, do you think the Americans will accept them? We don't think they will. Here is fresh tea. Please let us have some.'

A willowy and lovely Chinese girl had brought several pots of fresh tea and Chinese cookies. We drank the tea and turned to talk about the Chinese ballet and some new Chinese writers. Before I left I returned to my proposals. Again the Chinese talked among themselves. Ch'iao laughed in a high mocking tone. 'Show it to them with the improvements we have suggested. We tell you they will say, "No." But we appreciate what you are trying to do. We will always discuss the matter with you.' Three senior members of the delegation, led by Chang Han-fu, saw me to the front door, where another bunch of smiling, more junior Chinese waited to escort me to my car. Always they operate in groups.

A negotiation is an important matter when the United

States and several other 'capitalist' countries are ranged on the other side, and when Asian neutrals or nonaligned countries are present and must be duly considered. Besides, following the Mao dictum, there have to be enough members for each level in the hierarchy to hold its own discussions on the issues remitted to it. In 1954, too, their delegation at Geneva had been large and to Bandung in 1955 they took an enormous delegation. Moreover, at any conference there are times when each delegation must be represented at several simultaneous informal discussions, and to each of these the Chinese depute several diplomats. Though the major reason for this could be that it enables the delegation to function on the basis of intra-delegation discussion at each level of consideration of an issue, it certainly enables the closely knit Chinese to reassure themselves that no single member has talked or otherwise behaved in ways that could embarrass his government.

*

Growing American involvement in Indochina, the increasing commitment of US ground forces, and the decision of the Johnson administration to bomb North Vietnam into submission in 1965 posed serious problems for China.

In commenting on the American aggression the Chinese have carefully refrained from any suggestion that they would send troops to Vietnam.

DOCUMENT 38. EXTRACTS FROM 'ESCALATION MEANS GETTING CLOSER AND CLOSER TO THE GRAVE'. EDITORIAL IN *People's Daily*, 24 APRIL 1965 (*Peking Review*, 8, 18, 30 APRIL 1965, PP. 13–14)

The US imperialist war machine is operating at an increased tempo. It can be predicted that the Johnson Administration will continue to lay down its peace smokescreen. War expansion, peace fraud, and then war expansion again—these two tactics will be employed alternatively in a pattern of cyclical repetition. This is the customary practice of the Johnson Administration on the Vietnam question.

Let us take a look at the Johnson Administration's record over more than the past two months.

On February 7, big US air raids against North Vietnam started when the White House was trying strenuously to show that the United States 'seeks no wider war.' At about the same time, a US battalion of Hawk missiles was introduced into South Vietnam.

On February 18, the US State Department declared that the United States was exploring 'all avenues of peaceful settlement.' Immediately, Washington ordered the direct participation of the US air force in the assault against the South Vietnamese people's armed forces and decided to increase the number of puppet troops by another 100,000 and send several hundred more US military 'advisers.'

Shortly afterward, the United States announced the dispatching of two battalions of marines, the first contingent of marines to be sent to South Vietnam. What the United States was exploring turned out to be an avenue to war expansion.

On March 7, Rusk spread the speculation that for the United States the 'political channels' to the solution of the Vietnam question 'remain open.' Four days later, US planes began to extend their bombing deeper into the interior of North Vietnam. Then, six days afterward, 2,000 South Korean mercenaries arrived in South Vietnam. In fact, the United States was widening the channel to war further.

On March 25, Johnson issued a statement boasting that the United States 'will never be second in seeking a settlement.' Right after these high-sounding words were mouthed, US air strikes against North Vietnam went farther than the 20th parallel.

On April 7, Johnson, in his Baltimore address, expressed his willingness to conduct 'unconditional discussions' on the Vietnam question in order to achieve a 'peaceful settlement.' But only three days later, the United States sent its second contingent of two battalions of marines and a squadron of naval jet planes to South Vietnam. US planes even carried out provocation against China by intruding into the airspace over Hainan Island.

In face of this series of iron-clad facts, even the most slow-witted person will not believe that the Johnson Administration is really concerned about peace rather than expanding step by step its war of aggression in Vietnam. By its own increasingly truculent military actions, US imperialism has torn off its 'peaceful settlement' mask and slapped those who have made Herculean efforts to describe the US Government as 'restrained' and 'prudent' in the face.

Therefore, when Johnson in his April 17 statement talked glibly about 'window to peace' and 'come to the meeting room —we will be there,' we knew what US imperialism was up to. Sure enough, into the 'war room' of the US Pacific military command two days later walked McNamara, the US Defense Secretary, followed by a group of top-ranking military officers. The subject discussed was an even more adventurous step to expand the war.

For more than two months, the Johnson Administration has professed repeatedly that its military action of aggression against Vietnam is 'appropriate,' 'measured,' and 'carefully limited.' But the actual facts are that the United States, from sending 'advisers' to South Vietnam, has gone on to taking a direct part in the war; from aggression in the South to attacks on the North; from bombing raids south of the 18th Parallel to bombing raids north of the 20th Parallel; from day raids to round-the-clock raids; and from bombing of military targets to bombing of civilians. All this shows that what the Johnson Administration called 'appropriate,' 'measured,' and 'carefully limited' military action is a planned gradual expansion of the war.

A so-called theory of 'escalation' on the unleashing of an aggressive war is now prevalent among US ruling groups. They divide a war into a number of thresholds, each consisting of a number of rungs. They have advocated strengthening and expanding the use and threat of force according to these methods. The tactics used by the Johnson Administration are very similar to Hitler's gradual expansion of aggression before World War Two. The aim is nothing less than to slacken the vigilance of the world's people, so that they will be faced with a *fait accompli* by the US aggressor before they know it. While taking 'escalation' steps, the Johnson Administration continuously waves its olive branch in a vain attempt to demoralize its victims, hoodwink public opinion, and conceal its crimes of deliberately expanding the war. This is precisely what it is doing in Vietnam. . . .

If US imperialism refuses to withdraw all its armed forces from Vietnam, there will be no peace in Vietnam and Indochina, no matter how many times Johnson may repeat his words of 'peace.' The most important task of the people of Asia and the rest of the world today is to give resolute support to the Vietnamese people's just struggle against US aggression and for national salvation, to shatter Johnson's peace-talk schemes completely, curb his plans for escalating the war, and drive the US aggressors out of Vietnam.

(d) OUTER MONGOLIA

A significant comment on Mongolia was made by Mao Tse-tung on 10 July 1964 in reply to a question from Japanese Socialist delegates.

DOCUMENT 39. EXTRACT FROM 'CHAIRMAN MAO TSE-TUNG TELLS THE DELEGATION OF THE JAPANESE SOCIALIST PARTY THAT THE KURILES MUST BE RETURNED TO JAPAN', *Sekai Shuhu*, TOKYO, 11 AUGUST 1964 (D. J. DOOLIN, *Territorial Claims in the Sino-Soviet Conflict*, HOOVER INSTITUTION ON WAR, REVOLUTION AND PEACE, STANFORD UNIVERSITY, 1965, PP. 43-4)

The Head of the delegation of the staff of the Socialist Party on the island of Hokkaido, Tetsuo Ara, asked, 'At a time when we were kept in ignorance, the Kuriles were taken away from us in accordance with the Yalta Agreement and the Potsdam Declaration. We demand their return (by the Soviet Union) and, in this connection, would like to hear Chairman Mao's opinion.'

The following was said in reply: 'There are too many places occupied by the Soviet Union. In accordance with the Yalta Agreement, the Soviet Union, under the pretext of assuring the independence of Mongolia, actually placed the country under its domination. Mongolia takes up an area which is considerably greater than the Kuriles. In 1954, when Khrushchev and Bulganin came to China, we took up this question but they refused to talk to us. They (i.e., the Soviet Union) also appropriated part of Rumania. Having cut off a portion of East Germany, they chased the local inhabitants into West Germany.

They detached a part of Poland, annexed it to the Soviet Union, and gave a part of East Germany to Poland as compensation. The same thing took place in Finland. The Russians took everything they could. Some people have declared that the Sinkiang area and the territories north of the Amur River must be included in the Soviet Union. The Soviet Union is concentrating troops along its border.

'The Soviet Union has an area of 22 million square kilometres and its population is only 220 million. It is about time to put an end to this allotment. Japan occupies an area of 370,000 square kilometres and its population is 100 million. About a hundred years ago, the area to the east of (Lake) Baikal became Russian territory, and since then Vladivostok, Khabarovsk, Kamchatka, and other areas have been Soviet territory. We have not yet presented our account for this list. In regard to the Kurile Islands, the question is clear as far as we are concerned—they must be returned to Japan.'

*

Mao's remarks were in contrast to a statement on the Mongolian boundary by the Chinese Foreign Minister at a press conference a year later.

DOCUMENT 40. STATEMENT ON THE MONGOLIAN BOUNDARY. EXTRACT FROM FOREIGN MINISTER CHEN YI'S PRESS CONFERENCE, 29 SEPTEMBER 1965 ('VICE-PREMIER CHEN YI ANSWERS QUESTIONS PUT BY CORRESPONDENTS', FOREIGN LANGUAGES PRESS, PEKING, 1966, PP. 20–21)

On the Delimitation of the Sino-Mongolian Boundary

A correspondent from the Hongkong paper *Chin Pao* asked: The relationship between Outer Mongolia and China proper is closer than that between Tibet and China proper, whether viewed historically or from the standpoint of race, colour and culture. Tibet is part of China's territory, and all the more so is Outer Mongolia. Such being the case, why is it that the delimitation of the Sino-Mongolian boundary should have taken place?

In reply, Vice-Premier Chen Yi said: Tibet and the Mongolian People's Republic are two different matters, which should not be mentioned in the same breath. The Mongolian People's Republic proclaimed independence in 1924 following a revolution, whereas Tibet has always been a part of China's territory.

In 1945 Chiang Kai-shek's government concluded a treaty with the Government of the Soviet Union recognizing the Mongolian People's Republic. After its founding, New China succeeded to the commitment and recognized Mongolia as a socialist country. It is only natural and nothing strange for China and Mongolia to delimit the boundary between them in a friendly way.

There are Han chauvinists in China, who have always refused to recognize the Mongolian People's Republic. We are opposed to such Han chauvinism. Since its founding, New China has provided the Mongolian People's Republic with large amounts of aid. In recent years, the leading group of Mongolia has been following the Khrushchov revisionists in opposing China. But we do not cancel our aid to it on this account, because our New China is guided by Marxism-Leninism and Mao Tse-tung's thought, and we are not Khrushchov revisionists. It is for the Mongolian people themselves to decide whether co-operation with China is more in their interests. We do not impose our will on them.

(e) JAPAN

At the time of the signing of the peace treaty between Japan and the Allied Powers (8 September 1951) a separate Security Treaty provided for the continued defence of Japan by American forces. When, in 1958, the United States and Japan began negotiations to revise the Security Treaty the Chinese feared a revival of Japanese militarism.

DOCUMENT 41. CHINESE FOREIGN MINISTER CHEN YI'S STATEMENT ON REVISION OF JAPANESE-US SECURITY TREATY, 19 NOVEMBER 1958 (*China Today*, 3, 9, 1958, PP. 2–3)

It is by no means accidental that the United States has agreed to revise the Japanese-US 'security treaty' at the present moment. Having suffered successive defeats recently after entering the field itself in the Near and Middle East and particularly in the Taiwan Straits area, the United States is now anxious to find a capable helper in the Far East to bear the brunt for it, so that its plot of using Asians to fight Asians may be realized. Nor is it at all strange that Kishi should be willing to go with the United States into deep water. The Kishi Government, which is the concentrated expression of latent imperialism in Japan, imagines that by further collaborating with the United States, it would be able to revive Japanese militarism, suppress the dissatisfaction and resistance of the Japanese people, save Japan from its ever more serious economic crisis and realize the ambitions of Japanese monopoly capital to have a finger in Taiwan and to expand in the direction of Southeast Asia. But Kishi has totally miscalculated. The world of to-day is by no means the world of twenty years ago. The powerful Soviet Union and China are impregnable. The attempt of Japanese monopoly capital to carry out economic, political and military expansion in Southeast Asia by means of further military collusion with the United States is also bound to be frustrated. The awakened people of the Southeast Asian countries definitely will not tolerate Japanese plunder. Japanese expansion can have no other result but inciting the resolute opposition of the peoples of these countries, with itself ending in failure. If Kishi should refuse to come to his senses and be determined to play the accomplice in the United States aggression against China and the rest of Asia, he will be 'lifting a rock only to have his own toes squashed'.

Japan is a nation with a tradition of independence. The Japanese people are industrious, talented and brave. The Japanese people cannot possibly allow the United States to lord it over them for long. They resolutely demand the termination of the state of US occupation of Japan, the abrogation of the unequal treaties between the United States and Japan, and the establishment of relations of equality between Japan and the United States as between independent states. The Chinese people have always supported the Japanese people in their struggle for independence, peace and democracy, and heartily wish that Japan would become a country of peace and neutrality. The only bright future for the Japanese people lies in an independent, democratic, peace-loving and neutral Japan which has economic relations of equality and mutual benefit with other countries of the world, first of all with Asian countries, and together with them makes progress, enjoys prosperity and lives in peace.

Kishi's policy of leading the Japanese people to a dead end has evoked the ever stronger resistance of the Japanese people of all social strata. In order to deprive the Japanese people of democratic freedoms and pave the way for the revision of the Japanese-US 'security treaty', the Kishi Government is trying to force through the 'revision bill of police duties law'. The Japanese people have launched a powerful mass movement, unprecedented in its scale, to oppose this bill, to oppose the new military collusion between the US and Japanese reactionaries and to oppose the Kishi Government's policy of antagonizing China. Sensible people in the Liberal Democratic Party are also expressing ever greater discontent with Kishi's reactionary policy. The Chinese people have a sincere sympathy for and support the Japanese people in their just struggle to attain independence and safeguard democracy. Although the struggle will be long and the path tortuous, the US imperialists and their accomplices will surely suffer final defeat and the Japanese people will surely win ultimate victory.

*

A new Treaty of Mutual Co-operation and Security between Japan and the United States was finally signed in 1960, and ratified by Prime Minister Kishi, in the face of strong public demonstrations in Japan. Kishi's resignation in July 1960 was welcomed in China. China's policy was to woo sympathetic elements in Japan while developing commercial relations.

DOCUMENT 42. COMMENT ON SINO-JAPANESE RELATIONS. EXTRACT FROM FOREIGN MINISTER CHEN YI'S PRESS CONFERENCE, 29 SEPTEMBER 1965 ('VICE-PREMIER CHEN YI ANSWERS QUESTIONS PUT BY CORRESPONDENTS', FOREIGN LANGUAGES PRESS, PEKING, 1966, P. 18)

The Japanese correspondents asked about the prospects of Sino-Japanese relations. Vice-Premier Chen Yi replied: A lot has been said on this question by leaders of our country, so I will only give a brief answer here. If the present Japanese Government stops tailing after the United States, pursues an independent policy and renounces its anti-Chinese policy, possibilities will increase for the normalization of Sino-Japanese relations. At present the Sato cabinet is politically following the US anti-Chinese policy, while economically it wants to reap gains from Sino-Japanese trade. Such a policy is self-contradictory and cannot help normalize Sino-Japanese relations. It is up to Japan to remove this obstacle. Out of consideration for the traditional friendship between the great nations of peoples of China and Japan, the Chinese Government is willing to carry on trade between the two countries on the present level, but it is impossible to expand it.

The Japanese nation is full of promise, and the Japanese love peace. They demand the liquidation of US imperialist control and the dismantling of US bases in Japan. We have deep sympathy with their demands.

PART IV

China and the Third World

Immediately after Liberation, the Chinese were conscious that their example would have significance for other oppressed peoples, but were too preoccupied with their own problems to give more than expressions of sympathy except where, as in Vietnam, their own security was at stake. As more and more ex-colonial states achieved independence under nationalist non-communist regimes the emphasis of Peking's propaganda shifted from 'armed struggle' to 'peaceful co-existence' as highlighted at the Bandung conference. In the later 1950s it became apparent that the Bandung policy had failed to undermine American power and influence in South and East Asia (indeed the United States had begun to expand its influence), the dispute with India became acute, and the Chinese pressed their Soviet allies unsuccessfully to lead the struggle against imperialism. At about this time, Peking embarked on a more radical policy towards the new and underdeveloped states. In competition with both Soviet and American influence, the Chinese attempted in the first years of the 1960s to create a third force dedicated less to peaceful co-existence than to militant anti-imperialism.

The Chinese sought to play an influential role in the Afro-Asian People's Solidarity Organization which was formed in December 1957 in Cairo. At that time there was sympathy for Egypt, which had been the first Middle Eastern country to recognize Peking (in 1956), and China supported, in the cause of anti-imperialism and anti-Americanism, the Arab aims for the liberation of Palestine. However, in 1958, when Nasser, having formed the United Arab Republic, took steps to restrict the growth of communism in Syria, the Chinese began to cultivate the Algerians. They supplied the Algerian National

Liberation Front with arms, and gave recognition to the Front's provisional government during the years of struggle with France. Peking upheld the Algerians as a model for insurgency in the Third World and after the victory of Ben Bella in 1962 Algeria became a centre of Chinese influence in North Africa.

China's militant approach to national liberation movements undoubtedly reflected the Maoist rather than the less Maoist component in the Chinese leadership. Moreover it was appropriate in the dispute with the USSR for the Chinese to emphasize their own experience in resisting imperialist domination and exploitation. In the compromise agreement at Moscow in 1960 the Chinese contribution put stress on the importance of the class struggle in the capitalist countries, and on the national liberation movements in the colonial and dependent countries.

In 1964 the Chinese redefined their concept of the Intermediate Zone (analogous to the western term, the Third World). This had been originally described by Mao in 1946 as consisting of the vast area between the United States and the Soviet Union comprising capitalist, colonial and semi-colonial countries which he said the United States would have to subjugate before it could attack the Soviet Union. The 1964 definition divided the zone into two parts (see Document 52). Different tactics would be required in different areas. The first intermediate zone, the underdeveloped countries, would be responsive to calls for armed struggle against imperialism and neo-colonialism, while to the second intermediate zone, the advanced capitalist countries, China would stress the need for resistance to oppressive ruling classes and for national struggle against US imperialism.

The Chinese line was to play down the role of the 'national bourgeoisie' in the anti-imperialist struggle and to decry the value of aid from the developed capitalist states, although such views were not readily acceptable in many of the emerging nations. Moreover when the Chinese began to expect Afro-Asian states to show their friendship to China by opposing Soviet revisionism as well as American imperialism, they lost the support of those who were not on the extreme left. The countries of the Third World saw little benefit to themselves in the Sino-Soviet dispute.

The states of Latin America, underdeveloped and dominated

by the United States, might appear on first consideration to be a favourable area for the penetration of Chinese influence. In fact Peking has made little impression in Central and South America. One problem has been that the Communist parties have tended to be weak, ineffective and pro-Soviet. China's efforts have been directed to gaining the support of the communists of Latin America in the dispute with Moscow, and, when that failed, to creating reliable splinter parties. That policy succeeded to a limited degree in Brazil, Peru, Colombia, Chile and Haiti. It is a measure of China's failure to win over Latin American communist parties that in 1966 at the Tricontinental Conference held at Havana, China insisted that the Afro-Asian People's Solidarity Organization should keep its own identity rather than merge in an Afro-Asian-Latin American People's Solidarity Organization, in which pro-Soviet Latin American parties would be represented.

In the case of Cuba, China initially showed great interest in Castro's rise, as an example of the success of left-wing guerrilla warfare, and diplomatic relations and an aid programme were established in 1960. During the Cuban missile crisis Chinese propaganda exploited Khrushchev's failure but subsequently Chinese–Cuban relations deteriorated in the light of Castro's continued willingness to accept Soviet aid and of Peking's attempts to spread anti-Soviet propaganda inside Castro's regime.

In comparison with the Western Powers and the Soviet Union China has been able to give only a small amount of aid to the underdeveloped parts of the world. Nevertheless the total amount of China's foreign aid commitment in the period 1954 to 1964 has been roughly equal to the size of Soviet credits received by China, while interest rates have generally been lower than those charged by the Soviet Union. Most of China's aid has gone to the smaller communist states, notably North Korea and North Vietnam. China gave in aid to the Third World countries in the period 1956 to 1959 an average of $30 million a year distributed to seven countries, Cambodia, Ceylon, Indonesia, Nepal, the United Arab Republic and Yemen. However, in the years after 1960 the average annual value of aid rose to $125 million distributed among twenty-one countries of the Third World.

Not surprisingly China has emphasized the principle of self-help. This was an important theme of Chou En-lai's appeal to the new states of Africa during his extensive tour of that continent, December 1963 to February 1964. Chou, while stressing the rapid economic growth of China, was anxious not to give the impression that China was speedily becoming an economically developed power with no feeling for Africa's economic problems. China, he said, had always followed the line of 'taking agriculture as the foundation and industry as the leading factor'. China's 'Eight Principles of Economic Aid' were intended to encourage projects which required small investment while yielding quick results (Document 49).

In the case of armed uprisings China has consistently waited for the revolutionaries to demonstrate a measure of effectiveness before advancing its support. To insist that each revolutionary movement is fundamentally dependent on its own efforts makes sense when China's potentiality for giving aid is relatively small, and it also helps to preclude the backing of a lost cause. China's approach to the civil war in the Congo in 1964 exemplifies this policy. The Chinese press stridently denounced the imperialists and their mercenaries in the Congo while denying that China was intervening. Thus the thesis that 'revolution cannot be exported' was maintained, and there is evidence that in July 1964 the Chinese insisted that the Congolese insurgents should win at least one province as a condition for receiving aid. Bearing in mind Mao's stress on the importance of political objectives in guerrilla warfare and on the need for party leadership, the Chinese may well have doubted whether the Congolese were politically advanced enough to succeed.

The set-backs to the Congolese revolutionaries did not dim the optimism radiated by Chou En-lai when he addressed the National People's Congress in December 1964. The victory of the Algerian people was 'a brilliant example for the national-liberation movement in Africa'. The Congolese would ultimately win 'by . . . persisting in their long struggle'. China had given increasing aid to the socialist states and to newly-independent countries and, Chou En-lai insisted, would also support 'countries which are not yet independent in winning their independence'. The implication was that as China's economic situation improved she would increase her material support for national liberation movements.

Chou En-lai's wooing was intended to achieve consummation in a second conference of Afro-Asian states in 1965. The conference was postponed three times and finally abandoned. The fall of Ben Bella at the moment when the Chinese delegation en route to the conference had already reached Cairo was one cause of postponement. The other fundamental disagreements which finally doomed the conference were on policy in Vietnam, on the Chinese nuclear weapons programme which was not universally welcomed, and the Chinese insistence that the Soviet Union be excluded from the conference (see Document 50). It is possible that Mao himself insisted on this condition, disruptive though it was likely to be. The virtual cancellation of the conference on 1 November 1965 was a major diplomatic blow for China.

Another set-back had occurred in October when an attempted *coup* in Indonesia failed. Peking had been supporting President Sukarno's foreign policy in his confrontation with Britain and Malaysia, and had encouraged him at home in building a communist-led popular organization to check the power of the army. An abortive attempt by the Indonesian Communist Party, with the approval of Sukarno, to destroy the army's leaders, provoked a reaction in which half a million people died and the pro-Chinese Indonesian Communist Party was driven underground.

By the end of 1965, on the eve of the Cultural Revolution, China's Third World strategy had met with little success and was beginning to be counter-productive. Certain African leaders, for example Hamani Diori of Niger, Maurice Yameogo of Upper Yalta, and Hastings Banda of Malawi, issued warnings against the spread of Chinese influence in Africa. During the Cultural Revolution the fervent militancy emanating from Peking appalled many of Africa's leaders. The temporary outcome, albeit with important exceptions as in the case of Tanzania, was the weakening of Chinese influence. Subsequently, since 1969, relations between China and the Third World have improved, marked by a noticeably 'soft', non-aggressive and undemanding, policy line from Peking.

(a) THE CHINESE EXAMPLE

An editorial article in *People's China* February 1950 commemorating 'The Day of International Solidarity with the Youth and Students Fighting against Colonialism' organized by the World Federation of Democratic Youth, discussed the value of the Chinese example to other peoples struggling for national independence.

DOCUMENT 43. EXTRACTS FROM 'CHINA'S REVOLUTION AND THE STRUGGLE AGAINST COLONIALISM', *People's China*, 1, 4, 16 FEBRUARY 1950, PP. 4–5

The victory of the Chinese people has proved to the world that by following correct revolutionary lines colonial or semi-colonial peoples can defeat their imperialist rulers and gain true national independence.

The Chinese people have behind them a 110-year history of struggle against imperialism. Since the Opium War of 1840, they have had to fight against various types of imperialist encroachment—British 'free trade' and 'gunboat diplomacy'; the Americans' 'Open Door Policy' and intervention by 'mediation'; Japanese military aggression; etc. Because of the Chinese people's extremely abundant and varied experiences in fighting colonialism, and because of the resounding victory that has crowned their efforts, they are in a position to present many valuable lessons from China's successful revolution to all oppressed peoples who are struggling against colonialism.

The victorious history of the Chinese revolution has proved, first of all, that in colonial and semi-colonial countries, the working class must take the initiative in moulding a vast national united front directed against the imperialists and their local henchmen. It must mobilize into this front all classes, political parties and groups, organizations and individuals who are willing to oppose the colonial rulers and their running dogs. The corner-stone for this united front must be the staunch alliance of the working class and the broad peasant masses. And in order to form such an alliance, the working class must formulate a revolutionary agrarian program, based on the concrete conditions of the given country and the demands of the peasantry; and the workers must then fight shoulder-to-shoulder with the peasants to put this program into effect.

The working class must simultaneously unite with the broad masses of the petty bourgeoisie (especially with the revolutionary intelligentsia) for this class is also bitterly opposed to imperialism. Since the national bourgeoisie in colonies and semi-colonies are also oppressed by imperialism, they too can constitute a revolutionary force during the period of anti-imperialist struggle and can ally themselves with the working class under certain conditions and to a certain extent. Only the feudal landlord class (especially the big landlords) and the comprador bourgeois class, which both rely upon imperialism for their continued existence, are mortal enemies of the national liberation movement. Therefore, generally speaking, the working class can rally together all people in such countries except feudal landlords and comprador bourgeoisie and then lead them in the common fight against the imperialists and their henchmen. But unless such a broad national united front is mobilized, the working class, which is always a small minority of the population in economically undeveloped countries, cannot possibly lead the liberation movement to victory. . . .

In order to be able to assume leadership of the national liberation movement and to rally all these other classes around it, the working class and its Communist Party must be well-organized, well-disciplined and well-integrated with the masses. The Party must thoroughly master the theory of Marxism-Leninism and apply it to the concrete and objective conditions it confronts.

In colonies and semi-colonies, the Party cannot avoid drawing a high proportion of petty bourgeois elements into its ranks. Therefore it must conduct an unceasing ideological struggle against the disruptive traits inherent to this class, and especially against subjectivism, whether it takes the form of dogmatism or empiricism. This can only be done by skilfully employing criticism and self-criticism, an indispensable weapon in unifying the Party's own ranks, and by strengthening the leadership of the working class within the Party.

It is equally important for the Party and all revolutionary forces to comprehend that patriotism cannot be genuine patriotism unless it is integrated with proletarian internationalism. Their own experiences of struggle have convinced the Chinese people that only by leaning to one side, the side of the world democratic and peace-loving forces headed by the Soviet Union, can any country either achieve or maintain genuine independence.

This above point is of especial significance for the people of Southeast Asia, who are increasingly threatened by the conspiracies of Wall Street. American imperialism has taken to ranting with great noise and hypocrisy about 'national independence' for the 'backward countries', thus hoping to confuse the politically naive into thinking that independence is something which the imperialists can bestow upon them. But Titoism in Yugoslavia has already shown the world that bourgeois nationalism can only lead back into the clutches of imperialism, which is precisely why we find American spokesmen advocating this brand of 'nationalism'.

The history of the Chinese revolution has also proved that in colonies and semi-colonies, where the ruling classes are backed and armed by imperialist arsenals, the people cannot attain their liberation without an armed struggle. The people are faced with only the choice of organizing their own army to defend their interests or of being crushed by the mercenaries and traitors hired by the imperialists.

Now everybody realizes that without the heroic People's Liberation Army the Chinese people could not have attained their national liberation. However, it cannot be over-emphasized that the PLA would not have acquired its present invincible strength if it had not always been intimately linked with the broad masses of the peasants and with all the anti-imperialist forces in the country. Had the PLA adopted a purely military outlook, had it not gained the whole-hearted support of the people by fighting for the cause of the agrarian revolution and national independence, then the PLA could never have defeated the combined forces of domestic reaction and American imperialism.

This, of course, does not mean that armed struggle need not be co-ordinated with other forms of struggle. In those areas where the imperialists and their lackeys have a strong concentration of forces, it may not be possible to take up arms with any assurance of success. In such cases, the liberation movement should take on the form of legal and illegal mass struggles, which must, however, be co-ordinated with the armed struggle proceeding in other more favourable environments.

These are the major lessons to be drawn from the great victory of the Chinese people. These lessons can, with judicious adaptation, be applied by all colonial and semi-colonial peoples in their fight against colonialism for national independence.

*

The following extract from an article by Lu Ting-yi, a Member of the Central Committee of the CCP and director of the Party's Propaganda Department, is an early claim that Mao Tse-tung's theory of revolution is an extension of Marxism-Leninism with particular significance for the colonial and semi-colonial countries.

DOCUMENT 44. EXTRACT FROM LU TING-YI, 'THE WORLD SIGNIFICANCE OF THE CHINESE REVOLUTION', *People's China*, 4, 1, 1 JULY 1951, PP. 10–12

The victory of the Chinese people's revolution is a new victory of Marxism-Leninism. The integration of the universal truth of Marxism-Leninism with the concrete practice of the Chinese revolution constitutes Comrade Mao Tse-tung's theory of the Chinese revolution.

In the revolutionary movement of the colonial and semi-colonial countries, the most fundamental problem is one of the leadership of the revolution. If the revolutionary movement comes under the leadership of the political party of the bourgeoisie or the petty bourgeoisie, the revolution will fail, or will be liquidated or betrayed. It is only under the leadership of the working class that the revolution can win real victory.

The bourgeoisie in the colonial and semi-colonial countries can generally be divided into two categories.

The bureaucratic capitalists or the comprador capitalists are closely linked up with foreign imperialism and domestic feudal forces, and are the enemy which has to be overthrown by the people's democratic revolution.

The national bourgeoisie, who are repressed and squeezed

out by imperialism and feudalism, have fewer ties or no ties at all with foreign imperialism. They may participate in the people's democratic revolution or remain neutral. The working class in colonial and semi-colonial countries must pay close attention to the peasants, because they are the natural and most reliable ally of the working class. It must pay close attention to the petty bourgeoisie, because they are a reliable ally of the working class. It must also pay close attention to the national bourgeoisie, and unite them in a common struggle against imperialism. The working class in colonial and semi-colonial countries can and must lead the national bourgeoisie; it cannot and must never allow the national bourgeoisie to lead the revolution. This is because in the era of imperialism, with the exception of the working class, 'no other class in any country can lead any genuine revolution to victory.' . . .

The future development of New China will lead to socialism and Communism. China will take a path different from that of Japan which, after the Meiji Restoration, became an imperialist country and later on an actual colony of American imperialism. China will also take a path different from that of Turkey, which since the Kemal Revolution has become a satellite and henchman of the imperialist aggressive bloc. In the light of the great victory of the people's democratic revolution in China guided by Marxism-Leninism and Comrade Mao Tse-tung's theory of the Chinese revolution, all the bourgeois democratic movements of the old type in the history of Asia—such as the Meiji Restoration in Japan, the Kemal Revolution in Turkey, the Gandhiist movement in India, etc.—become pale and colourless. The victory in China of Marxism-Leninism and Comrade Mao Tse-tung's theory of the Chinese revolution will help the people of the Asian countries to free themselves from the influence of bourgeois democracy of the old type, resolutely take the path of the new democratic revolution of the people, and, after the victory of the people's democratic revolution, continue their march forward towards a better social system— the system of socialism and Communism.

Comrade Mao Tse-tung's theory of the Chinese revolution is a new development of Marxism-Leninism in the revolutions of the colonial and semi-colonial countries and especially in the Chinese revolution. This theory has significance not only for

China and Asia—they are of a universal significance for the world Communist movement. They are indeed a new contribution to the treasury of Marxism-Leninism. . . .

The prototype of the revolutions in imperialist countries is the October Revolution.

The prototype of the revolutions in colonial and semi-colonial countries is the Chinese Revolution.

(b) PEACEFUL CO-EXISTENCE

From 1951 onwards Chinese foreign policy began to place less emphasis on armed struggle, and to seek accommodation with the non-aligned states of Asia and Africa. India, with considerable influence in both the newly independent states and Western circles, was a key country in the move towards a policy of 'peaceful co-existence'. Sino-Indian discussions beginning in late 1953 resulted in an agreement in April 1954. India recognized the Chinese position in Tibet, and China and India agreed on the *Panch Shila* or Five Principles. In June 1954 Chou En-lai visited New Delhi while the Geneva Conference was in recess and a joint statement was issued reaffirming the Five Principles. It may be noted that the wording in reference to equality, mutual benefit and mutual respect for territorial integrity and sovereignty, is almost idential with the conditions for establishing diplomatic relations proclaimed by Mao in 1949 (Address to the Preparatory Meeting of the New Political Consultative Conference, 15 June 1949), and referred to in his speech of 30 June (Document 2).

The Five Principles have been included in virtually every treaty made by the People's Republic since 1954, an illustration of the enthusiasm of China's leaders for freely negotiated mutually advantageous agreements as the basis of international order.

DOCUMENT 45. THE FIVE PRINCIPLES OF CO-EXISTENCE. EXTRACT FROM JOINT STATEMENT BY THE PRIME MINISTERS OF INDIA AND CHINA ISSUED IN NEW DELHI, 28 JUNE 1954

Recently India and China have come to an agreement in which they laid down certain principles which should guide the relations between the two countries. These principles are:

1 Mutual respect for each other's territorial integrity and sovereignty;
2 Non-aggression;
3 Non-interference in each other's internal affairs;
4 Equality and mutual benefit; and
5 Peaceful co-existence.

The Prime Ministers reaffirmed these principles and felt that they should be applied in their relations with other countries in Asia as well as in other parts of the world. If these principles are applied not only between various countries but also in international relations generally, they would form a solid foundation for peace and security and the fears and apprehensions that exist today would give place to a feeling of confidence.

*

Peking's accommodating approach in the mid-fifties to the countries of the Third World was clearly demonstrated at the Bandung Conference of twenty-nine Asian and African nations in April 1955. The three Asian members of SEATO (formed in September 1954), the Philippines, Thailand and Pakistan, were present.

DOCUMENT 46. EXTRACT FROM SPEECH BY CHOU EN-LAI BEFORE THE FULL CONFERENCE OF AFRO-ASIAN COUNTRIES AT BANDUNG, 19 APRIL 1955 (SUPPLEMENT TO *People's China*, 16 MAY 1955, PP. 11–13)

In our conference we should seek common ground among us, while keeping our differences. As to our common ground, the conference should affirm all our common desires and demands. This is our main task here. As to our differences, none of us is asked to give up his own views, because difference in viewpoints is an objective reality. But we should not let our differences hinder us from achieving agreement as far as our main task is concerned. On the basis of our common points, we should try to understand and appreciate the different views that we hold.

Now first of all I would like to talk about the question of different ideologies and social systems. We have to admit that among our Asian and African countries, we do have different ideologies and different social systems. But this does not prevent us from seeking common ground and being united. Many independent countries have appeared since the Second World War. One group of them are countries led by the Communist Parties; another group of them are countries led by nationalists. There are not many countries in the first group. But what some people dislike is the fact that the 600 million Chinese people have chosen a political system which is socialist in nature and led by the Chinese Communist Party and that the Chinese people are no longer under the rule of imperialism. The countries in the second group are greater in number, such as India, Burma, Indonesia and many other countries in Asia and Africa. Out of the colonial rule both of these groups of countries have become independent and are still continuing their struggle for complete independence. Is there any reason why we cannot understand and respect each other and give support and sympathy to each other? There is every reason to make the five principles the basis for establishing friendly co-operation and good neighbourly relations among us. We Asian and African countries, with China included, are all backward economically and culturally. In as much as our Asian–African Conference does not exclude anybody, why could not we understand each other and enter into friendly co-operation?

Secondly, I would like to talk about the question as to whether there is freedom of religious belief. Freedom of religious belief is a principle recognized by all modern nations. We Communists are atheists, but we respect all those who have religious belief. We hope that those who have religious belief will also respect those without. China is a country where there is freedom of religious belief. There are in China, not only seven million Communists, but also tens of millions of Islamists and Buddhists and millions of Protestants and Catholics. Here in the Chinese Delegation, there is a pious Imam of the Islamic faith. Such a situation is no obstacle to the internal unity of China. Why should it be impossible in the community of Asian and African countries to unite those with religious belief and those without? The days of instigating religious strife should have passed, because those who profit from instigating such strife are not those among us.

Thirdly, I would like to talk about the question of the so-called subversive activities. The struggle of the Chinese people against colonialism lasted for more than a hundred years. The national and democratic revolutionary struggles led by the Chinese Communist Party finally achieved success only after a strenuous and difficult course of thirty years. It is impossible to relate all the sufferings of the Chinese people under the rule of imperialism, feudalism and Chiang Kai-shek. At last, the Chinese people have chosen their state system and the present government. It is by the efforts of the Chinese people that the Chinese revolution has won its victory. It is certainly not imported from without. This point cannot be denied even by those who do not like the victory of the Chinese revolution. As a Chinese proverb says: 'Do not do unto others what you yourself do not desire.' We are against outside interference; how could we want to interfere in the internal affairs of others? Some people say: There are more than ten million overseas Chinese whose dual nationality might be taken advantage of to carry out subversive activities. But the problem of dual nationality is something left behind by old China. Up to date, Chiang Kai-shek is still using some very few overseas Chinese to carry out subversive activities against the country where the overseas Chinese are residing. The People's Government of new China, however, is ready to solve the problem of dual nationality of overseas Chinese with the governments of countries concerned. Some other people say that the autonomous region of Tai people in China is a threat to others. There are in China more than forty million national minorities of scores of nationalities. The Tai people and the Chuang people, who are of the same stock as the Tai people, number almost ten million. Since they do exist we must grant them the right of autonomy. Just as there is an autonomous state for Shan people in Burma, every national minority in China has its autonomous region. The national minorities in China exercise their right of autonomy within China, how could that be said to be a threat to our neighbours?

On the basis of strict adherence to the five principles, we are prepared now to establish normal relations with all the Asian and African countries, with all the countries in the world, and first of all, with our neighbouring countries. The problem at present is not that we are carrying out subversive activities against the governments of other countries, but that there are people who are establishing bases around China in order to carry out subversive activities against the Chinese Government. For instance, on the border between China and Burma, there are in fact remnant armed elements of the Chiang Kai-shek clique who are carrying out destructive activities against both China and Burma. Because of the friendly relations between China and Burma, and because we have always respected the sovereignty of Burma, we have confidence in the Government of Burma for the solution of this problem.

The Chinese people have chosen and support their own government. There is freedom of religious belief in China. China has no intention whatsoever to subvert the governments of its neighbouring countries. On the contrary, it is China that is suffering from the subversive activities which are openly carried out without any disguise by the United States of America. Those who do not believe in this may come to China or send someone there to see for themselves. We take cognizance of the fact that there are doubts in the mind of those who do not yet know the truth. There is a saying in China: 'Better seeing once than hearing a hundred times.' We welcome the delegates of all the participating countries in this Conference to visit China, at any time they like. We have no bamboo curtain, but there are people who are spreading a smokescreen between us.

The 1,600 million people of Asia and Africa wish our conference success. All the countries and peoples of the world who desire peace are looking forward to the contribution which the conference will make towards the extension of the area of peace and the establishment of collective peace. Let us, the Asian and African countries, be united and do our utmost to make the Asian-African Conference a success.

*

In a subsequent speech Chou En-lai elaborated China's understanding of the Five Principles in seven points, and declared China's willingness to negotiate with the United States.

DOCUMENT 47. EXTRACTS FROM SPEECH BY CHOU EN-LAI BEFORE THE POLITICAL COMMITTEE OF THE BANDUNG CONFERENCE, 23 APRIL 1955 (*New York Times*, NEW YORK, 25 APRIL 1955)

The points on which we all agree are no longer five. They are seven. I hope we can all agree. With this basis of seven points we on our part would like to give our assurances here that we will carry them out. China is a big country and China is led by the Chinese Communist Party. So some people feel that we will not carry them out. So we give you our assurances and we hope that other delegations will do likewise.

The first point We respect each other's sovereignty and territorial integrity. We will adhere to this principle. Our relations with Burma have proved that we have respected the sovereignty of Burma. As to respect for territorial integrity, it is stated that China will not and should not have any demand for territory. We have common borders with four countries. With some of these countries we have not yet finally fixed our border line and we are ready to do so with our neighbouring countries. But before doing so, we are willing to maintain the present situation by acknowledging that those parts of our border are parts which are undetermined. We are ready to restrain our government and people from crossing even one step across our border. If such things should happen, we would like to admit our mistake.

As to the determination of common borders which we are going to undertake with our neighbouring countries, we shall use only peaceful means and we shall not permit any other kinds of methods. In any case, we shall not change this.

The second point is abstention from aggression and threats against each other. We shall also abide by this principle. There is fear of China on the part of our neighbours, Thailand and the Philippines. Since we lack mutual understanding, it is quite natural that they have this fear. But during our contacts this time, we have made assurances to Prince Wan of Thailand and General Romulo of the Philippines that we will not make any aggression or direct threats against Thailand or the Philippines. We also told Prince Wan of Thailand that even before diplomatic relations are established between our countries, we welcome a delegation from Thailand to visit our province of

Yunnan and see if we have any aggressive designs against others. We have told Prime Minister U Nu that we would very much like to pay a visit with him to that border region, but unfortunately we have no time now. We will see next time.

There is a notion that China has aggressive designs on the Philippines. We also welcome a delegation from the Philippines to visit our coastal regions, especially Fukien and Kwangtung provinces, and to see for themselves whether we are carrying out any activities for the purposes of directing threats against the Philippines.

The third point Abstinence from interference or intervention in the internal affairs of one another. This is a question with which the Indo-China states are most concerned. During the time of the Geneva Conference we made assurances to Cambodia and Laos. We have also told Mr Eden, the then Foreign Secretary, and Mr Molotov about our assurances. Later we also told Prime Minister Nehru and Prime Minister U Nu about our assurances. This time again we make our assurances to the delegations of Cambodia and Laos. We earnestly hope that these two countries will become peace-loving countries, peace-loving countries like India and Burma. We have no intention whatsoever to interfere in the internal affairs of these two neighbouring states of ours. This is our policy toward all countries. We are merely mentioning these two countries as examples.

The fourth point Recognition of equality of races. This point needs no explanation: we have always regarded that different races are equal. New China has not practised any discrimination.

The fifth point Recognition of the equality of all nations, large and small. We attach special importance to this question because we are a big nation. It is easy for big nations to disregard small nations and have no respect for small nations. This is the result of tradition. We are constantly examining our behaviour towards small nations. If any delegation here finds that a representative of China does not respect now any of the countries which are represented here, please bring this point out. We will be glad to accept the criticism and rectify mistakes.

The sixth point Respect for the rights of the people of all countries to choose freely a way of life as well as political and economic systems. We think that this is acceptable to all. The Chinese people have chosen a way of life as well as political and economic systems in new China. We will not allow any outside interference.

We on our part respect the way of life as well as the political and economic systems chosen by other people. For instance, we respect the way of life and political and economic systems chosen by the American people. We have also told the delegation of Japan that we respect the choice made by the Japanese people. When the Japanese people chose the Yoshida Government we recognized that Government as representing the Japanese people. Now the Japanese have chosen a Hatoyama Government, and we recognize that Government as representative of the Japanese people. The Chinese Prime Minister said the same thing to all the delegates when they visited China.

Point seven The abstention from doing damage to each other. Our relations should be mutually beneficial to each other, and one side should not do damage to each [*sic*] other. For instance, in our trade, it must be equally and mutually beneficial to one another; neither side should ask for privileges or attach conditions. China can give the assurance that in its dealings with the countries represented here and other countries which are not represented here, when entering into peaceful co-operation with all countries, when having economic and cultural intercourse with those countries, she will not ask for privileges or special conditions. We will go on an equal basis. . . .

As to the relations between China and the United States, the Chinese people do not want to have war with the United States. We are willing to settle international disputes by peaceful means. If those of you here would like to facilitate the settlement of disputes between the United States and China by peaceful means, it would be most beneficial to the relaxation of tension in the Far East and also to the postponement and prevention of a world war.

(*c*) THE INTERMEDIATE ZONE: THE EVOLUTION OF A POLICY?

The article from which the next document is extracted is a good example of Peking's radical line in the 1960s and its

167

verbal crusade on behalf of national liberation movements. The article is a polemic against the Soviet attitude to revolutionary wars (cf. Document 23) and attacks Soviet policies in Algeria and the Congo.

DOCUMENT 48. EXTRACTS FROM 'APOLOGISTS OF NEO-COLONIAL-ISM', BY THE EDITORIAL DEPARTMENTS OF *People's Daily* AND *Red Flag* (*Peking Review*, 6, 43, 25 OCTOBER 1963, PP. 7–14)

The national-liberation movement has entered a new stage. . . .

In the new stage, the level of political consciousness of the Asian, African and Latin American peoples has risen higher than ever and the revolutionary movement is surging forward with unprecedented intensity. They urgently demand the thorough elimination of the forces of imperialism and its lackeys in their own countries and strive for complete political and economic independence. The primary and most urgent task facing these countries is still the further development of the struggle against imperialism, old and new colonialism, and their lackeys. This struggle is still being waged fiercely in the political, economic, military, cultural, ideological and other spheres. And the struggles in all these spheres still find their most concentrated expression in political struggle, which often unavoidably develops into armed struggle when the imperialists resort to direct or indirect armed suppression. It is important for the newly independent countries to develop their independent economy. But this task must never be separated from the struggle against imperialism, old and new colonialism, and their lackeys.

Opposition to Wars of National Liberation

The history of the eighteen years since World War II has shown that wars of national liberation are unavoidable so long as the imperialists and their lackeys try to maintain their brutal rule by bayonets and use force to suppress the revolution of oppressed nations. These large-scale and small-scale revolutionary wars against the imperialists and their lackeys, which have never ceased, have hit hard at the imperialist forces of war, strengthened the forces defending world peace and effectively prevented the imperialists from realizing their plan of launching a world war. Frankly speaking, Khrushchov's clamour about the need to 'put out' the sparks of revolution for the sake of peace is an attempt to oppose revolution in the name of safe-guarding peace.

Proceeding from these wrong views and policies, the leaders of the CPSU not only demand that the oppressed nations should abandon their revolutionary struggle for liberation and 'peace-fully coexist' with the imperialists and colonialists, but even side with imperialism and use a variety of methods to extinguish the sparks of revolution in Asia, Africa and Latin America.

Take the example of the Algerian people's war of national liberation. The leadership of the CPSU not only withheld sup-port for a long period but actually took the side of French imperialism. Khrushchov used to treat Algeria's national inde-pendence as an 'internal affair' of France. Speaking on the Algerian question on October 3, 1955, he said, 'I had and have in view, first of all, that the USSR does not interfere in the internal affairs of other states.' Receiving a correspondent of *Le Figaro* on March 27, 1958, he said, 'We do not want France to grow weaker, we want her to become still greater.'

To curry favour with the French imperialists, the leaders of the CPSU did not dare to recognize the Provisional Govern-ment of the Republic of Algeria for a long time; not until the victory of the Algerian people's war of resistance against French aggression was a foregone conclusion and France was compelled to agree to Algerian independence did they hurriedly recognize the Republic of Algeria. This unseemly attitude brought shame on the socialist countries. Yet the leaders of the CPSU glory in their shame and assert that the victory the Algerian people paid for with their blood should also be credited to the policy of 'peaceful coexistence'.

Again let us examine the part played by the leaders of the CPSU in the Congo question. Not only did they refuse to give active support to the Congolese people's armed struggle against colonialism, but they were anxious to 'co-operate' with US imperialism in putting out the spark in the Congo.

On July 13, 1960, the Soviet Union joined with the United States in voting for the UN Security Council resolution on the dispatch of UN forces to the Congo; thus it helped the US imperialists use the flag of the United Nations in their armed intervention in the Congo. The Soviet Union also provided the UN forces with means of transportation. In a cable to Kasavubu and Lumumba on July 15, Khrushchov said that 'the United Nations Security Council has done a useful thing'. Thereafter, the Soviet press kept up a stream of praise for the United Nations for 'helping the Government of the Congolese Republic to defend the independence and sovereignty of the country', and expressed the hope that the United Nations would adopt 'resolute measures'. In its statements of August 21 and September 10, the Soviet Government continued to praise the United Nations, which was suppressing the Congolese people.

In 1961 the leaders of the CPSU persuaded Gizenga to attend the Congolese parliament, which had been convened under the 'protection' of UN troops, and to join the puppet government. The leadership of the CPSU falsely alleged that the convocation of the Congolese parliament was 'an important event in the life of the young republic' and 'a success of the national forces'.

Clearly these wrong policies of the leadership of the CPSU rendered US imperialism a great service in its aggression against the Congo. Lumumba was murdered. Gizenga was imprisoned, many other patriots were persecuted, and the Congolese struggle for national independence suffered a setback. Does the leadership of the CPSU feel no responsibility for all this? . . .

Against the 'Theory of Racism' and the 'Theory of the Yellow Peril'

Having used up all their wonder-working weapons for opposing the national-liberation movement, the leaders of the CPSU are now reduced to seeking help from racism, the most reactionary of all imperialist theories. They describe the correct stand of the CPC in resolutely supporting the national-liberation movement as 'creating racial and geographical barriers', 'replacing the class approach with the racial approach', and 'playing upon the national and even racial prejudices of the Asian and African peoples'. . . .

In the last analysis, the national question in the contemporary world is one of class struggle and anti-imperialist struggle. Today the workers, peasants, revolutionary intellectuals, anti-imperialist and patriotic bourgeois elements and other patriotic and anti-imperialist enlightened people of all races—white, black, yellow or brown—have formed a broad united front against the imperialists, headed by the United States, and their lackeys. This united front is expanding and growing stronger. The question here is not whether to side with the white people or the coloured people, but whether to side with the oppressed peoples and nations or with the handful of imperialists and reactionaries.

*

Chou En-lai made an extensive tour of Africa 14 December 1963 to 4 February 1964. Accompanied by Foreign Minister Chen Yi, ten important officials and forty others, he visited the United Arab Republic, Algeria, Morocco, Tunisia, Ghana, Mali, Guinea, Sudan, Ethiopia and Somalia. The Chinese hoped to rally support for a projected second 'Bandung' Conference, explain Chinese opposition to the test ban treaty, show China in a good light in contrast to the USSR, and to expound China's principles in giving economic aid.

DOCUMENT 49. EXTRACTS FROM CHOU EN-LAI'S 'REVOLUTIONARY PROSPECTS IN AFRICA EXCELLENT' SPEECH AT A MASS RALLY HELD IN MOGADISHU, SOMALIA, 3 FEBRUARY 1964 (*Peking Review*, 7, 7, 14 FEBRUARY 1964, PP. 6–8)

In each of the African countries we visited, we have deeply felt the African people's strong desire to promote the unity and solidarity of African countries in order to remove the obstacles caused by the colonialists' artificial division of Africa. This is a just desire which is fully understandable. A foundation for the unity and solidarity of African countries will be built when every new emerging African country endeavours to consolidate its national independence, safeguard its state sovereignty, develop its national economy and culture and strengthen its defence capability, and actively supports other African peoples in their fight for independence and freedom. The Summit Conference of African States held last May has made important contributions towards the promotion of the African people's cause of unity against imperialism. We are convinced that with the development of the African people's united struggle against imperialism and through persistent and unremitting efforts, final victory can certainly be won for the cause of unity and solidarity among African countries in the way chosen by the African peoples themselves.

The imperialists will of course never be reconciled to their defeat in Africa. They do not like to see the African people standing up and becoming masters of their own house. Nor do they like to see the independent development and prosperity of the African countries. Some old colonialists are continuing their bloody suppression of the African peoples fighting for independence and freedom; others have resorted to neo-colonialist tactics in an attempt to maintain their colonial rule; still others have again revealed their ferocious features as old colonialists after their neo-colonialist tactics were seen through by the masses. The neo-colonialists are even more sinister and cunning. They are now stepping up their infiltration and expansion in the political, military, economic and cultural fields by hypocritical means, trying hard to step into the shoes of the old colonialists and place the new emerging African countries under their control. The imperialists and old and new colonialists are employing all sorts of despicable means to sow discord and create disputes among African countries in an attempt to defeat them one by one so as to sabotage the African people's cause of unity against imperialism. . . .

We Asian and African peoples are brothers sharing the same life-breath and destiny. Imperialism and old and new colonialism are our common enemies. It is our common fighting task to win and safeguard national independence and develop national economy and culture. In the face of the arch enemy, it is necessary for us to strengthen our solidarity and co-operation continuously. Since the First Asian-African Conference in 1955 tremendous development has taken place in the Asian-African peoples' cause of unity against imperialism. Now the time is ripe for the convening of a second Asian-African conference and active preparation should be made for it. We are convinced that the convocation of this conference will make new contributions towards the further promotion of the Asian-African peoples' cause of unity against imperialism and of economic co-operation.

In order to consolidate their national independence, it is necessary for the new emerging Asian-African countries to develop their national economies and gradually remove the state of poverty and backwardness caused by colonial domination. In order to develop their national economies, it is necessary for the Asian and African countries to rely, first of all, on their own efforts, on the strength of their own peoples and on the full use of their own resources. Self-reliance does not preclude foreign aid and it is also necessary to have economic co-operation among all friendly countries. The important thing is that all foreign aid and economic co-operation should conform to the principle of equality and mutual benefit with no privileges and conditions attached. This aid and co-operation should really help to develop the independent national economy and should not be a means to control and manacle the Asian-African countries.

China's Eight Principles in Providing Economic Aid

In providing economic aid to other countries, the Chinese Government has always strictly abided by the following eight principles: One, the Chinese Government always bases itself on the principle of equality and mutual benefit in providing aid to other countries. It never regards such aid as a kind of unilateral alms but as something mutual and helpful to economic co-operation. Two, in providing aid to other countries, the Chinese Government strictly respects the sovereignty and independence of the recipient countries, and never attaches any conditions or asks for any privileges. Three, China provides economic aid in the form of interest-free or low-interest loans and extends the time limit for the repayment when necessary so as to lighten, as far as possible, the burden of the recipient countries. Four, in providing aid to other countries, the purpose of the Chinese Government is not to make the recipient countries dependent on China but to help them embark step by step on the road of self-reliance and independent economic development. Five, the Chinese Government tries its best to help the recipient countries build projects which require less investment while yielding quicker results so that the recipient governments may increase their income and accumulate capital. Six, the Chinese Government provides the best quality equipment and material of its own manufacture at internal market prices. If the equipment and material provided by the Chinese Government are not up to the agreed specifications and quality, the Chinese Government undertakes to replace them. Seven, in giving any particular technical assistance, the Chinese Government will see to it that the personnel of the recipient country fully master such technique. Eight, the experts and technical personnel dispatched by China to help in construction in the recipient countries will have the same standard of living as the experts and technical personnel of the recipient country. The Chinese experts and technical personnel are not allowed to make any special demands or enjoy any special amenities.

At present, the mutual aid and economic co-operation between Asian-African countries are still limited in scale. However, inasmuch as we share the same experience and are in similar positions and so best understand each other's needs, our mutual aid and economic co-operation are dependable, conformable to actual needs, equitable and of mutual benefit, and helpful to the independent development of various countries. Along with the development of national construction in Asian-African countries, there is no doubt that this mutual aid and economic co-operation will continuously expand in scope and increase in quantity.

*

The second Bandung type conference of Afro-Asian states scheduled to take place in March 1965, was postponed firstly to May then to June, then to November and finally dropped altogether. China was against allowing any representatives of the United Nations to the Conference, and also opposed the participation of the Soviet Union on the grounds that it was by tradition a European country.

DOCUMENT 50. ON THE SECOND AFRICAN-ASIAN CONFERENCE.
EXTRACT FROM FOREIGN MINISTER CHEN YI'S PRESS CONFERENCE,
29 SEPTEMBER 1965 ('VICE-PREMIER CHEN YI ANSWERS QUESTIONS
PUT BY CORRESPONDENTS', FOREIGN LANGUAGES PRESS, PEKING
1966, PP. 9–13)

Vice-Premier Ch'en Yi said: The African-Asian Conference is a
meeting of the heads of state or government of the more than
sixty African and Asian countries which have won independence. If this conference can develop the Bandung spirit and
discuss the questions of fighting imperialism and colonialism
and of the national-liberation movement of the world, I believe
it will be of great significance in international life. The conference should support the people of Viet Nam, Laos, the Congo
(Leopoldville), the Dominican Republic, Angola, Mozambique, Portuguese Guinea, South Africa, the Arab people of
Palestine, and the people of South Yemen, Malaya, Singapore
and North Kalimantan in their struggles against the aggression
of the imperialists, colonialists and neo-colonialists headed by
the United States. The Chinese Government has always stood
for holding the conference along these lines and making it a
success.

US imperialism dislikes this conference very much and is
trying to sabotage it by every means. It is anticipated that the
first item on the agenda after the opening session will be the
condemnation of US imperialism for its aggressions throughout
the world. If this is done, the Bandung spirit will be raised to a
new level. If it fails to make an open denunciation of US
imperialism but only opposes imperialism and colonialism in
general terms, then it will not have much significance.

Recently, a cabinet minister of a certain country told me that
some newly independent countries could not openly denounce
US imperialism at the African-Asian Conference because of
their need for US aid to solve the bread question. On the other
hand, some other Afro-Asian countries hold that the first and
foremost task of the African-Asian Conference is to denounce
US imperialism, otherwise there will be no sense in convening
the conference. These two tendencies are now engaged in a
struggle. China firmly sides with those that stand for condemnation of US imperialism. This position of China's will

never change. For without adopting resolutions condemning US imperialism, the African-Asian Conference will disappoint the people of Asia, Africa and Latin America. To hold such a conference would be a waste. As for the bread question, it is my view that if one relies on US aid, one will get less and less bread, while relying on one's own efforts one will get more and more. So far as certain countries are concerned, the more they denounce US imperialism the more bread they will probably get from it, otherwise they will not get any. Such is the character of US imperialism—bullying the weak-kneed and fearing the strong.

I have told the leaders of some Afro-Asian countries: since many Afro-Asian countries are receiving aid and loans from the United States and other countries, thus incurring ever-increasing burdens, it may be advisable to adopt a resolution at the African-Asian Conference declaring the cancellation of all debts which Afro-Asian countries owe to the United States. If this can be done, the debts owed to China may also be cancelled. They said this was a very good idea and could be considered.

In order to sabotage the African-Asian Conference, the imperialists are trying to hook it up with the United Nations. The Bandung Conference has enjoyed high prestige among the people of the world precisely because, having nothing to do with the United Nations, it was free from UN influence and contributed to the anti-imperialist and anti-colonialist cause of the people of the world independently and outside the United Nations. If the conference is to be linked with the United Nations, it will be tantamount to discarding the Bandung spirit. The Chinese Government is firmly against this.

To invite a representative of the United Nations or anyone from it to the African-Asian Conference would mean, in effect, to bring the United States into the conference. Is it not ludicrous to invite agents of US imperialism to an anti-imperialist conference?

The Chinese Government is resolutely against the participation of U Thant, Secretary-General of the United Nations, in the African-Asian Conference. Everybody is clear about the role U Thant is playing. He is not the head of the United Nations; the head of the United Nations is the United States.

Not being the head of any Afro-Asian state, what qualifications has he to participate in the African-Asian Conference?

The United Nations has excluded China for 16 years. China cannot sit together with its representative. The Chinese Government does not force other countries to boycott UN meetings, nor should others force us to sit together with a representative of the United Nations. Otherwise, it would be running counter to the Bandung spirit. Joint struggle against imperialism is possible only when no one imposes his will on others. The invitation for U Thant to attend the African-Asian Conference was issued before Ben Bella's fall. I am thankful to President Houari Boumedienne because he showed sympathy with China's stand and said he would try to find a solution to this problem.

The Chinese Government categorically states that no representative of the United Nations should be admitted to the African-Asian Conference.

As for inviting the Soviet Union to the African-Asian Conference, the Chinese Government is firmly opposed to it. Whether historically or politically, the Soviet Union is by tradition a European country, and there is no reason for its participation in the African-Asian Conference. The Soviet Union did not ask for participation in the First Asian-African Conference. At that time, Prime Minister Nehru openly declared that the Soviet Union, a European country, was not to be invited. Last year, India demanded Soviet participation, but the 22 countries failed to reach agreement, which means in effect the rejection of the demand for Soviet participation in the African-Asian Conference. Khrushchov stated last year that the Soviet Union would not put forward its request, if its participation would not conduce to Afro-Asian solidarity.

DOCUMENT 51. EXTRACT FROM B. D. LARKIN, *China and Africa 1949–1970*, UNIVERSITY OF CALIFORNIA PRESS, BERKELEY, 1971, PP. 156–8

China has advocated armed struggle in three types of African states. In self-acknowledged colonies and in white-supremacist states the enemy is evident. A general call for armed action in such states costs China little. If an indigenous group opts for armed struggle, Peking can support it with few reservations. China has also advocated armed struggle in some African states which are already independent and are not white-supremacist states. In such cases China treads very cautiously and appears to be a follower, not a leader.

Where opposition to an existing government does not serve China's purpose, where the government deals with China and appears to have the capacity to crush or contain opposition, China has withheld support from oppositionists. Before publicly encouraging struggle in a named country, Peking must envision a clear advantage. The record of her public commitments in Africa warrants the conclusion that she has supported armed struggle only if it promised to advance a radical purpose, and if the group to be overthrown was an inviting target. These cases have not required subtle political discrimination on China's part. Even more important, China publicly urges armed struggle only if it will probably be begun regardless of what China says or—better yet—if it is already under way.

If armed struggle is not suited to every case, why does China dwell upon armed struggle in her comment on Africa? China seeks to hasten the development of political opposition groups and guide them toward conceptions of action closely akin to her own. She must say what is distinctive about China's experience. If oppositionists are choosing among alternative patterns of action, China will lose by default if her pattern is not advertised. A revolutionary army conducting protracted struggle is the hallmark of the Chinese style; since it was not present in the Russian revolution, Peking can make some claim to originality for her revolutionary model. China must talk about armed struggle to advance her model. She seeks to avoid two dangers: unreasonable jeopardy to useful inter-governmental ties, and ill-chosen attachment to half-hearted oppositionists. She moves from the general to the specific only when her conditions are met. Her revolutionary posture is clear, but inter-governmental relations go on and she is sparing in her concrete support to oppositionists.

Armed struggle can be undertaken by anyone. China's indiscriminate general celebration of revolutionary war must influence some Africans to undertake violence even though Peking has no contacts with them and would not jeopardize other interests for their sake. China probably looks upon such violence with favor. China's prescription for revolution can succeed if it is tried. Therefore, though Peking may stop short of linking her prestige to small-scale violence which has little chance of success, every organized radical opposition can potentially grow in scale and win public Chinese support. The CCP has repeatedly emphasized that revolution is the best school for training revolutionaries. Moreover, once armed struggle is under way, it is an example to others who may also profit by the instability it breeds in adjacent territories.

China's mode, complete only in retrospect, is too elaborate for the actual conditions of social and political organization which prevail in many African countries. Rather than withdraw her model, China apparently has elected to guide African radicals across the transitional period until conscious Maoist struggle is possible. It is as if some Chinese foresee a process in two stages: first, draw scattered oppositionists into some form of organization and action (preferably armed action); second, transform a radical nationalist organization into a group borrowing heavily from the Chinese revolutionary model. At some time in the future an indigenous Maoist party will be required, but until then the CCP can provide strategic doctrinal, and organizational guidance. Chinese guidance need not be detailed or direct. No special political or military sophistication is required to follow the cues found in Chinese publications. The Chinese can have occasional contacts with opposition leaders, who may meet with Chinese embassy and NCNA representatives or visit China. If the oppositionists undertake armed struggle, castigate imperialism, and support China on some key issues Peking might conclude that the situation was maturing. China's wariness toward unproven groups (whose actions could cost China important diplomatic and economic assets) would persist. Where China would like to see large-scale opposition to existing authority develop, Chinese leaders may believe that their guidance spells the difference between determination and discouragement among the revolutionaries.

China wants a 'new democratic revolution' in Africa, but there are few Africans whose ideological purity she trusts. Their number will grow, CCP leaders probably believe, but in the meantime China will stand in their stead. The very special rendering of Marxism-Leninism to which China is now committed narrows the ranks of Africans who would meet Peking's ideological standards, with the result that there is no sign that China is passing an ideological baton to Africa. China could retire from the transitional role more quickly if she were ideologically less demanding. China remains guardian of orthodoxy herself, however, and opens the united front to all Africans equally. The relationship between the CCP and African radicals is clarified if one considers a worldwide united front of which China is the proletarian hegemon.

*

The 'intermediate zone' originally described in 1946 as consisting of the whole area between the US and the USSR was redefined in January 1964. The new definition distinguished a second intermediate zone consisting of the advanced capitalist countries which were 'subjected' to the United States. This pronouncement, issued during the Sino-French negotiations for the exchange of full diplomatic recognition, was clearly related to De Gaulle's determination to develop an independent foreign policy free from American domination.

DOCUMENT 52. ON THE INTERMEDIATE ZONE. EXTRACT FROM EDITORIAL IN *People's Daily*, 21 JANUARY 1964 (*Peking Review*, 7, 4, 24 JANUARY 1964, P. 7)

It can thus be seen that the US imperialist attempt to seize the intermediate zone is bound to run up against the opposition of all the peoples and countries in that region. This vast intermediate zone is composed of two parts. One part consists of the independent countries and those striving for independence in Asia, Africa and Latin America; it may be called the first intermediate zone.

The second part consists of the whole of Western Europe, Oceania, Canada, and other capitalist countries; it may be called the second intermediate zone. Countries in this second intermediate zone have a dual character. While their ruling class are exploiters and oppressors, these countries themselves are subjected to US control, interference and bullying. They therefore try their best to free themselves from US control. In this regard, they have something in common with the socialist countries and the peoples of various countries. By making itself antagonistic to the whole world, US imperialism inevitably finds itself tightly encircled.

*

The first intermediate zone was the subject of Lin Piao's famous article in September 1965. Apart from its obvious intention of scoring a point in the contest with Moscow, this article was an extreme example of the Chinese tendency to see the whole world in the light of their own experience, and of their assumption that the triumph of revolutionary forces is inevitable.

We must remember that in 1965 the crisis of the Cultural Revolution was approaching in China, and at the same time there was frightening evidence of American eagerness to take the offensive on her borders. The masquerade of the 'Tonkin Gulf Incident' was followed by the bombardment of North Vietnam and in February 1965 by full-scale American air attacks on North Vietnam. The Americans began to pour in large numbers of troops to shore up the regime in South Vietnam.

It was assumed by many in the West that Lin's statement heralded new aggressive moves by China. On the contrary, in the context of America's forward policy in 1965 it could be read as a reminder to the people of Vietnam and elsewhere that China's policy of letting them fight their own battles was unchanged.

DOCUMENT 53. EXTRACTS FROM LIN PIAO, 'LONG LIVE THE VICTORY OF PEOPLE'S WAR', *People's Daily*, 2 SEPTEMBER 1965 (*Peking Review*, 8, 36, 3 SEPTEMBER 1965, PP. 9–30)

The history of the people's war in China and other countries provides conclusive evidence that the growth of the people's revolutionary forces from weak and small beginnings into strong and large forces is a universal law of development of class struggle, a universal law of development of people's war. A people's war inevitably meets with many difficulties, with ups and downs and setbacks in the course of its development, but no force can alter its general trend towards inevitable triumph.

Comrade Mao Tse-tung points out that we must despise the enemy strategically and take full account of him tactically.

To despise the enemy strategically is an elementary require-ment for a revolutionary. Without the courage to despise the enemy and without daring to win, it will be simply impossible to make revolution and wage a people's war, let alone to achieve victory.

It is also very important for revolutionaries to take full account of the enemy tactically. It is likewise impossible to win victory in a people's war without taking full account of the enemy tactically, and without examining the concrete condi-tions, without being prudent and giving great attention to the study of the art of struggle, and without adopting appropriate forms of struggle in the concrete practice of the revolution in each country and with regard to each concrete problem of struggle. . . .

It must be emphasised that Comrade Mao Tse-tung's theory of the establishment of rural revolutionary base areas and the encirclement of the cities from the countryside is of outstanding and universal practical importance for the present revolutionary struggles of all the oppressed nations and peoples, and particu-larly for the revolutionary struggle of the oppressed nations and peoples in Asia, Africa and Latin America against imperialism and its lackeys.

Many countries and peoples in Asia, Africa and Latin America are now being subjected to aggression and enslave-ment on a serious scale by the imperialists headed by the United States and their lackeys. The basic political and economic con-ditions in many of these countries have many similarities to those that prevailed in old China. As in China, the peasant question is extremely important in these regions. The peasants constitute the main force of the national-democratic revolution against the imperialists and their lackeys. In committing aggression against these countries, the imperialists usually begin by seizing the big cities and the main lines of communica-tion, but they are unable to bring the vast countryside com-pletely under their control. The countryside, and the countryside alone, can provide the broad areas in which the revolutionaries can manoeuvre freely. The countryside, and the countryside alone, can provide the revolutionary bases from which the revolutionaries can go forward to final victory. Precisely for this reason, Comrade Mao Tse-tung's theory of establishing revolutionary base areas in the rural districts and encircling the cities from the countryside is attracting more and more attention among the people in these regions.

Taking the entire globe, if North America and Western Europe can be called 'the cities of the world', then Asia, Africa and Latin America constitute 'the rural areas of the world'. Since World War II, the proletarian revolutionary movement has for various reasons been temporarily held back in the North American and West European capitalist countries, while the people's revolutionary movement in Asia, Africa and Latin America has been growing vigorously. In a sense, the contemporary world revolution also presents a picture of the encirclement of cities by the rural areas. In the final analysis, the whole cause of world revolution hinges on the revolutionary struggles of the Asian, African and Latin American peoples who make up the overwhelming majority of the world's population. The socialist countries should regard it as their internationalist duty to support the people's revolutionary struggles in Asia, Africa and Latin America. . . .

Defeat US Imperialism and its Lackeys by People's War

Since World War II, US imperialism has stepped into the shoes of German, Japanese and Italian fascism and has been trying to build a great American empire by dominating and enslaving the whole world. It is actively fostering Japanese and West German militarism as its chief accomplices in unleashing a world war. Like a vicious wolf, it is bullying and enslaving various peoples, plundering their wealth, encroaching upon their countries' sovereignty and interfering in their internal affairs. It is the most rabid aggressor in human history and the most ferocious common enemy of the people of the world. Every people or country in the world that wants revolution, independence and peace cannot but direct the spearhead of its struggle against US imperialism. . . .

Viet Nam is the most convincing current example of a victim of aggression defeating US imperialism by a people's war. The United States has made south Viet Nam a testing ground for the suppression of people's war. It has carried on this experiment for many years, and everybody can now see that the US aggressors are unable to find a way of coping with people's war. On the other hand, the Vietnamese people have brought the power of people's war into full play in their struggle against the US aggressors. The US aggressors are in danger of being swamped in the people's war in Viet Nam. They are deeply worried that their defeat in Viet Nam will lead to a chain reaction. They are expanding the war in an attempt to save themselves from defeat. But the more they expand the war, the greater will be the chain reaction. The more they escalate the war, the heavier will be their fall and the more disastrous their defeat. The people in other parts of the world will see still more clearly that US imperialism can be defeated and that what the Vietnamese people can do, they can do too.

History has proved and will go on proving that people's war is the most effective weapon against US imperialism and its lackeys. All revolutionary people will learn to wage people's war against US imperialism and its lackeys. They will take up arms, learn to fight battles and become skilled in waging people's war, though they have not done so before. US imperialism like a mad bull dashing from place to place, will finally be burned to ashes in the blazing fires of the people's war it has provoked by its own actions.

(d) INDONESIA

Indonesian relations with China have been complicated by the presence of the large Chinese minority in Indonesia, by the role of the PKI (Indonesian Communist Party) and by the Sino-Soviet dispute. Chinese policy was to cultivate good relations with President Sukarno who was respected for his anti-imperialism and for his attempts to maintain amicable relations with the PKI. When a serious rebellion, supported by the United States, occurred in Sumatra in 1958, China gave Sukarno's government financial aid and political support. However, good relations were impaired in 1959 when the

Indonesians introduced repressive measures against the Chinese community. In 1960–61 attempts were made to settle the problem. At that time the Soviets were promising substantial military and economic aid to Indonesia, and Sukarno was anxious to be on good terms with both China and the Soviet Union. When Sukarno embarked on a policy of 'confronting' the Federation of Malaysia (created in 1963) he failed to get the support of the Soviet Union, which was anxious not to compromise its current efforts for *détente* with the Western powers. Djakarta moved closer to Peking; tangible rewards in 1965 included a Chinese credit of $50 million and support for Indonesia's decision to leave the United Nations.

The PKI, at first neutral in the ideological war between Peking and Moscow, moved after 1963 towards closer identification with the CCP. By 1965 Sukarno had clearly shown his preference for the radical left wing (including the PKI) in Indonesian politics, an orientation which was resented by the leaders of the army.

Of the attempted *coup* of 30 September–1 October 1965 there is, as yet, no clear and completely acceptable explanation. It is not unlikely that the PKI's attack on the generals was to forestall a right-wing plot against Sukarno's regime. The failure of the *coup* was followed by severe anti-Communist and anti-Chinese repression. Sukarno was unable to intercede effectively to protect the victims of the army's wrath, nor was he able to prevent a major shift in Djakarta's foreign policy. In 1966 the new right-wing government terminated the 'confrontation' with Malaysia, obtained promises of US aid, curtailed trade with China and closed the consulate in Peking. In spite of this rapid deterioration in relations the CPR did not adopt a completely hard line towards Indonesia until July 1967. In September 1966 the PKI had analysed its own 'faults' in a public statement and had begun to advocate a new 'Maoist' programme of revolution. It is not clear why the Chinese waited until July 1967 before openly advocating armed struggle in Indonesia. It may be that doubts as to the suitability of Indonesian conditions for successful 'people's war' were cast aside temporarily by China's left-wing at the height of the Cultural Revolution.

DOCUMENT 54. EXTRACTS FROM 'PEOPLE OF INDONESIA, UNITE AND FIGHT TO OVERTHROW THE FASCIST REGIME', EDITORIAL IN *Red Flag*, NO. 11, JULY 1967 (ENGLISH TRANSLATION PUBLISHED BY FOREIGN LANGUAGES PRESS, PEKING, 1968, PP. 1–10)

After staging the counter-revolutionary 1965 *coup d'état*, the Suharto-Nasution Right-wing military clique, faithful lackey of US imperialism and anti-communist ally of Soviet revisionism, established a fascist dictatorship of unprecedented ruthlessness in Indonesia.

For the past year or more, it has followed an out and out traitorous, dictatorial, anti-communist, anti-China and anti-popular counter-revolutionary policy.

It has imposed a white terror in Indonesia on an unprecedented scale, slaughtered several hundred thousand Communists and revolutionary people and thrown into prison another several hundred thousand fine sons and daughters of the Indonesian people. All Indonesia has been turned into one vast hell. By engaging in bloody suppression, it attempts in vain to wipe out the Indonesian Communist Party and stamp out the Indonesian revolution. . . .

At present, the Indonesian Communists and revolutionary people are regrouping their forces for a new battle. The August 17, 1966 statement of the Political Bureau of the Central Committee of the Indonesian Communist Party and the Self-Criticism it endorsed in September, which were published by the magazine *Indonesian Tribune* not long ago, are a call to the Indonesian Communists and the Indonesian working class, peasants, revolutionary intellectuals and all anti-imperialist, anti-feudal revolutionary forces to unite and engage in a new struggle. . . .

In these two documents, the Political Bureau of the Indonesian Communist Party sums up the experience and lessons of the Party in leading the Indonesian people's revolutionary struggle, criticizes the Right opportunist errors committed by the leadership of the Party in the past, points out the road for the Indonesian revolution and lays down the principles for future struggle. . . .

The documents criticize the slogan of 'national co-operation with the "Nasakom" as the core' and hold that such a statement obscures the class content of the united front. In its effort to establish a united front with the national bourgeoisie, the Party leadership in the past abrogated the independent role of the proletariat and turned it into an appendage of the national bourgeoisie. It put the three components of Marxism on a par with the 'three components of Sukarno's teachings' and in an unprincipled way recognized Sukarno as 'the great leader of the revolution'. The Party's erroneous attitude towards Sukarno was a major manifestation of its loss of independence within the united front.

They point out that an arduous task lies ahead in the building up of the Indonesian Communist Party. It must be built into a Marxist-Leninist Party free from all forms of opportunism, one that resolutely opposes legalism, subjectivism and modern revisionism. . . .

After summing up the historical experience of the Indonesian revolution, the Statement and the Self-Criticism of the Political Bureau of the Central Committee of the Indonesian Communist Party comes to this important conclusion:

> To win victory for the people's democratic revolution, the Indonesian Marxist-Leninists must hold aloft the Three Banners of the Party, namely:
> The first banner, the building of a Marxist-Leninist Party which is free from subjectivism, opportunism and modern revisionism.
> The second banner, the armed people's struggle which in essence is the armed struggle of the peasants in an anti-feudal agrarian revolution under the leadership of the working class.
> The third banner, the revolutionary united front based on the worker-peasant alliance under the leadership of the working class.

The conclusion drawn by the Political Bureau of the Indonesian Communist Party concerning the 'Three Banners' conforms with Marxism-Leninism, Mao Tse-tung's thought, and will play an important guiding role in the Indonesian revolution.

The road pioneered by Comrade Mao Tse-tung for the Chinese revolution is the road by which '*political power grows out*

of the barrel of a gun', the road of relying on the peasants, establishing rural revolutionary bases, encircling the cities from the
rural areas and finally capturing the cities. . . .

At present, the white terror in all its severity continues to
reign over Indonesia. The Indonesian Communist Party is faced
with an extremely difficult and complex task. The Party's
struggle is undergoing a major change: a switch from the cities
to the countryside, from peaceful struggle to armed struggle,
from legal to illegal, from open to secret. For a Party, whose
main work over a long period of time was open and legal
activity in the cities, this change is not easy indeed. It is bound
to meet many difficulties. But the objective realities of the
revolutionary struggle compel people to make the change and
compel them to learn armed struggle, and there is no alternative for them but to master it. In fact, as long as they are
resolute and surmount all difficulties, there is no doubt that
they can do so.

Comrade Mao Tse-tung says:

A revolutionary war is a mass undertaking; it is often not a
matter of first learning and then doing, but of doing and
then learning, for doing is itself learning. There is a gap
between the ordinary civilian and the soldier, but it is no
Great Wall, and it can be quickly closed, and the way to
close it is to take part in revolution, in war.

We are convinced that the Indonesian Marxist-Leninists,
guided by the invincible Marxism-Leninism, Mao Tse-tung's
thought, will surmount obstacle after obstacle, effect this
historic change and lead the Indonesian people on to the long
march for winning victory in the revolution.

PART V

Foreign Relations during the Cultural Revolution

There is no simple explanation of the Great Proletarian Cultural Revolution, but it is generally assumed to have been concerned essentially with internal affairs. The years 1966 to 1969 during which the Cultural Revolution was at its height were a time of introspection, tinged with xenophobia, when China's relations with the outside world were distorted and uneasy.

After Mao Tse-tung relinquished the Chairmanship of the Republic in favour of Liu Shao-chi in 1959, Liu had increasingly been accepted as the leader of a policy of moderation and restraint in a period of recovery after the set-backs associated with the Great Leap Forward. To Mao, however, the rise of Liu and his followers seemed a threat to the realization of true socialism. Mao sought support particularly from the leaders of the PLA, and notably Marshal Lin Piao, the hero of the Korean War who was appointed Minister of Defence in 1959. The years between 1962 and 1966 may be viewed as a preliminary to the Cultural Revolution. The Socialist Education Movement was started in 1962 and blossomed in Autumn 1964 with the 'Four Clean-ups', a campaign concerned with inculcating in the masses and junior cadres a revived spirit of enthusiasm for a classless society and with encouraging maximum economic production. Initially directed at the countryside, the movement was then turned into the cities, and a number of intellectuals and artists were disgraced for unrevolutionary and revisionist work.

In May 1965 the step was taken of theoretically abolishing all ranks in the PLA and insignia and uniforms were changed to combat élitism. In November 1965 the Shanghai newspaper *Wen-hui Pao* published an article, instigated by Mao himself, which criticized the playwright Wu Han, the Deputy Mayor of Peking, on the grounds that his play *Hai Jui Dismissed from Office* was a covert attack on Mao. This article was later hailed as the first bugle call of the Cultural Revolution. The downfall of Peng Chen, Mayor of Peking and Chairman of the Peking Municipal Party Committee, followed in June 1966. By August others had fallen, notably Lu Ting-yi Minister of Culture and Lo Jui-ching Chief of Staff of the PLA. Liu Shao-chi himself came under attack as 'China's Khrushchev', the 'top Party person in authority taking the capitalist road'. At about this time schools and colleges were closed, and students were encouraged to travel about China. The ferment of public denunciations, big character posters and Red Guard rallies began to characterize the Chinese scene from August 1966. On the 18th of that month in Tien An Men Square, Mao and his close comrade-in-arms Lin Piao welcomed and encouraged a mass rally of a million young people. A '16 point decision' adopted on 8 August 1966 was intended to provide guidelines and keep the revolution under control. The violence, chaos, and bloodshed of the ensuing months led eventually to the restoration of order by the PLA. Army personnel took the lead in Revolutionary Committees established at all levels and in all institutions across China.

The turmoil of the Cultural Revolution reached its height in the summer of 1967. In April Chen Yi, Vice-Premier and Foreign Minister, was openly criticized by Red Guards for his 'revisionist foreign policy'. All but one of China's ambassadors abroad had been recalled and the result was an almost complete breakdown in normal diplomatic relations. At the beginning of 1967 Red Guards in Macao had virtually taken control of the small Portuguese enclave. Similar agitation in Hong Kong in the summer of 1967 was successfully resisted. In Peking Red Guards demonstrated against foreign legations; the office of the British Chargé d'Affaires was burned down and the Chargé d'Affaires was placed under house arrest. The Reuters Correspondent Anthony Grey was subjected to what can only be described as mob violence, and held virtually incommunicado for twenty-six months. In London the Chinese staff at the

Chargé d'Affaires office exchanged blows with London police-men on duty in Portland Place (Document 58).

In the Foreign Ministry in Peking, Red Guards took charge temporarily from the senior officials and despatched instruc-tions to overseas posts. China was at odds with almost all governments in the Communist as well as the non-Communist world. The issue of *Peking Review*, 14 July 1967, referred to disputes with eight different countries (Britain, Soviet Union, United States, Burma, Indonesia, India, Nepal, the Ivory Coast) and with the United Nations. The Chinese press began openly to support a peasant rebellion in West Bengal as a prelude to revolution throughout India, although ironically the rebels were challenging a United Front Government in West Bengal in which the Left Wing of the Indian Communist Party was the most powerful force. In the case of Burma, the carefully cultivated friendship of years was abruptly broken in mid-summer 1967. Previously Sino-Burmese relations had been a model of China's policy of peaceful co-existence with non-Com-munist countries. Burma had been the first non-Communist state to recognize the People's Republic; the common frontier had been amicably defined in 1960 and Peking had made a development loan in 1961. Ne Win had been welcomed in Peking and Chinese leaders had made official visits to Rangoon. The incident which destroyed this happy relationship began when the Burmese government forbade children to wear Mao badges in school; minor incidents led to riots and bloodshed, and within a few days Peking was denouncing the Ne Win government and calling for its overthrow at the hands of the Burmese Communist Party.

The only explanation for this apparently abrupt shift in policy is that temporarily the uncontrolled emotionalism of the Cultural Revolution had spilled over. The case of Burma is an extreme example but it highlights the fact that for a time the Maoist enthusiasts saw no limits to the spread of their new revolutionary fervour beyond the boundaries of China. Whereas previously Chinese approval of revolutionary move-ments abroad had been given to non-Communists as well as Communist organizations and particularly to those that seemed to be the most effective, now, at the height of the Cultural Revolution, foreign revolutionary movements were judged by the extent to which they showed their identity with the ideology of Chairman Mao.

The abortive rising led by Che Guevara in Bolivia in March 1967 was ignored by the Chinese press, presumably because Guevara's approach to revolution was different in several ways from the Chinese model, and in the context of the Cultural Revolution could be seen as a challenge to the relevance of Mao Tse-tung's thought.

Attacks on Liu Shao-chi included the charge that he was in favour of the liquidation of struggle with the United States and the Soviet Union, and did not give enough support to revolutionary movements in the developing world. Such criticism need not be taken too seriously. While it was undoubtedly convenient to blame Liu Shao-chi for past failures, his influence in the years immediately prior to the Cultural Revolution was largely in home affairs. It was Mao himself who was particularly identified with foreign policy in the period 1963–5.

It should be noted that the Cultural Revolution was far from totally disrupting China's development. One impressive achievement was the testing of China's first hydrogen bomb on 17 June 1967. In September 1967 China committed herself to the largest extension of Third World aid to date by signing an agreement to build and finance the Tanzania–Zambia railway. China has meticulously maintained her timetable for the surveying and construction of this railway. Major building operations began in 1970 and it is likely that the project will be completed in 1975.

By 1969 the period of the Cultural Revolution was drawing to a close although its effects and the long-term changes it has wrought remain incalculable. It was in 1969 that the dispute with the USSR flared up with a new violence and there was armed confrontation along the Ussuri River and on the border of Sinkiang (Document 60). The Chinese began to denounce the Soviets as 'social-imperialists', meaning that they were socialists who were behaving like an imperialist power. When a world communist conference was held at Moscow in June 1969, China was absent.

*

The following extracts from a book published in 1970 comment on the Chinese tendency to see foreign relations in terms of their own outlook and experience. This analysis is particularly pertinent to the period of the Cultural Revolution.

DOCUMENT 55. EXTRACTS FROM R. L. WALKER, 'PEKING'S APPROACH TO THE OUTSIDE WORLD' IN F. N. TRAGER AND W. HENDERSON (EDS), *Communist China, 1949–1969. A Twenty Year Appraisal*, NEW YORK UNIVERSITY PRESS, 1970, PP. 287–90

If we are to understand Chinese Communist foreign policy and its goals, we must also appreciate the extent to which the Chinese 'internalize.' Others have noted that the Chinese tend to judge in Chinese terms, but much more than this is involved. China is a country of such vastness, such grandeur, such scope, that it attracts full-time internal attention. Any Chinese leadership is likely to be concerned with foreign policy primarily in relation to internal developments; and Peking's foreign policy has constantly reflected the ebb and flow of the political fortunes of those who lead the nation. To a good Chinese nationalist, there is no subject more worthy of study than China itself—and exclusive study at that. It is not surprising that foreign policy is frequently subordinated to internal considerations. Further, internal problems and attitudes are projected onto the outside world, particularly by a leadership that is attempting to justify its position to its own people and to maintain its grandeur. Thus Peking claims that:

Today the attitude toward Chairman Mao Tse-tung and Mao Tse-tung's thought is the touchstone and the dividing line between the revolutionaries and the pseudo-revolutionaries, and the true Marxists-Leninists and the counter-revolutionary revisionists.

That the world could believe such a proposition is obviously absurd to many intellectuals in mainland China today, but not to those who have operated within the Maoist totalitarian mold. China's internalization and her relatively unreal approach to the outside world have intensified over the years of the Mao regime; the process has been largely a result of, and has been accelerated by, the growth of the cult of Mao Tse-tung. Within the framework of this personality cult, it becomes increasingly clear that the outside world can have little impact on Peking. The leadership interprets the whole panorama of international affairs in such a way as to glorify Mao; and in any case, the wide spectrum of domestic activities in China commands overwhelming attention as the items of first importance and magnitude....

Political leaders and scholars outside China have urged that we judge the mainland regime by its actions rather than its words. But the words are taken seriously by their authors; they are part of an overall operational code, and an essential ingredient of the guiding rationale for action. It would be a grave mistake not to take at least some of Peking's words, some of the polemics, some of the litany of abuse seriously. In this connection, it is worth pointing out that over the first two decades of Communist rule in China, techniques of analysis which have been successfully employed by the Kremlinologists in studying Soviet foreign policy have also proved useful in relation to Chinese Communist foreign policy. The omission, for example, of a single word of abuse in a list of adjectives preceding the name of the United States can signal the downgrading of a current anti-American campaign.

Another factor, linked to the totalitarian mode of operation and to some of the institutions of Marxism-Leninism, has been the growing intensity of the Maoist cult. This has involved an attempt to tap Chinese national pride with the assertion that China itself has now produced one of the world's greatest Communist leaders. The acceptance of Mao and his thought has become a basis for many of Peking's judgments in the projection of its foreign policy. This feature of its approach to the outside world reached ludicrous proportions in the late 1960s in the claims that were advanced for the scientific relevance of the Thought of Mao Tse-tung for all people everywhere. Despite some doubt as to whether the urbane and sophisticated Chinese people really accepted these assertions of the infallible and all-embracing truth of Maoist teachings, Chairman Mao himself remained in a central position as the guiding spirit behind what his colleagues did and said toward the outside world.

The outside world may have reason for worry about the foreign policy implications of the Maoist cult. The mystical and magical qualities attributed to Mao and his thought are reminiscent of the manner in which the Japanese emperor was treated by the militarists in the years immediately preceding World War II. During the second decade of Communist rule on the mainland, the works of Mao Tse-tung, his picture, and even parades in his honor assumed an almost sacred character; and any defacing of likenesses of the Great Helmsman, whether in India or Italy or Switzerland, could lead to serious diplomatic incidents.

*

The article from which the following extracts are taken was obviously intended as a warning to revisionists in China. The references to the world significance of the Cultural Revolution are very generalized comments and reflect the mounting ideological turmoil in China in August 1966.

DOCUMENT 56. EXTRACTS FROM 'THE GREAT CULTURAL REVOLUTION IS AN ISSUE OF PRIME IMPORTANCE FOR THE DESTINY, PROSPECT, AND OUTLOOK OF OUR PARTY AND COUNTRY AND ALSO AN ISSUE OF PRIME IMPORTANCE FOR THE WORLD REVOLUTION', *Liberation Army Daily*, 6 JUNE 1966 (*Carry the Great Proletarian Revolution Through to the End*, FOREIGN LANGUAGES PRESS, PEKING, 1966)

Over the past sixteen years, there has been one struggle after another on the ideological and cultural fronts, each more profound than the one before. Far from being isolated and accidental phenomena, these struggles are manifestations of the deepening class struggle in China and abroad. A handful of representatives of the bourgeoisie, constantly and stubbornly trying to assert themselves, have been desperately holding on to their bourgeois ideological stronghold and engaging in frantic anti-Party and anti-socialist activities. Make trouble, fail, make trouble again, fail again, till their doom—that is the logic of all reactionaries. This handful of bourgeois representatives is certainly no exception to the rule.

We know from the historical experience of the proletarian revolution that the basic question in every revolution is that of state power. We conquered the enemy in the country and seized state power by the gun. They can all be overthrown, be it imperialism, feudalism or the bureaucrat capitalist class; millionaires, billionaires and trillionaires can be toppled, whoever they may be. And their property can be confiscated. However, confiscation of their property does not amount to confiscation of the reactionary ideas in their minds. Daily and hourly they are always dreaming of a comeback, dreaming of restoring their lost 'paradise.' Although they are only a tiny percentage of the population, their political potential is quite considerable and their power of resistance is out of all proportion to their numbers.

Socialist society emerges out of the womb of the old society. It is not at all easy to eradicate the idea of private ownership formed in thousands of years of class society and the forces of habit and the ideological and cultural influence of the exploiting classes associated with private ownership. The spontaneous forces of the petty bourgeoisie in town and country constantly give rise to new bourgeois elements. As the ranks of the workers grow in number and extent, they take in some elements of the complex background. Then, too, a number of people in the ranks of the Party and state organizations degenerate following the conquest of state power and living in peaceful surroundings. At the same time, on the international plane the imperialists headed by the United States and the reactionaries of various countries are trying hard to eliminate us by using the counterrevolutionary dual tactics of threats of war and 'peaceful evolution.' And the modern revisionist group with the leadership of the Soviet Communist Party as the center is also trying by hook or by crook to topple us. If we were to forget about class struggle and drop our guard in these circumstances, we would be in danger of losing state power and allowing capitalism to make a comeback. . . .

The first socialist country, the Soviet Union was dragged by Khrushchev revisionism on to the road of capitalist restoration. Now all the oppressed people and oppressed nations of the whole world place their hopes on the revolutionary New China. Under the leadership of the Party's Central Committee, holding high the great red banner of Marxism-Leninism, of Mao Tsetung's thought, persisting in their firm stand against imperialism, modern revisionism, and reactionaries of various countries, and greatly deflating the enemy's arrogance and boosting the morale of the people, the Chinese people have set a brilliant example for the people of the whole world. Our country has become the base of the world revolution. Our Party has become the standard bearer of the world revolution. Mao Tse-tung's thought is the beacon of the world revolution. If these anti-Party and anti-socialist elements made China change its color, who can say how many more of the oppressed people in all countries would die, how much more suffering they would have to endure and by how many years the victory of the world revolution would be delayed.

By their anti-Party and anti-socialist activities, the handful of representatives of the bourgeoisie interacted internationally with imperialism, modern revisionism, and all reactionaries. And their exposure is a serious blow to the class enemy abroad; it removed a hidden time bomb inside our Party. With the deepening of China's great Cultural Revolution, the propaganda machinery of the imperialists, modern revisionists and all reactionaries has gone into top gear and they are bombarding us with their anathemas. By negative example, this proves the great significance of this struggle of ours.

*

In January 1963 as the Sino-Soviet dispute was reaching a climax Mao wrote a reply to a poem written by his close friend Kuo Mo-jo. Some of the allusions in Mao's poem are obscure but it is believed that the 'flies' symbolize Mao's opponents in China, the 'ants' are the leaders of the Soviet Union and the 'mayflies' are the US government. At the time it was written the poem was not widely known, but in November 1966 at the height of the Cultural Revolution, it was published on the front page of China's leading newspapers.

DOCUMENT 57. A REPLY TO KUO MO-JO, TO THE MELODY 'THE FULL RIVER IS RED'. A POEM BY MAO TSE-TUNG (*Chinese Literature*, NO. 5, FOREIGN LANGUAGES PRESS, PEKING, MAY 1966, P. 13)

On this tiny globe
A few flies dash themselves against the wall.

Humming without cease,
Sometimes shrilling,
Sometimes moaning.
Ants on the locust tree assume a great nation swagger
And mayflies lightly plot to topple the giant tree.
The west wind scatters leaves over Changan,
And the arrows are flying, twanging.

So many deeds cry out to be done,
And always urgently;
The world rolls on,
Time presses.
Ten thousand years are too long,
Seize the day, seize the hour!

The Four Seas are rising, clouds and waters raging,
The Five Continents are rocking, wind and thunder roaring.
Away with all pests!
Our force is irresistible.

*

The exuberance of the Cultural Revolution was apparently shared by the staff of the Chinese Chargé d'Affaires office in London. Their action was reported with approval in Peking.

DOCUMENT 58. THE *Peking Review* COMMENTS ON AN INCIDENT IN PORTLAND PLACE (*Peking Review*, 10, 29, 14 JULY 1967, P. 40)

Protest Against Anti-China Provocation in Britain

While millions upon millions of people throughout the world hail China for having successfully exploded its first hydrogen bomb, US and British imperialism, modern revisionism and all reactionaries mortally fear and deeply hate this great victory achieved by the Chinese people under the guidance of the invincible thought of Mao Tse-tung. With the connivance of the British Government and incited by the official propaganda machine, a handful of anti-China elements, in the name of the 'campaign for nuclear disarmament', created disorders and provocations in front of the Chinese Chargé d'Affaires Office in London on June 18 and 27. They were sternly rebuked by members of the office on both occasions.

A handful of ruffians, catering to the needs of US and British imperialism and the Soviet revisionist leading clique, carried out another provocation in front of the Chinese Chargé d'Affaires Office on the evening of July 4. Some of them went so far as to burn a copy of *Quotations From Chairman Mao Tse-tung*, which is most treasured by the revolutionary people of the world and regarded by them as a powerful weapon against imperialism, revisionism and all reactionaries. Staff members of the Chinese Chargé d'Affaires Office, who have enormous love for the great leader Chairman Mao, immediately rushed out to stop the ruffians' shameless crime, and managed to seize evidence of the crime on the spot.

The incident was a new and grave political provocation engineered by British imperialism against the great Chinese people. On July 5, Chinese Chargé d'Affaires *ad interim* Shen Ping lodged the most serious and most emphatic protest with the British Foreign Office.

*

The following document describes one of the dramatic incidents which seriously disturbed China's relations with foreign states during the Cultural Revolution. It should be noted that the Chinese have since attributed the attack on the mission to extremist elements acting in defiance of authority and have apologized and made restitution.

DOCUMENT 59. 'MOB BURNS BRITISH MISSION IN PEKING' (FROM THE *Guardian*, 23 AUGUST 1967, P. 1)

Mob Burns British Mission in Peking
Stiff Retaliation Against Chinese in Britain

Strong action against Chinese diplomatic staff in Britain was taken by Whitehall last night after a Chinese mob had invaded the British mission in Peking yesterday. The mission's office building was destroyed.

The residence of the British chargé d'affaires, Mr Donald Hopson, which is near the chancery, was not destroyed, but the furniture was taken out and smashed. Reports made it clear that Mr Hopson was safe, as were the British staff of his mission and their families, who were being looked after in other embassies friendly to Britain. None of the staff was seriously injured, though some appeared to have received rough treatment.

The reports were received at the Foreign Office through a friendly diplomatic mission in Peking. Earlier, the Foreign Office had lost radio contact with the mission after receiving from it a message saying 'They're breaking in.' It was assumed that its wireless transmitter had fallen into Chinese hands or been put out of working order.

The Chinese chargé d'affaires in London, Mr Shen Ping, was summoned to the Foreign Office late last night and was told by Mr George Thomson, the Minister of State, that Britain was taking these measures:

No Chinese diplomats or officials may leave Britain without a special exit visa;

Chinese diplomats must not travel more than five miles from Marble Arch unless two days' notice is given;

The Chinese mission cannot use its diplomatic wireless until British wireless links with Peking are restored.

The attack on the mission came about two hours after the expiry of the Chinese 48-hour ultimatum to the British Government on the subject of the banning in Hongkong of three pro-Peking newspapers and the detention of 53 Chinese who had taken part in demonstrations in the colony.

China demanded that the three newspapers should be allowed to resume publication and that the detained Chinese should be released. The British Government refused to accept the Note containing these demands, on the grounds that it was couched in offensive language and threatened 'serious' consequences.

The mission in Peking had already been in a state of semi-siege during the weekend. On Sunday there were demonstrations both inside and outside the mission, entailing the presentation of 'petitions' and some stone-throwing. Demonstrations had continued early on Monday, when the premises of the mission were reported to be under strong police and military guard.

'Admit Guilt'

And yesterday morning the Chinese domestic and outside staff of the mission assembled and demonstrated on its terrace, while a crowd was milling about outside its gates. Mr Hopson was surrounded and hemmed in by the Chinese members of the staff when he went on to the terrace and was called upon to 'bow his head and admit his guilt'.

The members of the staff also demanded that he should accept and transmit to the British Government a written protest against British rule in Hongkong. Mr Hopson and the British executive members of his staff spent over two hours trying to reason with the Chinese employees.

At the end of that time their demand for an act of obeisance and admission of guilt was withdrawn. Mr Hopson agreed to accept the written protest. He was then standing close to the main gate of the mission and in plain view of the crowd outside —presumably to demonstrate to them that his Chinese staff had carried out the orders which were obviously given to them by higher authority.

Later there came reports of the invasion of the mission. There was no precise information about who may have been in the building at the time. The total of British staff working there is 25, of whom 10 are executive members. There are 29 'dependants' in all, including wives, children, and British domestic staff in British households.

Mr Hopson and his family would normally have been in the residence, which is directly across the road from the mission, while other members of the staff live about a quarter of a mile away in the diplomatic compound for foreign diplomats from various countries.

According to the diplomatic reports in London, the doyen of the diplomatic corps in Peking, the United Arab Republic's Ambassador, had been trying to see the Chinese Foreign Minister, Chen Yi, to protest about the incidents, but so far had not been able to do so.

In London last night extra police were guarding the Chinese

Legation in Portland Place. All the windows in the four-storey building were shuttered, and all was quiet outside.

Trial Continues

Meanwhile in Hongkong the trial of five pro-Peking newspaper executives continued calmly yesterday as the time limit in China's ultimation to Britain was expiring. The whole day was spent reading out charges against the five, who, according to agency reports were led into court in a file with their hands on each other's shoulders.

The defendants held up the proceedings on Monday by shouting protests at their arrest, but there were no disorders in court yesterday, though, in another part of the colony, a terrorist bomb exploded in the Hilton Hotel.

*

The Cultural Revolution had produced even more vehement Chinese attacks on the Soviet leadership. By 1969 there was no abatement of Sino-Soviet antagonism; on the contrary there was a state of serious military confrontation. One of the most widely publicized of the armed clashes on the border took place in March 1969 over a disputed island in the Ussuri river.

DOCUMENT 60. A CHINESE COMMENT ON AN INCIDENT ON THE USSURI RIVER BOUNDARY. EXTRACT FROM 'DOWN WITH THE NEW TSARS', FOREIGN LANGUAGES PRESS, PEKING, 1969, PP. 9–11

Soviet Revisionist Renegade Clique Directs Soviet Frontier Guards to Intrude Flagrantly into China's Territory Chenpao Island

On March 2 the Soviet modern revisionist renegade clique directed Soviet frontier guards to intrude flagrantly into the area of Chenpao Island, Heilungkiang Province, China, and outrageously open cannon and gun fire, killing and wounding many Chinese frontier guards. The Chinese frontier guards were compelled to fight back in self-defence. This extremely grave incident of armed provocations deliberately created by the Soviet revisionist renegade clique is another grave crime perpetrated by it against the Chinese people and once again reveals its fiendish features as social-imperialism.

At about 09:00 hours on March 2, large numbers of fully armed soldiers, together with armoured vehicles, a lorry and a command car, sent by the Soviet frontier authorities, flagrantly intruded into the area of Chenpao Island which is indisputably Chinese territory, and carried out provocations against the Chinese frontier guards who were on normal patrol duty on the island. At that time, the Chinese frontier guards, showing very great restraint, repeatedly warned the intruding Soviet soldiers and ordered them to stop their provocations and withdraw from the Chinese territory. However, the intruding Soviet soldiers refused to heed these warnings and became even more truculent. At 09:17 hours, the intruding Soviet soldiers outrageously opened up with cannon and gun fire on the Chinese frontier guards. Having reached the end of their forbearance, the Chinese frontier guards were compelled to fight back in self-defence, giving the intruders, who were committing provocations, their deserved punishment and triumphantly safeguarding our country's sacred territory.

This extremely grave armed conflict single-handedly created by the Soviet revisionist renegade clique is by no means an isolated incident. For a long time, the Soviet revisionist renegade clique, ignoring the repeated warnings of the Chinese Government, has time and again encroached upon China's territory and her air space and created incidents involving bloodshed on many occasions. During the ice-bound session in the more than two years between January 23, 1967 and March 2 this year, Soviet frontier guards intruded into the area of Chenpao Island on sixteen occasions, and on several occasions wounded Chinese frontier guards who were on normal patrol duty, and looted arms and ammunition. Between the end of November 1967 and January 5, 1968, the Soviet revisionist renegade clique sent Soviet frontier guards on eighteen occasions to intrude into the area of Chilichin Island, north of Chenpao Island, Heilungkiang Province, China, disrupting Chinese people's production and on many occasions killing and wounding Chinese people engaged in productive labour. Soviet frontier guards also intruded into the area of Kapotzu Island, south of Chenpao Island, Heilungkiang Province, China, on many occasions. And, on a still greater number of occasions, Soviet military planes intruded into China's air space over Heilungkiang Province.

The criminal activities of the Soviet revisionist renegade clique in deliberately encroaching upon China's territory and creating incidents involving bloodshed one after another have glaringly exposed the vicious features of the clique, which for a long time has collaborated with US imperialism, frenziedly opposed China and practised social-imperialism and social-fascism. These grave crimes of the clique have aroused the utmost indignation of the Chinese armymen and civilians. The Chinese people sternly warn the Soviet revisionist renegade clique: The 700 million Chinese people, tempered in the great proletarian cultural revolution, are not to be trifled with. China's sacred territory brooks no violation. If you should wilfully cling to your reckless course and continue to provoke armed conflicts along the Sino-Soviet border, you will certainly receive resolute counter-blows from the 700 million Chinese people who are armed with Marxism-Leninism-Mao Tse-tung Thought!

PART VI

Foreign Relations since the Cultural Revolution

There have been dramatic turns in China's foreign relations since the Cultural Revolution. With Mao aging, the fractionally (three years) younger Chou En-lai has emerged as the steadying central figure. It is likely that history will show that it was Chou En-lai above all who charted China on a new course after 1970. It may also be seen that the currents in which he had to steer were inexorably moving towards world-wide realignment.

The simple fact was that the United States had no permanent interest in maintaining its aggressive posture towards China. Americans have been a long time recognizing the weakness of their inflexible position. They have taken even longer to admit their defeat in Indochina. But given the demonstrated limitations of American power, and the apparently irreconcilable differences between China and the Soviet Union, a diplomatic revolution has become possible.

Nixon's victory in the 1968 election did not, ostensibly, presage a change in American policy. Commenting on the President's inaugural address, the *People's Daily* of 27 January 1969 accused Nixon of using tactics of political deception to cover military aggression (Document 61). Certainly the United States appeared unrepentant, as it set about extending the war in Indochina, firstly engineering a coup in Cambodia followed by an invasion by South Vietnamese troops, and later instigating the invasion of Laos, where the CIA had long held power in the non-'liberated' areas. This latter escalation in a country contiguous with China prompted a warning from China. The

People's Daily (14 February 1971) treated with contempt the American claim that action in Laos did not threaten China in an article entitled 'Don't Lose Your Head, Nixon' (Document 63).

By March it was clear that the South Vietnamese attacks had failed to fulfil American hopes. When Nixon made his foreign policy report to Congress on 25 February he dealt with the problem of China, and spoke of the need to draw China into a constructive relationship with the world community, and particularly with the rest of Asia. He added that the US was prepared to establish a dialogue with Peking. For some months Washington had been seeking through various unofficial channels to ascertain whether the President would be welcome to visit China. A sign that Peking was ready to reciprocate moves towards better relations with the US came in April 1971 when the American table-tennis team was invited to tour China.

In July Dr Henry Kissinger visited Peking secretly for talks with Chou En-lai, an event which was announced on page 1 of the *People's Daily* (16 July 1971), and which paved the way for President Nixon's sensational visit to Peking in February 1972.

Meanwhile American suggestions of a 'two Chinas' solution to the United Nations seat problem were rebutted by strongly worded statements in the Chinese press (Document 64). When the issue came before the General Assembly on 25 October 1971 there was an overwhelming vote for the admission of China and the expulsion of the delegates from Taiwan. Representatives of the People's Republic headed by Chiao Kuan-hua took seats in the assembly of the United Nations.

Gaining their legitimate rights in the UN was both a tangible and symbolic achievement for the CPR. A number of nations (twenty during the year 1972), no doubt encouraged by Nixon's visit, hastened to establish or restore diplomatic relations with Peking. Cultural exchanges and the visits of distinguished western statesmen signalled the beginning of a new era. The Chinese, twenty-three years after Liberation, had cause for satisfaction. The people who, in Mao's words, first 'stood up' in 1949 had at last won wide recognition and universal respect.

Between China and the Soviet Union there has been no diminution of mutual hostility. The Soviet-Indian Friendship Treaty (August 1971) and Soviet support for India in the

Bangladesh war have been cited as evidence that the Soviet Union intends to use India to extend its 'aggressive' influence in Asia (Document 67). The Soviets have retorted that the Chinese policy of colluding with America while intensifying propaganda against the Soviet Union does not reflect the true interests and wishes of the Chinese people. In 1973 Soviet proposals for a non-aggression treaty and Brezhnev's statement that the Soviet Union had 'absolutely no territorial claims against the People's Republic of China' met with no sympathetic response from Peking. A *People's Daily* article of 31 December 1973, reviewing the past year, warned that the Soviet Union intended to make inroads into areas previously under US domination; specifically that the Soviets had expansionist designs on Western Europe. Peking's pronouncements indicate that Soviet 'revisionism' has replaced American 'imperialism' as the chief enemy.

(a) 'RAPPROCHEMENT' AND RECOGNITION

DOCUMENT 61. EXTRACT FROM 'CONFESSION IN AN IMPASSE', BY COMMENTATOR, *People's Daily*, 27 JANUARY 1969 (FOREIGN LANGUAGES PRESS, PEKING, 1969)

Lyndon Johnson has stepped down and Richard Nixon has taken over. This happened in the last year of the 1960s. On January 20, this jittery chieftain of US imperialism delivered an 'inaugural address' amid angry roars from the American people. No sooner had it been broadcast than it drew gloomy public comments in the capitalist world to the effect that the address made in a 'cold grey plaza' was 'very low keyed' and 'vague', and the tone 'more muted than bold', that it reflected 'almost super-human difficulties' and 'near-insuperable difficulties' and was 'a grim warning'. In short, even in the capitalist world it was keenly felt that the 'low keyed' address reflected the difficulties of US imperialism which finds itself at the end of its rope and is closer to its doom. It was a confession by the US imperialists (and, in fact, by the Soviet revisionist clique of renegades and all the reactionaries as well) that they are beset with difficulties both at home and abroad and are in an impasse.

The US monopoly capitalist class thrust Nixon into power

with an eye to extricating the imperialist system from crisis. The event had been intended to be a joyful occasion. But it was run like a funeral. Secret service men and police ringed Nixon with protective cordons and even the platform from which he made his inaugural speech was screened off by bullet-proof glass. The Western press ridiculed Nixon's inaugural address as a 'speech made from a glass cage'. However, it serves as excellent teaching material by negative example for the revolutionary people throughout the world. It enables us to see more clearly the very weak, paper-tiger nature of US imperialism and helps us recognize the counter-revolutionary tactics that US imperialism is going to adopt.

Chairman Mao has pointed out:

> All reactionary forces on the verge of extinction invariably conduct desperate struggles. They are bound to resort to military adventure and political deception in all their forms in order to save themselves from extinction.

An outstanding feature of Nixon's address was that US imperialism is relying more on the tactics of political deception to cover up its military aggression. Nixon said: 'In these difficult years, America has suffered from a fever of words. . . .' His address was typical of precisely this 'fever of words'.

What are the 'words' Nixon juggled with? First, 'unity'; second, 'peace' and third, 'spirit'.

Confronted by unprecedentedly fierce class contradictions at home, the rapidly mounting consciousness of class struggle of the American working class, students and other youth and the oppressed Black people, and the vigorously growing revolutionary mass movement of broad sections of the people, Nixon had to admit that US imperialism is in 'the valley of turmoil' (which should read: the angry torrents of the people's revolution). In mortal fear, he cried out in alarm: 'We are torn by division. . . .' The 'division' between the American people, who account for more than 95 per cent of the population, on the one hand and the monopoly capitalist class which oppresses and exploits them and its political system on the other, is an excellent one. This 'division' marks the people's awakening. It shows the big progress of the proletariat and broad sections of the oppressed people in the United States in their class struggle against US imperialist ruling circles. It augurs a great proletarian revolution and will finally send US imperialism into the 'valley'. Nixon's fear of 'division' reflects the alarm of the bourgeoisie at the great revolutionary forces of the people. What is to be done? Nixon shouts himself hoarse for 'unity', for all to 'go forward together' and for things 'to be done by government and people together', and so on and so forth. How could there be 'unity' between the masses of Black people and the racists, between the workers and the capitalists and between the broad masses and the reactionary ruling circles? Nixon wants to 'go forward together' with the American people. Doesn't that mean 'going forward' to 'the valley of turmoil' which spells doom to imperialism? It is enough to make you laugh your head off to hear a wolf, while devouring a sheep, tell it: 'Let's do it together!' This clumsy deception of class conciliation fully shows Nixon's feeling of impotence when confronted by 'division', that is, by the revolutionary struggle of the oppressed people, and, therefore, he could only utter nonsense to deceive people in a vain effort to lessen the wrath of the American people and give himself some consolation.

*

From the summer of 1969 the United States began to explore the possibilities of improving relations with China. The Nixon administration suggested publicly that tensions might be eased and proposed the re-opening of the ambassadorial talks in Warsaw, suspended during the Cultural Revolution. The talks began in January 1970 only to be immediately broken off after the US backed invasion of Cambodia (30 April 1970). Perhaps the Americans hoped by alternating military threats with a conciliatory approach to urge the Chinese into a dialogue which would end their problems in Southeast Asia. The US administration went ahead with the gradual removal of trade embargoes against China, eased restrictions on American travel to China, and began to convey messages that an invitation to Nixon to visit Peking would be welcome.

DOCUMENT 62. A CONVERSATION BETWEEN CHAIRMAN MAO AND EDGAR SNOW, DECEMBER 1970 (EXTRACT FROM E. SNOW, *The Long Revolution*, HUTCHINSON, LONDON, 1973, PP. 171–3, 174)

[Chairman Mao said]... between Chinese and Americans there need be no prejudices. There could be mutual respect and equality. He said he placed high hopes on the peoples of the two countries.

If the Soviet Union wouldn't do (point the way), then he would place his hopes on the American people. The United States alone had a population of more than 200 million. Industrial production was already higher than in any other country, and education was universal. He would be happy to see a party emerge there to lead a revolution, although he was not expecting that in the near future.

In the meantime, he said, the Foreign Ministry was studying the matter of admitting Americans from the left, middle, and right to visit China. Should rightists like Nixon, who represented the monopoly capitalists, be permitted to come? He should be welcomed because, Mao explained, at present the problems between China and the USA would have to be solved with Nixon. Mao would be happy to talk with him, either as a tourist or as President.

I, unfortunately, could not represent the United States, he said; I was not a monopoly capitalist. Could I settle the Taiwan question? Why continue such a stalemate? Chiang Kai-shek had not died yet. But what had Taiwan to do with Nixon? That question was created by Truman and Acheson.

It may be relevant to mention—and this was not a part of my talk with Chairman Mao—that foreign diplomats in Peking had been aware that messages were being delivered from Washington to the Chinese government by certain go-betweens. The purport of such communications was to assure Chinese leaders of Mr Nixon's 'new outlook' on Asia. Nixon was firmly determined, it was said, to withdraw from Vietnam as speedily as possible, to seek a negotiated international guarantee of the independence of Southeast Asia, to end the impasse in Sino-American relations by clearing up the Taiwan question and to bring the People's Republic into the United Nations and into diplomatic relations with the United States.

Two important Frenchmen were in China in 1970. The first was André Bettencourt, the minister of planning, the second was Maurice Couve de Murville, premier under De Gaulle's regime. M. Couve de Murville completed arrangements for a visit to China by General de Gaulle which was to have occurred this year. It was to General de Gaulle, I was authoritatively informed, that Mr Nixon had first confided his intention to seek a genuine *détente* with China. Some people had anticipated that De Gaulle, during his visit, would play a key role in promoting serious Sino-American conversations. Death ruled otherwise. Chairman Mao's tribute to the General, sent to Mme de Gaulle, was the only eulogy which he was known to have offered for any non-Communist statesman since Roosevelt died.

Meanwhile, other diplomats had been active. The head of one European mission in Peking, who had already made one trip to see President Nixon, returned to Washington last December. He bypassed the State Department to confer at the White House, and was back in China in January. From another and unimpeachable diplomatic source I learned, not long before my departure from Peking in February, that the White House had once more conveyed a message asking how a personal representative of the President would be received in the Chinese capital for conversations with the highest Chinese leaders. About the same time, I was enigmatically told by a senior Chinese diplomat who had formerly maintained quite the opposite, 'Nixon is getting out of Vietnam.'

I must once more stress that none of the above background information was provided to me by Mao Tse-tung.

As we talked, the Chairman recalled to me once again that it was the Japanese militarists who had taught revolution to the Chinese people. Thanks to their invasion, they had provoked the Chinese people to fight and had helped bring Chinese socialism to power.

I mentioned how Prince Sihanouk had told me a few days before that 'Nixon is the best agent for Mao Tse-tung. The more he bombs Cambodia, the more Communists he makes. He is their best ammunition carrier,' said the Prince. Yes, Mao agreed. He liked that kind of help. . . .

Referring once again to the United States, Chairman Mao

said that China should learn from the way America developed, by decentralizing and spreading responsibility and wealth among the fifty states. A central government could not do everything. China must depend upon regional and local initiatives. It would not do (spreading his hands) to leave everything up to him.

*

In February 1971 the United States instigated the invasion of Laos by the South Vietnamese.

DOCUMENT 63. 'DON'T LOSE YOUR HEAD, NIXON', BY COMMENTATOR IN *People's Daily*, 20 FEBRUARY 1971 (*Peking Review* 14, 9, 26 FEBRUARY 1971, P. 6)

US imperialist chieftain Richard Nixon made a speech reeking with gunpowder at his February 17 press conference. Keeping silent for about ten days after the massive invasion of Laos by US imperialism, Nixon finally came forward with wild war-cries, openly revealing his diabolical warmonger features.

Nixon minced no words in making several points clear:

1 To achieve their goal of aggression, the US-puppet troops invading Laos on a massive scale 'will stay' there 'if it takes a longer time'.

2 The Saigon puppets themselves can 'make decisions' on invading Viet Nam.

3 As long as he considers the US forces in south Viet Nam 'threatened', he will 'take strong action' and is not going to 'place any limitation upon the use of air power' of the United States.

4 'There will be Americans in south Viet Nam and enough Americans', as long as the so-called US prisoner-of-war issue is not settled.

In this way, Nixon in fact told the whole world that he is wilfully continuing to carry out the criminal plan of persisting in and expanding the war of aggression in Indochina. He is not only prepared to stick to its mad course in Laos, but also plans to step up bombing raids on north Viet Nam further, and even unleash the Saigon puppet troops to mount, with the coordination of the US aggressor troops, surprise attacks on the Democratic Republic of Viet Nam, thus expanding the war of aggression in Viet Nam and the rest of Indochina to a still larger scale. Showing his ferocious features, Nixon has indeed reached the height of arrogance.

Nixon's mad talk has again proved to the world that US imperialism wants to hang on in south Viet Nam, and the so-called 'troop withdrawal from Viet Nam' is only a ruse aimed at deception. By using this ruse, US imperialism yesterday extended the flames of the war of aggression to Cambodia; and resorting to the same ruse again, it spreads the flames of aggressive war to Laos today. Nixon had the cheek to say that this rotten trick was the fixed policy of his government and declared that he would continue to pursue it. This only shows that the Nixon government is bent on going down the road of expanding its war of aggression in Indochina.

For the Nixon government to wilfully 'escalate' the war in Indochina in a big way is highly dangerous. The US bourgeois press has pointed out that he is taking the road the Truman administration took in Korea many years ago. But Nixon claimed that US imperialist actions of enlarging the aggression 'present no threat' to China and said: 'I do not believe' that China has 'any reason . . . to react to it.' Nixon's attempt to tie the hands of the Chinese people in supporting the Laotian people and the other peoples in Indochina in their war against US aggression and for national salvation can never succeed.

Laos is not in Northwest Europe or South America, but in north Indochina. She and China are linked by the same mountains and rivers and have a common boundary of several hundred kilometres. Nixon should not lose his head and forget such common knowledge of geography. By spreading the flames of aggressive war to the door of China, US imperialism certainly poses a grave threat to China. The Chinese people cannot be indifferent to such rabid acts of aggression on the part of US imperialism. The Chinese people have rich experience in struggle against US imperialism and we know very well how to deal with the US aggressors. We must warn Nixon once again that the 700 million Chinese people will never let you run amuck in Indochina.

Though it shows its teeth and claws and adopts an insolent

air, US imperialism is in reality only a paper tiger putting up a death-bed struggle. The Nixon government's reactionary policy of persisting in expanding the war in Indochina started with the aim of injuring others only to end up by ruining itself, as the law of development which governs all reactionary policies shows. US imperialism will certainly suffer the consequences of its frantic war adventures.

*

Meanwhile the American *démarche* continued. In February 1971 the term the 'People's Republic of China' was used for the first time in a US official document and in March Nixon hinted that he was prepared to see China in the United Nations, but not at the expense of displacing the Republic of China (Taiwan). Such a solution, recognizing 'two Chinas', had long been anathema to the Chinese. They had spoken against it when Kennedy had seemed to favour the 'two successor states' formula in 1961 and they did so again.

DOCUMENT 64. OPPOSING A 'TWO CHINAS' SOLUTION, COMMENTATOR IN *People's Daily*, 4 MAY 1971 (*Peking Review*, 14, 19, 7 MAY 1971, PP. 13–14)

[The] claim that the sovereignty over Taiwan and the Penghu Islands is a question subject to 'international resolution' or to be resolved on the basis of so-called 'agreements arrived at between the two governments' of China is not only preposterous, but a flagrant interference in China's internal affairs. It is crystal clear that Taiwan and the Penghu Islands are an integral part of China's territory and the question of 'international resolution' does not exist at all. The Chinese people will never permit the US Government to play with the plots of 'two Chinas' or 'one China, one Taiwan'. When and how the Chinese people liberate Taiwan is entirely China's internal affair, and no foreign country has any right to interfere.

Our great leader Chairman Mao has pointed out: The Chinese people 'are determined to liberate Taiwan, to safeguard the national sovereignty and territorial integrity of China.' The US armed forces must pull out of Taiwan and the Taiwan Straits. The US aggressors have to pull out in any case and are not allowed to behave otherwise. China's sacred territory Taiwan and the Penghu Islands must be returned to the embrace of the motherland.

*

Dr Henry Kissinger's visit to Peking in July 1971 was to prepare the way for the visit of President Nixon in February 1972. As Chou En-lai explained: Nixon wanted to come and the Chinese were willing to talk with him because if you do not talk with the head who else should you talk with? Nevertheless the volte-face implied in accepting the arch-enemy of communism as an honoured guest has caused soul-searching in China. Almost certainly the invitation was a victory for veteran conciliator Chou En-lai, and signified the growing strength of the moderates after the Cultural Revolution. It may also be related to the mysterious demise of Lin Piao, Mao's heir apparent, in a plane travelling away from Peking across Mongolia in September 1971.

It is likely that the announcement of Nixon's proposed visit helped to swing the UN vote in favour of seating the People's Republic. The probability of a vote in China's favour may also have given urgency to American negotiations with China.

Following Kissinger's visit to Peking the Secretary of State, William Rogers, announced that the US would support action at the United Nations calling for the seating of the People's Republic while opposing 'any action to expel the Republic of China or deprive it of representation in the UN'. He emphasized that the expulsion of the Republic of China was an important question, i.e. requiring a two-thirds majority vote. Statements from Taipeh showed the Nationalists reacting equally strongly against the idea of two Chinas.

On 25 October 1971 the General Assembly adopted by a large majority a resolution demanding both the admission of the People's Republic and the expulsion of the Nationalists. Thus the Nixon visit, five months before it occurred, had already helped to produce one important and tangible gain for the Chinese.

DOCUMENT 65. EXTRACTS FROM SPEECH BY CHIAO KUAN-HUA, CHAIRMAN OF THE DELEGATION OF THE PEOPLE'S REPUBLIC OF CHINA AT THE PLENARY MEETING OF THE 26TH SESSION OF THE UN GENERAL ASSEMBLY, 15 NOVEMBER 1971 (EXTRACTS FROM 'IRRESISTIBLE HISTORICAL TREND', FOREIGN LANGUAGES PRESS, PEKING, 1971, PP. 4–15)

Mr President,
Fellow Representatives,

First of all, allow me, in the name of the Delegation of the People's Republic of China, to thank Mr President and the representatives of many countries for the welcome they have given us.

Many friends have made very enthusiastic speeches expressing their trust in as well as encouragement and fraternal sentiments for the Chinese people. We are deeply moved by this, and we shall convey all this to the entire Chinese people.

It is a pleasure for the Delegation of the People's Republic of China to be here today to attend the 26th Session of the General Assembly of the United Nations and take part together with you in the work of the United Nations.

As is known to all, China is one of the founding members of the United Nations. In 1949, the Chinese people overthrew the reactionary rule of the Chiang Kai-shek clique and founded the People's Republic of China. Since then, the legitimate rights of China in the United Nations should have gone to the People's Republic of China as a matter of course. It was only because of the obstruction by the United States Government that the legitimate rights of the People's Republic of China in the United Nations were deprived of for a long time and that the Chiang Kai-shek clique long repudiated by the Chinese people was able to usurp China's lawful seat in the United Nations. This was a gross interference in China's internal affairs as well as a wilful trampling on the Charter of the United Nations. Now such an unjustifiable state of affairs has finally been put right. . . .

We have consistently maintained that all countries, big or small, should be equal and that the Five Principles of Peaceful Coexistence should be taken as the principles guiding the relations between countries. The people of each country have the right to choose the social system of their own country according to their own will and to protect the independence, sovereignty and territorial integrity of their own country. No country has the right to subject another country to its aggression, subversion, control, interference or bullying. We are opposed to the imperialist and colonialist theory that big nations are superior to the small nations and small nations are subordinate to the big nations. We are opposed to the power politics and hegemony of big nations bullying small ones or strong nations bullying weak ones. We hold that the affairs of a given country must be handled by its own people, that the affairs of the world must be handled by all the countries of the world, and that the affairs of the United Nations must be handled jointly by all its member states, and the superpowers should not be allowed to manipulate and monopolize them. The superpowers want to be superior to others and lord it over others. At no time, neither today nor ever in the future, will China be a superpower subjecting others to its aggression, subversion, control, interference or bullying.

The one or two superpowers are stepping up their arms expansion and war preparations and vigorously developing nuclear weapons, thus seriously threatening international peace. It is understandable that the people of the world long for disarmament and particularly for nuclear disarmament. Their demand for the dissolution of military blocs, withdrawal of foreign troops and dismantling of foreign military bases is a just one. However, the superpowers, while talking about disarmament every day, are actually engaged in arms expansion daily. The so-called nuclear disarmament which they are supposed to seek is entirely for the purpose of monopolizing nuclear weapons in order to carry out nuclear threats and blackmail. China will never participate in the so-called nuclear disarmament talks between the nuclear powers behind the backs of the non-nuclear countries. China's nuclear weapons are still in the experimental stage. China develops nuclear weapons solely for the purpose of defence and for breaking the nuclear monopoly and ultimately eliminating nuclear weapons and nuclear war. The Chinese Government has consistently stood for the complete prohibition and thorough destruction of nuclear weapons and proposed to convene a summit conference of all countries of the world to discuss this question and, as the first step, to reach an agreement on the non-use of nuclear weapons. The Chinese Government has on many occasions declared, and now on behalf of the Chinese Government, I once again solemnly declare that at no time and under no circumstances will China be the first to use nuclear weapons. If the United States and the Soviet Union really and truly want disarmament, they should commit themselves not to be the first to use nuclear weapons. This is not something difficult to do. Whether this is done or not will be a severe test as to whether they have the genuine desire for disarmament.

We have always held that the just struggles of the people of all countries support each other. China has always had the sympathy and support of the people of various countries in her socialist revolution and socialist construction. It is our bounden duty to support the just struggles of the people of various countries. For this purpose, we have provided aid to some friendly countries to help them develop their national economy independently. In providing aid, we always strictly respect the sovereignty of the recipient countries, and never attach any conditions or ask for any privileges. We provide free military aid to countries and peoples who are fighting against aggression. We will never become munition merchants. We firmly oppose certain countries trying to control and plunder the recipient countries by means of 'aid'. However, as China's economy is still comparatively backward, the material aid we have provided is very limited, and what we provide is mainly political and moral support. With a population of 700 million, China ought to make a greater contribution to human progress. And we hope that this situation of our ability falling short of this wish of ours will be gradually changed.

Mr President and fellow representatives,

In accordance with the purposes of the United Nations Charter, the United Nations should play its due role in maintaining international peace, opposing aggression and interference and developing friendly relations and co-operation among nations. However, for a long period the one or two superpowers have utilized the United Nations and have done many things in contravention of the United Nations Charter against the will of the people of various countries. This situation should not continue. We hope that the spirit of the United

Nations Charter will be really and truly followed out. We will stand together with all the countries and peoples that love peace and uphold justice and work together with them for the defence of the national independence and state sovereignty of various countries and for the cause of safeguarding international peace and promoting human progress.

DOCUMENT 66. THE NIXON VISIT. JOINT COMMUNIQUÉ AGREED BY THE CHINESE AND US SIDES IN SHANGHAI, 27 FEBRUARY 1972

President Richard Nixon of the United States of America visited the People's Republic of China at the invitation of Premier Chou En-lai of the People's Republic of China from February 21 to February 28, 1972. Accompanying the President were Mrs Nixon, US Secretary of State William Rogers, Assistant to the President Dr Henry Kissinger, and other American officials.

President Nixon met with Chairman Mao Tse-tung of the Communist Party of China on February 21. The two leaders had a serious and frank exchange of views on Sino-US relations and world affairs.

During the visit, extensive, earnest and frank discussions were held between President Nixon and Premier Chou En-lai on the normalization of relations between the United States of America and the People's Republic of China, as well as on other matters of interest to both sides. In addition, Secretary of State William Rogers and Foreign Minister Chi Peng-fei held talks in the same spirit.

President Nixon and his party visited Peking and viewed cultural, industrial and agricultural sites, and they also toured Hangchow and Shanghai where, continuing discussions with Chinese leaders, they viewed similar places of interest.

The leaders of the People's Republic of China and the United States of America found it beneficial to have this opportunity, after so many years without contact, to present candidly to one another their views on a variety of issues. They reviewed the international situation in which important changes and great upheavals are taking place and expounded their respective positions and attitudes.

The Chinese side stated: Wherever there is oppression, there is resistance. Countries want independence, nations want liberation and the people want revolution—this has become the irresistible trend of history. All nations, big or small, should be equal; big nations should not bully the small and strong nations should not bully the weak. China will never be a super-power and it opposes hegemony and power politics of any kind. The Chinese side stated that it firmly supports the struggles of all the oppressed people and nations for freedom and liberation and that the people of all countries have the right to choose their social systems according to their own wishes and the right to safeguard the independence, sovereignty and territorial integrity of their own countries and oppose foreign aggression, interference, control and subversion. All foreign troops should be withdrawn to their own countries. The Chinese side expressed its firm support to the peoples of Viet Nam, Laos and Cambodia in their efforts for the attainment of their goal and its firm support to the seven-point proposal of the Provisional Revolutionary Government of the Republic of South Viet Nam and the elaboration of February this year on the two key problems in the proposal, and to the Joint Declaration of the Summit Conference of the Indochinese Peoples. It firmly supports the eight-point program for the peaceful unification of Korea put forward by the Government of the Democratic People's Republic of Korea on April 12, 1971, and the stand for the abolition of the 'UN Commission for the Unification and Rehabilitation of Korea'. It firmly opposes the revival and outward expansion of Japanese militarism and firmly supports the Japanese people's desire to build an independent, democratic, peaceful and neutral Japan. It firmly maintains that India and Pakistan should, in accordance with the United Nations resolutions on the India-Pakistan question, immediately withdraw all their forces to their respective territories and to their own sides of the ceasefire line in Jammu and Kashmir and firmly supports the Pakistan Government and people in their struggle to preserve their independence and sovereignty and the people of Jammu and Kashmir in their struggle for the right of self-determination.

The US side stated: Peace in Asia and peace in the world requires efforts both to reduce immediate tensions and to eliminate the basic causes of conflict. The United States will work for a just and secure peace: just, because it fulfils the aspirations of peoples and nations for freedom and progress; secure, because it removes the danger of foreign aggression. The United States supports individual freedom and social progress for all the peoples of the world, free of outside pressure or intervention. The United States believes that the effort to reduce tensions is served by improving communication between countries that have different ideologies so as to lessen the risks of confrontation through accident, miscalculation or misunderstanding. Countries should treat each other with mutual respect and be willing to compete peacefully, letting performance be the ultimate judge. No country should claim infallibility and each country should be prepared to re-examine its own attitudes for the common good. The United States stressed that the peoples of Indochina should be allowed to determine their destiny without outside intervention; its constant primary objective has been a negotiated solution; the eight-point proposal put forward by the Republic of Viet Nam and the United States on January 27, 1972 represents a basis for the attainment of that objective; in the absence of a negotiated settlement the United States envisages the ultimate withdrawal of all US forces from the region consistent with the aim of self-determination for each country of Indochina. The United States will maintain its close ties with and support for the Republic of Korea; the United States will support efforts of the Republic of Korea to seek a relaxation of tension and increased communication in the Korean peninsula. The United States places the highest value on its friendly relations with Japan; it will continue to develop the existing close bonds. Consistent with the United Nations Security Council Resolution of December 21, 1971, the United States favors the continuation of the ceasefire between India and Pakistan and the withdrawal of all military forces to within their own territories and to their own sides of the ceasefire line in Jammu and Kashmir; the United States supports the right of the peoples of South Asia to shape their own future in peace, free of military threat, and without having the area become the subject of great power rivalry.

There are essential differences between China and the United States in their social systems and foreign policies. However, the two sides agreed that countries, regardless of their social systems, should conduct their relations on the principles of respect for the sovereignty and territorial integrity of all states, non-aggression against other states, non-interference in the internal affairs of other states, equality and mutual benefit, and peaceful coexistence. International disputes should be settled on this basis, without resorting to the use or threat of force. The United States and the People's Republic of China are prepared to apply these principles to their mutual relations.

With these principles of international relations in mind the two sides stated that:

—progress toward the normalization of relations between China and the United States is in the interest of all countries;

—both wish to reduce the danger of international military conflict;

—neither should seek hegemony in the Asia-Pacific region and each is opposed to efforts by any other country or group of countries to establish such hegemony; and

—neither is prepared to negotiate on behalf of any third party or to enter into agreements or understandings with the other directed at other states.

Both sides are of the view that it would be against the interests of the peoples of the world for any major country to collude with another against other countries or for major countries to divide up the world into spheres of interest.

(b) BANGLADESH

A major international crisis in which China was bound to have a voice was the confrontation in 1971 between India and Pakistan over Bangladesh (formerly East Pakistan).

Common hostility to India has been a key element in Sino-Pakistan relations. As a member of SEATO Pakistan was anxious to emphasize that no hostility to China was intended. After the Sino-Indian War in 1962 there was speedy agreement on the Chinese border with Pakistan-held Kashmir.

A general improvement of communications included the establishment of an airline route in 1964. When, in 1965, Pakistan resorted to arms in its dispute with India over Kashmir, China gave some material aid and diplomatic support. Nevertheless President Ayub made a peace settlement, with Soviet mediation, in which he gained nothing in respect of Kashmir. The pro-Chinese Foreign Minister Mr Bhutto was dismissed in June 1966. Although after 1966 China delivered military equipment in substantial quantities to Pakistan, Ayub, to Peking's disgust, also accepted military and economic aid from the Soviet Union. It is likely that Ayub's decision in late 1969 not to run again for President and the re-emergence of Bhutto was welcomed in China. When after March 1971 the Pakistan army engaged in brutal repression in Bangladesh, Chinese disapproval was constrained by anxiety to prevent the break-up of Pakistan, and Peking gave Pakistan propaganda support. Soviet and Indian backing for Bangladesh, and the Soviet-Indian Friendship Treaty of August 1971, must have weighed heavily with China. The major Chinese statement was published on 16 December just after Pakistan and India had agreed on a cease-fire. Subsequently (31 January–2 February 1972) President Bhutto visited China and fresh grants of economic aid were announced.

DOCUMENT 67. BANGLADESH. EXTRACTS FROM STATEMENT OF THE GOVERNMENT OF THE PEOPLE'S REPUBLIC OF CHINA, 16 DECEMBER 1971 (SUPPLEMENT TO *Peking Review*, 14, 51, 17 DECEMBER 1971)

A large scale war of aggression against Pakistan was brazenly launched by the Indian Government on November 21, 1971 with the active encouragement and energetic support of the Government of the Soviet Union. This has gravely disrupted peace on the South Asian subcontinent, given a tremendous shock and caused serious anxiety to the people throughout the world. On December 7, the United Nations General Assembly adopted by the overwhelming majority of 104 to 11 with 10 abstentions a most urgent resolution which, being very magnanimous to India, calls upon India and Pakistan to bring about a cease-fire and withdraw their armed forces to their own side of the India-Pakistan borders. . . .

Ignoring the opposition of the overwhelming majority of the countries of the world, the Indian Government is continuing to expand its war of aggression, moving massive troops to press on the capital of East Pakistan, Dacca, blockading the ports and sea lanes in East and West Pakistan with its naval forces, and carrying out continuous wanton bombings with its air force against East and West Pakistan, stopping at nothing in committing most brutal atrocities. These acts have completely laid bare the wild ambitions of the Indian expansionists. Cherishing the pipe dream of a Greater Indian Empire, they want not only to swallow up East Pakistan, but also to destroy Pakistan as a whole. If a timely stop is not put to such aggression committed by the Indian Government, Pakistan will not be the only country to fall victim, inevitably other countries neighbouring on India will also be endangered. . . .

The Indian Government asserts that it has launched the war in order to realize the national aspirations of the people in East Pakistan and bring about the return of East Pakistan refugees to their homeland. This assertion is indeed absurd to the extreme. Many countries in the world have nationality problems, which need to be solved properly and reasonably in conformity with the desire and interests of the people but these are the internal affairs of the respective countries, which can be solved only by their own governments and people and in which no foreign country has the right to interfere. . . .

As for the question of the return of the East Pakistan refugees to their homeland, it should, and can only, be settled by India and Pakistan through consultation, and it is absolutely unjustifiable to resort to force. Has there not been much interflow of refugees between India and Pakistan over the past two decades and more since the India-Pakistan partition? Because of this conflicts have often occurred on the India–Pakistan borders. All these sufferings of the Indian and Pakistan peoples stem from the roots of trouble left over by the British Empire in carrying out India-Pakistan partition after World War II. Colonialism has brought calamities on us Afro-Asian peoples. Should this bitter lesson not be enough to arouse us to concentrating our national hatred on imperialism? Should we instead slaughter one another? . . .

The Soviet Government has played a shameful role in this war of aggression launched by India against Pakistan. The whole world has seen clearly that it is the back-stage manager of the Indian expansionists. For many years, the Soviet Government has been energetically fostering the Indian reactionaries and abetting India in its outward expansion. In last August the Soviet Union and India signed the treaty which is labelled as one of 'peace, friendship and co-operation' but is in substance a treaty of military alliance. They claimed that this treaty was not directed against any country, but actually it is precisely under their joint conspiracy that the subversion, interference and aggression against Pakistan have been intensified. Since the outbreak of the war of aggression the Soviet Union has stepped up its efforts in pouring a steady stream of arms and equipment into India to bolster and pep up the Indian aggressors. What makes people particularly indignant is that the representative of the Soviet Government in the UN Security Council has time and again used the veto to obstruct the cease-fire and troop withdrawal which are desired by the overwhelming majority of countries and the people all over the world. The Soviet Government has wantonly vilified China, alleging that it is China that has stirred up the conflict between India and Pakistan and 'set Asians to fight Asians'. Actually, it is the Soviet Government itself that has really and truly 'set Asians to fight Asians'. The purpose of the Soviet Union in so doing is known to all, that is, to further strengthen its control over India and thereby proceed to contend with the other super-power for hegemony in the whole of the South Asian sub-continent and the Indian Ocean and at the same time to foster India and turn it into a sub-superpower on the South Asian subcontinent as its assistant and partner in committing aggression against Asia. The present sudden invasion of Pakistan by India with the support of the Soviet Union is precisely a repetition on the South Asian subcontinent of the 1968 Soviet invasion and occupation of Czechoslovakia. . . .

The Chinese Government and people firmly support the Pakistan Government and people in their struggle against aggression, division and subversion; we not only are doing this politically, but will continue to give them material assistance. The Chinese Government firmly maintains that the December 7, 1971 resolution of the UN General Assembly must be carried out immediately.

*

Subsequently China used her veto in the UN Security Council for the first time to postpone the admission of Bangladesh to the United Nations.

DOCUMENT 68. EXTRACT FROM SPEECH BY CHIAO KUAN-HUA, CHAIRMAN OF THE DELEGATION OF THE PEOPLE'S REPUBLIC OF CHINA, AT THE PLENARY MEETING OF THE 27TH SESSION OF THE UN GENERAL ASSEMBLY, 3 OCTOBER 1972 (FOREIGN LANGUAGES PRESS, PEKING, 1972, PP. 6–8)

Mr President,

Now I wish to speak on the question of the Indo-Pakistan subcontinent. We all remember that last December in this very hall, the General Assembly at its 26th Session adopted by the overwhelming majority of 104 votes a resolution calling for ceasefire and troop withdrawal by India and Pakistan. Subsequently, the Security Council also adopted by 13 votes in favour and two abstentions a resolution demanding ceasefire, troop withdrawal and release of prisoners of war by all those concerned. However, while the relevant resolutions of the United Nations were not yet implemented, the Soviet Government and its followers raised at the Security Council last August the question of the admission of 'Bangladesh' into the United Nations. In disregard of the reasonable demand of many countries to postpone the consideration of the question, they insisted on a vote to compel China to use the veto. China's stand for postponing the consideration of this question does not mean that we are fundamentally opposed to the admission of 'Bangladesh' into the United Nations. China cherishes friendly sentiments for the people of East Bengal and has no prejudice against Mr Mujibur Rahman. We stand for postponing the consideration of this question, in order to promote a reconciliation among the parties concerned and the implementation of the UN resolutions, which are the very immediate concern. However, the Soviet Government has hurriedly pressed for UN admission of 'Bangladesh'. This is definitely not aimed at helping 'Bangladesh', but at forcing China to use the veto, maintaining and aggravating the tensions among the parties concerned on the subcontinent and white-washing its foul act of supporting the Indian Government in dismembering Pakistan last year. But its attempt will not succeed. If it had been national self-determination, it should have been the people of East Bengal solving their problems by themselves. Why should Indian troops have invaded East Pakistan? And why should the 90,000 and more Pakistani war prisoners and civilians have been taken to India?

After the admission of 'Bangladesh' has been vetoed, certain people are trying to bypass the Security Council and referring the question to the General Assembly for discussion. This is clearly done with ulterior motives. This will in no way help promote a reconciliation among the parties concerned on the subcontinent, not will it reflect honour on the country inciting such a move. China stands firm on principles. China considers that whether or not reasonable UN resolutions supported by the overwhelming majority of its members are implemented is a matter of principle affecting what direction the UN is heading for. And on matters of principle China will never retreat.

(c) POST-RECOGNITION POLICIES

Following the Nixon visit Sino-Japanese relations remained unsettled. Premier Sato's government made equivocal statements on the status of Taiwan which provoked ridicule in the Chinese press. With the retirement of Sato in July 1972 and the establishment of the Tanaka government, there were rapid moves to settle outstanding difficulties between the two countries. For China the *sine qua non* of an agreement was Japanese acceptance of 'three principles', i.e. that the CPR government was the sole legal government of China; that Taiwan was an inalienable part of Chinese territory, and that the Japan-Taiwan treaty should be abrogated. Public statements by the Tanaka government indicated acceptance of the 'three principles', and there were cultural exchanges which included a visit to China by the Japanese volleyball team. A Chinese invitation for Tanaka to visit Peking led to agreement and a joint statement heralding a new era in Sino-Japanese relations.

DOCUMENT 69. JOINT STATEMENT OF THE GOVERNMENT OF THE PEOPLE'S REPUBLIC OF CHINA AND THE GOVERNMENT OF JAPAN, 29 SEPTEMBER 1972 (FROM 'A NEW PAGE IN THE ANNALS OF SINO-JAPANESE RELATIONS', FOREIGN LANGUAGES PRESS, PEKING, 1972, PP. 15–18)

At the invitation of Premier Chou En-lai of the State Council of the People's Republic of China, Prime Minister Kakuei Tanaka of Japan visited the People's Republic of China from September 25 to 30, 1972. Accompanying Prime Minister Kakuei Tanaka were Foreign Minister Masayoshi Ohira, Chief Cabinet Secretary Susumu Nikaido and other government officials.

Chairman Mao Tse-tung met Prime Minister Kakuei Tanaka on September 27. The two sides had an earnest and friendly conversation.

Premier Chou En-lai and Foreign Minister Chi Pengfei had an earnest and frank exchange of views with Prime Minister Kakuei Tanaka and Foreign Minister Masayoshi Ohira, all along in a friendly atmosphere, on various matters between the two countries and other matters of interest to both sides, with the normalization of relations between China and Japan as the focal point, and the two sides agreed to issue the following joint statement of the two Governments:

China and Japan are neighbouring countries separated only by a strip of water, and there was a long history of traditional friendship between them. The two peoples ardently wish to end the abnormal state of affairs than has hitherto existed between the two countries. The termination of the state of war and the normalization of relations between China and Japan—the realization of such wishes of the two peoples will open a new page in the annals of relations between the two countries.

The Japanese side is keenly aware of Japan's responsibility for causing enormous damages in the past to the Chinese people through war and deeply reproaches itself. The Japanese side reaffirms its position that in seeking to realize the normalization of relations between Japan and China, it proceeds from the stand of fully understanding the three principles for the restoration of diplomatic relations put forward by the

Government of the People's Republic of China. The Chinese side expresses its welcome for this.

Although the social systems of China and Japan are different the two countries should and can establish peaceful and friendly relations. The normalization of relations and the development of good-neighbourly and friendly relations between the two countries are in the interests of the two peoples, and will also contribute to the relaxation of tension in Asia and the safeguarding of world peace.

1 The abnormal state of affairs which has hitherto existed between the People's Republic of China and Japan is declared terminated on the date of publication of this statement.

2 The Government of Japan recognizes the Government of the People's Republic of China as the sole legal government of China.

3 The Government of the People's Republic of China reaffirms that Taiwan is an inalienable part of the territory of the People's Republic of China. The Government of Japan fully understands and respects this stand of the Government of China and adheres to its stand of complying with Article 8 of the Potsdam Proclamation.

4 The Government of the People's Republic of China and the Government of Japan have decided upon the establishment of diplomatic relations as from September 29, 1972. The two Governments have decided to adopt all necessary measures for the establishment and the performance of functions of embassies in each other's capitals in accordance with international law and practice and exchange ambassadors as speedily as possible.

5 The Government of the People's Republic of China declares that in the interest of the friendship between the peoples of China and Japan, it renounces its demand for war indemnities from Japan.

6 The Government of the People's Republic of China and the Government of Japan agree to establish durable relations of peace and friendship between the two countries on the basis of the principles of mutual respect for sovereignty and territorial integrity, mutual non-aggression, non-interference in each other's internal affairs, equality and mutual benefit and peaceful coexistence. . . .

7   The normalization of relations between China and Japan is not directed against third countries. Neither of the two countries should seek hegemony in the Asia-Pacific region and each country is opposed to efforts by any other country or group of countries to establish such hegemony.

8   To consolidate and develop the peaceful and friendly relations between the two countries, the Government of the People's Republic of China and the Government of Japan agree to hold negotiations aimed at the conclusion of a treaty of peace and friendship.

9   In order to further develop the relations between the two countries and broaden the exchange of visits, the Government of the People's Republic of China and the Government of Japan agree to hold negotiations aimed at the conclusion of agreements on trade, navigation, aviation, fishery, etc., in accordance with the needs and taking into consideration the existing non-governmental agreements.

(Signed)
CHOU EN-LAI
Premier of the State
Council of the
People's Republic of China
(Signed)
CHI PENG-FEI
Minister of Foreign
Affairs of the
People's Republic of China

(Signed)
KAKUEI TANAKA
Prime Minister of Japan

(Signed)
MASAYOSHI OHIRA
Minister for Foreign
Affairs of Japan

Peking, September 29, 1972

*

The joint editorial of *People's Daily* and *Red Flag* on 1 October (National Day) 1972, stressed that China's policy of peaceful co-existence on the basis of the Five Principles was to be extended to countries 'in the second intermediate zone', even to countries previously hostile to China if they indicated a change of policy.

The reference to first and second intermediate zones, was elucidated in November, in a definition significantly different

230

from that of 1964 (see Document 52). Soviet revisionism has joined the same category as American imperialism. It is implied that a united Europe could better resist the two superpowers.

DOCUMENT 70. THE TWO INTERMEDIATE ZONES. EXTRACT FROM ARTICLE IN *Red Flag*, NO. 11, NOVEMBER 1972 (*Peking Review*, 15, 45, 10 NOVEMBER 1972)

Like two slices of bread with meat between them, the two superpowers—Soviet revisionism and US imperialism—are trying to sandwich other countries in various parts of the world. They not only plunder the small and medium-sized countries in Asia, Africa and Latin America, but also practise the 'jungle law' policy towards their 'allies' in Europe, Asia, North America and Oceania. The Soviet revisionists are sparing no effort to extend their sphere of influence to West Europe. Thus, between these two overlords and the socialist countries there exist two broad intermediate zones. The first intermediate zone includes the Asian, African and Latin American countries which have suffered from colonialist and imperialist aggression and oppression in the past and are today carrying on a valiant struggle against imperialism and colonialism and especially against the two superpowers. The second intermediate zone includes the major capitalist countries both in the West and in the East except the two superpowers. These countries too are subjected to the control, intervention and bullying of the two overlords to varying degrees, and the contradictions between these countries and the two superpowers are daily developing. The two superpowers' wild ambition to dominate the world and their aggressive activities have aroused the world's people to rise and fight against them. Countries in the first as well as in the second intermediate zones are getting united in different forms and different scopes to oppose the power politics and hegemonism of the superpowers. This is a trend of world history.

*

Taiwan is today a relatively prosperous country; its *per capita* income the second highest in Asia. Yet it cannot be for its material wealth, nor for the man-power of its 14 million population that China has set such store by its recovery. Taiwan has become the symbol of the struggle to complete the Revolution by casting out the last reactionary, foreign supported remnant on Chinese territory. Any remaining doubts about the legitimacy of the communist regime will be removed; for Chinese around the world there will be only 'one sun in the heaven' and Chiang Kai-shek's vision of a China reconstructed on its traditional basis will no longer exist as an alternative.

For the Taiwanese, if a majority would really prefer some sort of autonomous status, the future is not propitious. The principle of self-determination has not weighed heavily, it appears, with the Chinese in the case of Tibet. It is unlikely that the Taiwanese will enjoy a larger degree of local rule when in due course they rejoin the mainland. Meanwhile the tone of Peking's overtures to the leaders of the regime in Taipeh has been conciliatory but has not immediately produced a favourable response.

DOCUMENT 71. 'CHINA INVITES TAIWAN TO TALKS ON REUNITING NATION'—'TAIWAN SNUBS OFFER' (*Guardian*, 2–3 MARCH 1973)

China Invites Taiwan to Talks on Reuniting Nation

China's leaders last night invited the Taiwan Nationalists to join them in open or secret talks on reunifying China—seemingly the start of a diplomatic offensive after the visit here of President Nixon's special envoy, Dr Kissinger.

The olive branch was offered to the Nationalists by 80-year-old Fu Tso-yi, former Nationalist military commander of Peking, who defected to the Communists and handed over the capital without a fight in 1949, the year of Mao Tse-tung's victory.

Mr Fu's appeal, in the Taiwan Room of Peking's Great Hall of the People, China's Parliament, was published today in the *People's Daily*. Envoys here said that the former Kuomintang general was obviously speaking for Mao Tse-tung and Chou En-lai.

'It is now high time to unify the Motherland,' he said. 'Let us come together and talk, the sooner the better.'

Mr Fu, who is vice-chairman of the national committee of the Chinese People's Political Consultative Conference, said the Nationalists should send 'some people' to the mainland if they were not prepared to enter into formal talks right away.

They could come openly or secretly 'to have a look and visit relatives and friends,' he added. 'You can rest assured that the Government will keep the matter secret, keep its word, and guarantee your safety and freedom to come and go.'

Mr Fu said: 'Nixon has had the courage to see the error in containing China and realize that only when the US restores normal relations with China and coexists peacefully with her on the basis of the five principles [of peaceful coexistence] is it possible to maintain peace in the Asian and Pacific region and the world at large.'

Both the policy of the United States and the American attitude towards the Taiwan question had changed and this was clearly shown by two Sino-American communiqués after President Nixon's visit here last year and Dr Kissinger's talks here this February.

The US recognized Taiwan as part of China's territory, and the two countries had decided to establish liaison offices in each other's capitals, the former general said.

'Of late, Kissinger further said the US favoured the peaceful resolution of disagreements between the mainland and Taiwan. It is very obvious: how long can Taiwan rely on the US? Absolutely not long.'

In an oblique reference to the Soviet Union, which has reportedly made overtures to Taiwan, he said: 'It should be pointed out that if there are people, who although they see clearly that the US cannot be relied on yet dream of relying on someone else, this is not only absurd but absolutely impossible.

'Our military and administrative colleagues in Taiwan must not make a fresh error.'

Laio Cheng-chin, a prominent Peking figure in overseas affairs, said that the Peking Government would treat all patriots with respect and forgive them for their past wrongdoings 'however serious these were'. That was provided they now supported the Socialist Motherland and worked for China's unification.

A diplomat said the initiative was a 'logical consequence of the Kissinger visit though I am not saying it was done in the full knowledge of the United States.'

The speeches marked the '26th anniversary of the February uprising of the people of Taiwan province'.

Taiwan Snubs Offer

General Chiang Kai-shek's Government in Taiwan today snubbed Peking in reply to the Communists' latest appeals to the Nationalists to open formal or secret talks aimed at re-unifying China.

A Government spokesman, Federick Chien, said he did not want to dignify the statements from Peking. Any made there in connection with the status of Taiwan were absolutely 'not worthy of comment'.

*

During most of the years covered by this book, ex-CIA agent John Downey was a prisoner in China (see Document 13). Released on 12 March 1973 he was one of the beneficiaries of the new relationship between America and China.

DOCUMENT 72. 'FREED AMERICAN SPY LOOKS BACK ON MORE THAN 20 YEARS WASTED IN A CHINESE PRISON' (*The Times*, 14 MARCH 1973)

Mr John Downey, the American spy freed on Monday after more than 20 years' imprisonment in China, said today that he had been kept in leg irons during the first 10 months of his captivity and that Chinese officials had pried military information from him. But after the first months his treatment had met 'minimum standards'.

Mr Downey, now 42, who was freed by the Chinese so that he could hurry to the bedside of his critically ill mother, was speaking at his first press conference since his release.

He refused to describe the circumstances of his capture during the Korean war in November, 1952, the year after he was recruited by the Central Intelligence Agency while a student at Yale University.

But under questioning by more than 50 reporters, he said

that his aircraft, which also carried a second CIA agent, was shot down by the Chinese. Until today it had not been known whether the aircraft, which was reported to have been dropping supplies to Chinese nationalist guerrillas on the mainland, had crashed, been forced down or shot down.

Smiling, in good spirits and reporting that he felt 'great and full of pep', Mr Downey said he never lost hope during his long incarceration, but he had felt bitter at times and felt he had wasted 20 years of his life.

Would he do it again, a reporter asked, alluding to the spy mission?

'No', Mr Downey replied. Asked if the spy mission was 'worth it', he hesitated a second, then answered: 'No, it wasn't.'

Mr Downey, whose mother's condition has shown marked improvement since her son's arrival last night, refused to divulge the military information which he said the Chinese had extracted from him during his first 10 months in prison.

Nor would he say whether he thought he might have been released earlier had the United States Government conceded sooner that he was on a spy mission when he was captured.

For almost 20 years the Government—through the Truman, Eisenhower, Kennedy, Johnson and Nixon Administrations—had maintained that he was a civilian employee of the Army and that the aircraft was on a flight from Seoul to Tokyo.

Last January, however, President Nixon said Mr Downey was involved with the CIA. It was never made clear whether this statement was inadvertent or deliberate, but it is believed to have cleared the way for his release.

The Chinese released Mr Downey when President Nixon appealed personally to Mr Chou En-lai, the Chinese Prime Minister, after Mr Downey's mother had suffered a stroke last Wednesday.

Mr Downey said he had come away with mixed feelings about China. 'The conditions are not bad there and the people are better off than I expected.'

He said he underwent political indoctrination throughout his captivity. This had not changed his political thinking, 'although it changed my opinion of China somewhat'.

*

At the time of the Tenth Party Congress in August 1973 there were indications of a major policy debate. The targets of criticism were Lin Piao (who died after an attempted *coup* in 1971) and Confucius, symbol of reaction. It is likely that the debate was fundamentally concerned with domestic policy and with rivalry among the leadership. At the same time symptoms of the dispute have been seen in foreign relations. Attacks on Western music and, for example, the China film made by Antonioni, can be interpreted as an assertion that increasing diplomatic contacts with the West should not lead to a dilution of national and ideological standards. Early in 1974 China used force to protect its claim (disputed by South Vietnam) to the Hsisha Islands (the Paracels). Meanwhile verbal attacks on Soviet revisionism were maintained vigorously. In January a considerable propaganda stroke (chiefly for internal consumption) was achieved by the capture and subsequent expulsion of five Soviet spies.

DOCUMENT 73. EXTRACT FROM 'SOVIET REVISIONIST SPIES CAUGHT RED-HANDED' (*Peking Review*, 17, 5, 1 FEBRUARY 1974, PP. 14–15)

On the night of January 15 when the streets of Peking were thinning out, a light grey Volga limousine slipped out of the Soviet Embassy. Winding through streets and lanes, it sped towards the northeastern outskirts and suddenly pulled up at a dark place along Peihuantung Road about 4·5 kilometres from the city proper. Two persons, one tall, one short, cautiously got out of the car and headed for Hsipaho Bridge about 170 metres ahead, the tall one carrying a heavy travelling bag. They stopped at the northeastern corner of the bridge, which is about 30 metres long and 15 metres wide. Both looked around before they disappeared under the bridge one by one. The car, plate number shi (CD) 01-0044, left immediately in a northwest direction with one man and two women in it.

These people, five all told, were V. I. Marchenko, First Secretary of the Soviet Embassy in China, and his wife, Third Secretary U. A. Semenov and his wife, and A. A. Kolosov, interpreter in the Office of the Soviet Military Attaché. On leaving the Soviet Embassy, they took great pains to disguise themselves. Marchenko himself was at the wheel, his wife and Semenov's served as cover for Semenov and Kolosov who crouched and hid themselves inside the car. To avoid being noticed when the car stopped to drop the two men, the tail lights' circuit had been rewired so that they would not be on when the brake was applied. In the dark of the night, these people had hastily set out to do their dirty espionage business.

Taken on the Spot

U. A. Semenov, the tall man, and A. A. Kolosov, the short one, hid themselves under the bridge. The time was ten past nine. All was quiet in the fields of the Taiyangkung People's Commune. Only dogs were barking in a nearby village with a few motor vehicles speeding across Hsipaho Bridge every now and then.

Some 25 minutes later, two shadows suddenly appeared at the west end of the bridge. Loitering on the bridge for a while, they then walked to the northeast corner to give the password. This done, they went under the bridge. The two were the Soviet-dispatched agent Li Hung-shu and his accomplice. Li Hung-shu, the culprit, later confessed that as he went down under the bridge Semenov looked at him closely. It was only when the former repeated the password that Semenov grabbed and hugged him and called out in Russian: 'Dear Alen!' (Alen was the code name used by culprit Li Hung-shu for Semenov and Kolosov to check identities.) Li Hung-shu then handed Semenov a white gauze surgeon's mask which contained intelligence in secret writing sealed in a tiny plastic pouch and also pinshaped secret-writing instruments the Soviet revisionist espionage agency had instructed Li Hung-shu to return. Semenov in turn gave him the heavy travelling bag. By now, these enemies thought they had made it and were beside themselves with excitement. But they rejoiced too soon.

Just as these men hid themselves in a dark corner and were engaged in criminal activities against the Chinese people a red signal flare burst over Hsipaho Bridge. This was followed by illuminating flares as courageous militiamen and public security personnel closed in from all directions, rushing down to the bridge and shouting 'Catch the spies.'

The agents and spies under the bridge were in utter confusion. Semenov who sensed trouble, trying to destroy the criminal evidence instantly threw into the creek by him the white mask containing the intelligence he had just got from the agent Li Hung-shu. But it was too late. Semenov and the others were caught by Chinese public security personnel and militiamen on the spot—under Hsipaho Bridge, together with the travelling bag Semenov had passed to Li Hung-shu. The white mask jettisoned by Semenov was also fished out from the creek by our vigilant militiamen.

Conclusive Evidence

Semenov and the others, caught on the spot and terrified, were trembling like leaves. It was then that the two Soviet revisionist spies with a guilty conscience were found to have disguised themselves beforehand. Semenov had covered his Western-style suit with a blue cotton-padded overcoat usually worn by Chinese. Kolosov wore a blue Chinese suit, a blue cap and a pair of black cloth shoes. Both of them wore big surgeon's masks.

An angry crowd demanded: 'Who are you?' Semenov replied hurriedly in stuttering Chinese: 'I am from the Soviet Embassy,' at the same time producing his diplomatic identification card. This enraged the crowd even more and they asked: 'What are you people from the Soviet Embassy doing here under this bridge on the outskirts at this hour of the night?' The Soviet spy turned pale and was at a loss for an answer.

In the presence of the spies, Chinese public security personnel and militiamen opened on the spot Semenov's travelling bag intended for Li Hung-shu. Inside was a big parcel wrapped in a blanket with dark-grey and white designs. In the parcel were two oblong blue bags, and in the bags were a miniature radio composed of a high-speed transmitter and receiver (placed separately in two yellow metallic boxes, and the lid of each box was painted with a red cross and the Chinese characters 'serve the people' as a camouflage), an illustration showing how to install antennae, a chart showing radio communication frequencies and a timetable and the methods of contact set up by the Soviet espionage agency and a timetable for emergency contact, a 'directive' written in invisible ink from the Soviet espionage agency to Li Hung-shu and his accomplice, a copy of the programme for establishing a secret counter-revolutionary organization in China, two reactionary letters, two bottles of chemicals for developing copies of secret writing, eight packages of moisture-proof powder to protect the transmitter and receiver, a blank Chinese border pass forged by the Soviet revisionist espionage agency and a sample indicating how to fill it in, as well as 5,000 yuan Renminbi to be used as funds for espionage purposes, and Peking cloth, grain and flour coupons, and so on. Thus, with culprits and material evidence at hand, the crime was conclusively established.

Unable to deny the facts, the Soviet revisionist spies had to hang their heads. All this was filmed.

PART VII

Interpreting China's Foreign Policy: A Selection of Views

The following four documents represent contrasting views, published in the West, of the mainsprings and objectives of China's foreign policy. Apart from their intrinsic interest these extracts provide material for discussion and may be useful as guidelines for further analysis of the material in this book.

DOCUMENT 74. EXTRACTS FROM A. HUCK, *The Security of China*, CHATTO & WINDUS, LONDON, 1970, PP. 24–8

It would be absurd to argue that the Maoist rulers of China see the world in exactly the same way as the imperial mandarinate of earlier centuries but their political styles look increasingly alike: China is the source of all wisdom and correct political ideas. The content of the wisdom is, of course, very different. The old mandarinate was characterized by enormous complacency, the new by a basic insecurity which has been rationalized in an ideology of change. The old envisaged a permanent world order, essentially unchanging, the new envisages continual change. However, the concepts of a world order are in both cases primarily doctrinal. This is not to say that they are or were remote from any political reality. A doctrine must have *some* relation to reality if it is to function at all, but the relationship may be somewhat oblique. The traditional doctrine bore some relation to the realities of Chinese foreign relations during the Ch'ing dynasty, but not much. Similarly, Maoist doctrine bears some relation to the modern world: much of the world is in a transitional stage; many of the new states are unstable creations carved out of dead empires; many do have high revolutionary potential. In both cases, however, it would be naive to draw from such doctrinaire pictures of the world direct inferences about what Chinese policy would be in any specific case.

In the traditional view China lay at the centre of a basically stable world. The stability was not to be achieved by means of a balance of power as that idea has been understood in Europe. Indeed, the notion of a balance of power is essentially a European one, presupposing a system of nation-states with clearly defined boundaries, independent sovereign governments and equality of status. Stability in the Chinese view depended rather on the recognition of a natural order which corresponded roughly to the actual situation of Imperial China in her heyday. The heartland, the traditional Eighteen Provinces, was the seat of Han civilization. Beyond this, in roughly concentric zones, lay regions of different importance and interest to China. The contiguous non-Han regions of Korea, Manchuria, Mongolia, Chinese Turkestan, Tibet and Annam were clearly of the greatest importance. If these could not be brought under direct Chinese control they must at least accept some sort of Chinese suzerainty. On occasions of course the tables were turned and alien conquest dynasties like the Mongol and the Manchu dominated the Chinese heartland. The Ch'ing (Manchu) dynasty at its greatest extent regarded some areas like Mongolia as more or less incorporated territories, others, more distant, as tributary regions. The celebrated tribute system, whatever else it may have been, was certainly not a colonial system as that term has been understood in the West. . . .

This traditional Chinese view of a world order with China as its natural centre has been often enough described but how far it has had a continuing influence on how modern Chinese see the world has been hotly debated. Educated Chinese have come to terms with the idea of China as a modern nation-state in a world of nation-states but this has left unresolved the question of what constituted the territory of the modern Chinese state. The extent of the traditional area where China expected to have at least a formal primary position had been fairly well understood even if much of it had had no exact boundaries. Reference books published under both the Nationalists and the Communists have indicated it with some precision in maps. Although some variations occur these maps generally include within the 'Chinese' area Sakhalin, Korea, Formosa, most of British Borneo and the Sulu Archipelago, all of mainland South-East Asia, Assam, the Himalayan Kingdoms, Tibet, much of Soviet Middle Asia, Chinese Turkestan, all of Mongolia and part of the Soviet Far East. Beyond this lay what Ginsberg has called an Outer Asian Zone—Persia, India, Indonesia, the Philippines, Japan—countries relatively well known to the Chinese. Beyond that again lay all the rest of the world, 'in Chinese eyes largely undifferentiated'. It is often suggested that many Chinese still see the world essentially in terms of this model: a central China, an Asian periphery and an alien beyond. It is one thing however to assert that traditional models can have a long persistent effect on patterns of thought and quite another to suggest that they have a dominant influence on policy making. Nationalist and Communist alike have talked of their 'lost' territories, by which they have meant the large peripheral segments of the zone of primary Chinese concern which were detached by different imperial countries during the decline of the Ch'ing dynasty. The list of intrusions is formidable: Russia into her new Far East and Outer Mongolia, Japan into Korea, Formosa and later Manchuria and China herself, France into Indo-China, Britain into Burma and so on.

It does not follow that any modern Chinese state will want to regain all these 'lost' territories in the sense of incorporating them in a new Chinese Empire (whether Communist or not). Some of these territories were never formally administered by China and they certainly did not lie within a precisely defined Chinese boundary, whatever modern maps may show. The traditional Chinese state at many points did not have precise boundaries. It faded away into areas of less and less concern to China until the Great Unknown was reached. The problem for any modern Chinese state is precisely to determine some practicable boundaries. In the early nineteenth century there was no such thing as the internationally recognized boundary of China and the Chinese were not interested in such a concept. The re-establishment of something like the old order, however, would clearly be incompatible with the establishment of a modern nation-state. The first thing a modern state has to have is a clearly defined boundary, widely recognized, delimited on maps and demarcated, that is marked out on the ground, where possible. The establishment of such a boundary has not been an easy task for either Republican or Communist China and, where it has been agreed on, the problems of relations with the many different states on the other side of it have not disappeared.

On the face of it the Maoist picture of the world in revolutionary ferment is the antithesis of the traditional Chinese view of a stable world order with China at its centre. The two views are not however particularly difficult to reconcile. Both have a determined interest in removing alien (distant, foreign, 'imperialist') influence from the periphery of China. Traditionalists could see the successful accomplishment of this as the re-establishment of the old conditions for a secure China, revolutionaries as a set-back for the imperialists which strengthened the forces of Marxism-Leninism. In both cases, however, these guiding pictures should not be taken as identical with concrete policies: from a map which shows China as the centre of world revolutionary thought it does not allow that fomenting revolution will be the prime Chinese object in all dealings with foreign states; from a map showing 'lost' territories it does not follow that a modern Chinese state must be hell-bent on 're-gaining' them in the sense of including them within a territorial border which did not clearly exist before they were 'lost'.

DOCUMENT 75. EXTRACT FROM J. D. SIMMONDS, *China's World. The Foreign Policy of a Developing State,* COLUMBIA UNIVERSITY PRESS, 1970, PP. 227–8

China's total foreign policy over the last twenty years has been designed principally to protect the nation from its real or imaginary enemies. Although its major goal has consequently been generally negative, in that policy has often been simply reactive, China has at the same time pursued certain forward policies. It has attempted, and with a degree of success, to spread its influence throughout the six continents. It has established genuinely friendly relations with a number of countries, eroded the influence of the Soviet Union, campaigned against the United States, and gained some revolutionary respectability among the people of the world. If it has not always and everywhere met with unqualified success, it is not alone in this respect and in any case has probably achieved more than most nations in the last twenty years. On the whole it has, following the Maoist precept, employed its strategy skilfully within the national limitations. Revolutionary communism has been the principal ideological weapon with which it has sought to ensure its national interests. In short the state interests of China have overridden all others as they may be said to have done for the Soviet Union and the United States. Even the reiterated call to establish communism in China and the world would seem to be little more than an ideological expression of state interests.

The Albanian command to the world revolutionaries to support and protect China is another expression of Chinese state interests. The fundamental requirement of the Chinese state is the attainment of political consolidation, economic well-being, and military security. What is more particularly Chinese in this respect is the extent of the domestic pressures. These may have altered in form over the years but there is little to suggest that they have slackened, and even less that they will markedly decrease in the forseeable future. They may even intensify. Since 1949, consequently, the regime has consistently and with vigour made every effort to keep the lid on at home; to maintain control and momentum. One gigantic movement has followed another in rapid and regular succession. It is almost as though the masses have been deliberately subjected to perpetual shock to keep them off balance and make them more receptive or amenable to control. The regime's foreign policy likewise has been partly designed to fulfill this purpose; it has sought to maintain national credibility in a ceaseless external threat. The propaganda drives of two decades against the United States, and about a decade against Soviet revisionism, have been adroitly integrated into the overall domestic effort.

DOCUMENT 76. EXTRACT FROM I. C. OJHA, *Chinese Foreign Policy in an Age of Transition: The Diplomacy of Cultural Despair*, BEACON PRESS, BOSTON, 1969, PP. 21-5

Having passed through centuries as a great power and as the center of an international order, China was all the more humiliated by her defeats. Here China differs from India, which was ruled by foreigners for a millennium before regaining independence. India's memories of grandeur were dimmed by history and her national humiliation was softened by long practice. To China, whose independence was never totally lost, historical shame was recent enough to be galling. The Ottoman Empire presented still another picture, for Ataturk's statesmanship gave away all pretensions to the Empire and concentrated on the Turkish nation.

China was thus eager to regain her great-power status. This desire is often described as a peculiar heritage of Chinese history. A better explanation, however, lies in the drives of a nation trying to regain the power and status which its leaders consider appropriate to its size, population, geographical position, and historical heritage. To a considerable extent, this drive explains China's domestic and foreign policies of the twentieth century, including those of the Communist government. Whatever their ideological hue, foreign policy decision-makers have derived their ultimate motivation from the goal of regaining China's position as a great power. With the rise of mass nationalism the same goal has also motivated most of the Chinese people irrespective of political belief.

Nevertheless, this resurgent China is trying neither to dominate a resurrected East Asian world order nor to alter the diplomatic rules of the game. China now has world-wide pretensions. If and when Peking regains the status of a world power, its activities will never be confined to the East Asian periphery. Even if China succeeds in establishing a sort of Monroe Doctrine, her leaders will not withdraw their interest from the rest of the world. In any case, the East Asian world order cannot be revived and the tribute system cannot be reestablished.

The Chinese may not like all the rules of the present international order and may break many of them. Yet they can neither dominate the whole global system nor escape from it. In this case, history is irreversible. It has altered not only China and her periphery but the rest of the world as well. Just as the age of imperialism has bowed to the age of nationalism, so China as a Middle Kingdom has given way to China as a nation. If and when China develops superpower status, she will try to do all those things which other superpowers do.

The leaders of Communist China have not made their predecessors' mistake of giving foreign policy priority over domestic policy. They have realized the correct relationship between national power and the domestic base, between sociopolitical changes and economic modernization, and between the means and ends of power. Even the Cultural Revolution is attuned to the full mobilization of China's domestic base. The Chinese Communist government also understands that an inadequate domestic base places limits on the exercise of power. In spite of its verbal violence, Peking has in fact pursued a cautious foreign policy that accords with the continuing recognition of relative weakness. Concepts of people's war and self-reliance represent a clear-headed effort to strike the proper balance between a weak base and a vigorous foreign policy.

In contrast to most other nationalist movements, Communist China's leaders had at least some foreign policy experience before they came to power. Even outside of the international Communist movement they maintained contacts with foreigners. In the 1940s, for example, an almost full-fledged foreign office, functioning under Chou En-lai's leadership, operated through communications outlets in Hong Kong and elsewhere. The Communists had their own territorial power base as well as their own armies in the north-west. They also acquired experience from negotiating with the Nationalist government at Chungking. Finally, they maintained their own news agency with foreign correspondents who gained some idea of what the diplomatic world was all about.

Many top Chinese officials of the foreign ministry and the diplomatic corps received their initial training during this period. By contrast, the nationalist struggles of countries like India, while concerning themselves with foreign policy, gained no practical experience. Thus Nehru, the foreign policy expert of the Indian National Congress, had developed his own ideas about India's foreign policy after independence but had almost no experience with diplomatic negotiations.

Nevertheless, although greater than those of other newly independent countries, China's foreign policy experience was far from well rounded. To a great extent, it was colored by the need for Communist survival. Chinese Communist attitudes towards Japan, the Soviet Union, and Chiang Kai-shek practically determined their view of other powers. They naturally resented all those who supported Chiang.

The intense Chinese Communist preoccupation with anti-colonialism and anti-imperialism thus arises not only from the humiliations of modern Chinese history, but also from their intensely personal experience during twenty years of struggling for power. In this sense the Chinese leadership differs from the Soviets, who did not have to endure that bitter and prolonged period of civil war. Even their short civil war, as George F. Kennan has pointed out, gave rise to Soviet accusations of Western intervention and to considerable Soviet claustrophobia. In this light the bitter and resentful attitudes of Chinese foreign policy seem much more understandable.

The same twenty-year period also helps to explain why Communist China's leaders have sought to identify themselves with the cause of all other newly independent nations. Their preoccupation with imperialism and anticolonialism makes them see international relations in terms of the age of imperialism rather than the age of nationalism. For modern examples of imperialism they point to both the American presence in Asia and the Soviet invasion of Czechoslovakia. Their fear that a Soviet-American *entente* will divide up the world at China's expense is genuine. They do not even rule out the possibility of an invasion of China.

As they face a ring of American bases in Asia and a war in Vietnam, Chinese leaders conclude that the gunboat diplomacy which marked the age of imperialism lives on. For them, concessions wrung from the Opium Wars and American intervention in China's civil war (perpetuated by the protection of Taiwan) are part of the same spectrum.

For this reason they are naturally sympathetic to anyone who believes that the age of imperialism is not over. In other words, the search for historical continuities underlying Communist China's foreign policy would lead to the age of imperialism rather than to the Confucian past. On this point China does not significantly differ from the rest of the Third World, whose motive power springs from anti-imperialism rather than from semi-mythical golden ages.

Thus the historical sources of Communist China's conduct in international relations do not extend far into Chinese history. No one can deny that the Communists are Chinese. Yet they are a different kind of Chinese. They have accepted the need for modernization. They have realized that modernization cannot confine itself to armaments. They are prepared to make all the necessary sacrifices to make China a viable and influential nation. Aside from their efforts to establish their own legitimacy, they are also trying to create a new Chinese society and a new Chinese man.

DOCUMENT 77. EXTRACT FROM NEAL ASCHERSON, 'THE GREAT LEAP BACKWARDS?' *Observer*, 5 MARCH 1972

China, so the casual assumption runs, has emerged from its long isolation to play its full role in world politics. But has it? Just as China still regards herself, we are told, as that 'Middle Kingdom', to which all other human affairs and struggles are peripheral, so that American assumption may be dangerously egocentric. To a politician in southern Asia, the perspective could look different. Perhaps China is not really 'emerging' at all. Perhaps China is actually retreating from active involvement in world politics, and tying up dangerously loose ends in order to concentrate on her own affairs.

There are, it can be argued, two sorts of foreign policy. One is the 'offensive', the attempt to intervene in the affairs of other States in a sustained fashion—with force or with reconciling diplomacy—in order to bring about a change in the international relationships favourable to the initiator.

The other sort of foreign policy can be called the 'sortie'. From a walled city, the defenders sally out on a limited mission to demolish a threatening siege tower or even merely to cut down bushes that might one day shelter hostile archers. The object here is not to conquer or expand, but to guarantee the citizens security to carry on their own projects without interference.

A great deal of Chinese policy, since the triumph of the revolution in 1949, has been composed of sorties. Sometimes the image has been almost literal. In 1950 Chinese armies poured out over the Yalu River into Korea, and in 1962 they advanced through the Himalayas into India. They removed apparent threats to the integrity of China, and withdrew again when their purpose had been accomplished. Sometimes the sortie has been diplomatic: the Chinese participated in the 1954 Geneva conference on the future of Indo-China.

There followed a startling period of 'offensive'. This was the attempt—which began well before the Cultural Revolution and lasted for more than 10 years—to export and foment world revolution on the Maoist model.

This is the phase that is ending, giving way to a new period of 'sortie' diplomacy. This great contraction and transformation of Chinese foreign policy is shown by a confidential Chinese document dating from September 1967, just published in a Polish weekly.

The document, which reads like a battle report of expanding Asian revolution, was delivered by Yao Wen-yuan, one of the leaders of the Cultural Revolution in Shanghai. It describes how the banners of Mao Tse-tung's thought were carrying revolution to victory in Burma, in the Philippines, among the Naxalite guerrillas in eastern India and even in Japan.

All this has gone. In the last few years the Naxalites, the Maoist peasants of East Bengal led by the Maulana Bhashani, the pro-Chinese revolutionaries who rose in Ceylon, have looked in vain for Chinese support. Chinese enthusiasm for the war in Vietnam as a 'people's war' had noticeably declined long before President Nixon was able to visit Peking and bomb North Vietnam simultaneously.

Even in Eastern Europe, where the Chinese tried to manipulate every crisis from the Polish October of 1956 to the tensions between Russia and Romania in recent years, their activity has shrunk to radio propaganda and expanding trade. Albania, as a Chinese client, has begun to cut her losses and make non-ideological terms with Yugoslavia and Greece.

In the Bangladesh crises, China uneasily and ineffectively supported 'reactionary' Pakistan. A *rapprochement* with 'revisionist' North Korea has been under way since 1970. Chou En-lai recently told a French delegation that he had no intention of getting involved in the trap of a new Indo-China treaty. He seems to have told President Nixon in private that China no longer intends to use force even to take back Taiwan.

Mao insists that China does not wish to be a conventional, bullying 'great power'. Chou says that all international disputes can be settled by consultation.

What is happening? The Russian Press shouts that the Chinese are Trotskyists preparing war in order to achieve world revolution. This is probably the exact reverse of the truth, as Soviet history itself suggests. It is the 'Trotskyist' doctrine of world revolution as the condition of building socialism at home that China is now abandoning.

Instead, we have something much more like Stalin's 'socialism in one country' which succeeded Trotsky's vision: a foreign policy based on national rather than ideological needs, designed to keep China clear of foreign entanglement so that an undisturbed effort may be made to build an industrialized socialist economy at home. Fear of the Soviet Union no doubt plays its part. But so do last year's economic results: Chinese steel production rose by 18 per cent, pig iron production by 23 per cent, chemical fertiliser by over 20 per cent. This is the future China is now trying to protect.

A country that wants to be undisturbed must sally out to settle unresolved problems first. China might well have done so earlier. But Western reluctance, not Chinese isolationism, denied her a seat at the United Nations, embassies in many Western countries, perhaps even a presidential visit, for many years. President Nixon in Peking was not leading China out into the battlefield of world affairs. Whether he knew it or not, he was covering China's retreat.

Conclusion

Still prominent among those in power in Peking today are men who led China to Liberation in 1949. Mao and his comrades in arms have concentrated on consolidating and extending the revolution at home while seeking to gain security and win respect in the face of much hostility abroad.

This is not to say that the outlook of China's leaders has undergone no modifications. Expectations in the first flush of revolutionary success that China's example would be widely emulated have long since waned. Forced at times to modify its tactics in foreign affairs China has appeared to make shifts in its strategy but there has been much continuity. China's foreign policy objectives have been clearly defined and have, to date, been limited.

At the time of writing China still gives priority to the unfinished work of reuniting the country. The 'liberation' of Taiwan takes precedence over all other considerations, even the independence of Vietnam. Whether, its goals achieved, the People's Republic will intrude aggressively into world affairs remains to be seen. China's leaders have disclaimed great power chauvinism. At the United Nations they speak for the equality of small nations and stress non-interference and peaceful co-existence. In the case of any other country this might be taken as a mere platitude. In the case of the erstwhile self-contained 'Middle Kingdom' it merits consideration at its face value.

The Chinese welcome the expansion and growing integration of the European Common Market seeing it as potentially a fifth power with the US, USSR, China and Japan. As the Americans withdraw from their world-wide dominance there is the need for a new balance of forces which will forestall Soviet expansion. While attacking the supremacy of the two super-powers, the Chinese are presumably hoping for a modified world-order which will preserve the peace which China needs if it is to fulfil the objectives of its own development.

It is possible that in the increasingly interacting world of the future China will play a more dominant role commensurate with her potentially very great power. Directly or indirectly, China's influence must surely increase. The nature of that influence, the extent to which China will act conservatively or radically in world affairs, remains an open question.

Select Bibliography

(a) GENERAL

CHAI, WINBERG, *The New Politics of Communist China. Modernization Process of a Developing Nation*, Goodyear Publishing, California, 1972.

CLUBB, O. EDMUND, *Twentieth Century China*, Columbia University Press, 1965.

GOODSTADT, LEO, *Mao Tse-tung, The Search for Plenty*, Longman, London, 1972.

KAROL, K. S., *China, The Other Communism*, Heinemann, London, 1967.

MOSELEY, GEORGE, *China, Empire to People's Republic*, Batsford, London, 1968.

SCHRAM, STUART, *Mao Tse-tung*, Penguin, Harmondsworth, 1966.

SCHRAM, STUART, *The Political Thought of Mao Tse-tung* (first published 1963), Penguin, Harmondsworth, 1969.

SCHURMANN, FRANZ, *Ideology and Organization in Communist China*, University of California, 1966 (revised).

SCHWARTZ, BENJAMIN I., *Communism and China: Ideology in Flux*, Harvard University Press, 1968.

SNOW, EDGAR, *Red China Today. The Other Side of the River*, Penguin, Harmondsworth, 1970.

WALLER, D. J., *The Government and Politics of Communist China*, Hutchinson, London, 1970.

WAUNG, W. S. K., *Revolution and Liberation, A Short History of Modern China 1900–1970*, Heinemann Educational, London, 1971.

(b) FOREIGN RELATIONS

BARNETT, A. DOAK, *Communist China and Asia*, Vintage Books, Random House, New York, 1960.

CLUBB, O. EDMUND, *China and Russia, The 'Great Game'*, Columbia University Press, 1971.

FITZGERALD, STEPHEN, *China and the Overseas Chinese. A study of Peking's changing policy*, Cambridge University Press, 1972.

GITTINGS, JOHN, *Survey of the Sino-Soviet Dispute*, Oxford University Press, 1968.

GREENE, FELIX, *A Curtain of Ignorance—China, How America is Deceived*, Jonathan Cape, London, 1965.

GURTOV, MELVIN, *China and Southeast Asia—The Politics of Survival*, D. C. Heath, Lexington, Massachusetts, 1971.

HALPERN, A. M., 'China in the Postwar World', *China Quarterly*, no. 21, 1965.

HEVI, EMMANUEL JOHN, *The Dragon's Embrace. The Chinese Communists and Africa*, Pall Mall Press, London, 1967.

HINTON, HAROLD C., *Communist China in World Politics*, Macmillan, London, 1966.

HSIUNG, JAMES CHIEH, *Law and Policy in China's Foreign Relations*, Columbia University Press, 1972.

JOHNSON, CECIL, *Communist China and Latin America, 1959–1967*, Columbia University Press, 1970.

LARKIN, BRUCE D., *China and Africa 1949–1970*, University of California Press, 1971.

MAH, FENG-HWA, *The Foreign Trade of Mainland China*, Edinburgh University Press, 1972.

OJHA, ISHWER C., *Chinese Foreign Policy in an Age of Transition: The Diplomacy of Cultural Despair*, Beacon Press, Boston, 1969.

SIMMONDS, J. D., *China's World, The Foreign Policy of a Developing State*, Columbia University Press, 1970.

VAN NESS, PETER, *Revolution and Chinese Foreign Policy. Peking's Support for Wars of National Liberation*, University of California Press, 1970.

Index

Acheson, Dean, 37
Afghanistan, 108–9
Afro-Asian People's Solidarity
    Organization, 150, 152
Aigun, Treaty of (1858), 116
Aksai Chin Plateau, 107–8, 109
Albania, 28, 68–70, 98, 244, 249
Algeria, 98, 150–1, 168–9, 171
Ambassadorial talks, 56–61, 117,
    209
Angola, 175
Australia, 18
Austria, 116
Ayub, President, 223

Bac Bo Gulf incident, 98, 101,
    181
Banda, Hastings, 154
Bandaranaike, Mrs, 110
Bandung (Asian-African) Con-
    ference (1955), 11, 18, 55–6,
    141, 150, 161–7, 172
Bangladesh (formerly East Pakis-
    tan), 222–7, 249
Belgium, 116
Ben Bella, Ahmed, 151, 154, 177
Bettencourt, André, 211
Bhutan, 114–15, 121
Bhutto, Zulfikar, 223
Boumedienne, Houari, 177
Brazil, 152

Brezhnev, Leonid, 93–4, 207
Bulganin, Nikolai, 144
Bulgaria, 28
Burma: Chou En-lai's comments
    on, 162–6; hostility during
    Cultural Revolution, 191,
    249; Sino-Burmese border,
    108, 119–20, 124, 164, 242;
    Treaty of Friendship with
    CPR, 109, 126–7

Cairo Declaration, 34, 37, 55
Cambodia, 18, 110, 135–7, 152,
    166, 205, 209, 211, 220
Canada, 4, 68, 180
Castro, Fidel, 152
Central Intelligence Agency
    (CIA), 48–50, 205, 234–
    235
Ceylon, 110, 152, 249
Chang Han-fu, 140
Chen Chia-kang, 39
Chen Yi, 5, 12; in Cultural
    Revolution, 190, 201; on
    Japan, 146–9; on Mongolia,
    145–6; on Second Afro-
    Asian Conference (1965),
    175–7; on Sino-Indian con-
    flict, 128–33
Chenpao Island, see Ussuri
    River dispute

Chi Peng-fei, 12, 219, 228
Chiang Kai-shek, 2, 16–17, 19–23, 29, 35–6, 43, 49, 52–4, 146, 163, 216, 232, 247
Chiao Kuan-hua, 140, 206, 216–219, 226–7
Chile, 152
Chou En-lai, 3, 11–12, 15, 17, 30, 39–40, 43, 55–8, 65, 95, 160, 205–6, 215, 219, 228, 230, 232, 235, 246, 249–50; African tour, 153–4, 171–4; at Bandung (1955), 18–19, 161–7; at Geneva (1954), 134–7; on Sino-Indian border question, 107–9, 120, 122–6, 129
Churchill, Winston, 55
Colombia, 152
Colombo Conference (1962), 109–10
Colombo Proposals (on Sino-Indian border), 132
Common Market, see Europe
Confucius, 236
Congo, 97–8, 153, 168–70, 175
Couve de Murville, Maurice, 211
Cuban missile crisis, 69, 81, 97, 115, 152
Cuban Revolution, 78, 152
Cultural Revolution, 8–10, 13–14, 70, 113, 154, 189–204, 209, 246, 249
Czechoslovakia, 28, 247

Dalai Lama, 67, 108
De Gaulle, Charles, 1, 3, 180, 211
Diori, Hamani, 154
Dominican Republic, 175
Downey, John, 48–50, 234–5
Dulles, John, 18, 42–3, 51–5, 57–8, 64, 136

Economic aid, China's principles on giving, 153, 173–4, 218
Eden, Anthony, 166
Egypt, 150; see also United Arab Republic
Eisenhower, Dwight D., 57, 67, 82, 235
Ethiopia, 171
Europe, 231; Common Market, 251

Finland, 145
Five Principles of Co-existence, 13, 89, 107, 130–1, 160–1, 216–17, 230, 233
Formosa, see Taiwan
France, 3, 18, 24, 27, 116, 151, 169, 180, 242; Geneva Conference (1954), 135–136
Fu Tso-yi, 232–3

Gandhi, Mrs Indira, 110
Geneva Conference (1954), 18–19, 52, 110–11, 134–7, 141, 166
Geneva Conference on Laos (1961–2), 111, 137–41
Germany, 24, 116, 144–5
Ghana, 110, 171
Gizenga, Antoine, 170
Gomulka, Wladyslaw, 74
Great Britain, 24, 27–8; diplomatic relations with CPR, 3–4; Geneva Conference (1954), 137; hostility during Cultural Revolution, 190–1, 198–202; 'imperialist exploitation', 114–16, 155, 224, 242; Indonesia, 154; Laos Conference, 138; in SEATO, 18; status of Taiwan, 38, 54–5; status of

Tibet, 107; Test-ban Treaty, 82–4, 97; Tibet border, 124
'Great Leap Forward', 66, 68
Greece, 249
Grippa, Jacques, 91
Guevara, Che, 192
Guinea, 171

Haiti, 152
Harriman, Averell, 91
Ho Chi Minh, 136
Hong Kong, 8, 18, 69, 116–17, 190, 200–2, 246
Hopson, Donald, 200–1
Hsisha Islands, 7, 236
'Hundred Flowers' campaign, 65–6
Hungarian crisis (1956), 65
Hungary, 28
Hurley, Patrick J., 21

Ikeda, Hayato, 113
Ili, Treaty of (1881), 116
India, 6, 11, 13, 70, 136, 159, 162, 191, 206–7, 220–1, 242, 245–6, 249; Bangladesh, 222–7; Five Principles, 160–161; Sino-Indian disputes, 7, 67–9, 80–1, 99, 106–10, 117–26, 128–34
Indochina, 51–2, 70, 110–11, 134–44, 166, 205, 212–15, 220–1, 242, 249; see also Cambodia, Laos, Vietnam
Indonesia, 4, 68, 110, 152, 154, 162, 184–8, 191, 242
Intermediate Zone, 10, 151, 180–1, 230–1
Italy, 24, 116
Ivory Coast, 191

Jammu, 220–1

Japan, 9, 11, 14, 24, 30, 34, 37, 85, 112–16, 155, 159, 167, 183, 211, 220–1, 242, 247, 249, 251; diplomatic *rapprochement* with CPR, 227–230; Soviet Union, 113, 144–5; Taiwan, 34, 38, 55; trade with CPR, 113; treaties with United States, 38, 46, 55, 146–9
Johnson, Lyndon B., 141–4, 207, 235

Kasavubu, Joseph, 170
Kashmir, 108, 220–2
Kennan, George F., 247
Kennedy, John F., 115, 214, 235
Khamba revolt, 107
Khmer Issarak, 136
Khrushchev, Nikita, 6, 14, 66, 68–9, 75, 83, 86, 146, 152, 177; Algerian war, 169; Asian tour (1960), 68; Congo, 170; his fall, 70, 91–9, 102; Quemoy crisis (1958), 67; repudiation of Stalin, 65, 71–3; Sino-Indian war, 80–1, 109; visit to Peking (1954), 32, 64, 144
Kishi, Nobosuke, 113, 147–8
Kissinger, Henry, 4, 206, 215, 219, 232–4
Korea, 7, 137, 213, 241–2; mercenaries in Vietnam, 142; North Korea, 2–3, 16, 38, 40, 47–8, 95, 102, 152, 220, 249; South Korea, 16–17, 40–2, 47, 221
Korean War, 5, 11, 14, 16–18, 38–47, 51, 82, 234
Kurile Islands, 144–5
Kuznetsov, V. V., 83

Laio Cheng-chin, 233
Laos, 18, 110–11, 135–41, 166, 175, 205–6, 212–13, 220
Latin America, 78, 85, 104, 151–2, 168–9, 176, 180, 182–3, 231
Li Fu-chun, 32
Lin Piao, 10, 181, 189–90, 215, 236
Lisbon, Protocol of (1887), 116
Liu Shao-chi, 9, 189–90, 192
Lo Jui-ching, 190
Lu Ting-yi, 158–60, 190
Lumumba, Patrice, 170

Macao, 18, 116–17, 190
MacArthur, Douglas, 17, 37, 40, 42, 45, 47–8
McCarthy, Joseph, 16
MacMahon (McMahon) Line, 108, 119–25, 128–9, 131
McNamara, Robert, 105, 143
Mahendra, King of Nepal, 109
Malawi, 154
Malaya, 175
Malaysia, 154, 185
Mali, 171
Manchuria, 21–2, 34
Mao Tse-tung, 2, 5, 8–11, 15–16, 19–21, 22–4, 27, 67, 69, 86, 95, 98, 105, 189–90, 192, 197–8, 205, 208, 214, 219, 228, 232, 251; cult of Chairman Mao, 65, 193–5, 198–9; on guerrilla warfare, 151–3; 'Hundred Flowers' campaign, 65–6; on Mongolia, 112, 144–5; on nuclear warfare, 74–5, 81–2, 89–90; on 'People's War', 182–3, 187–8; on procedure at conferences, 139; on proposed Afro-Asian Conference (1965), 154; on Soviet borders, 144–5; talk with Edgar Snow, 193–5; his 'theory of the Chinese revolution', 159–60
Marshall Plan, 28
Mendès-France, Pierre, 135–6
Menon, Krishna, 130
Mikoyan, A. I., 92
Molotov, V. M., 135, 166
Mongolian People's Republic, 28, 92–4, 106, 112, 144–146
Morocco, 171
Moscow Meeting (November 1957), 66, 73–4, 96
Moscow Meeting (November 1960), 75–80, 96, 151
Mozambique, 175

Nanking, Treaty of (1842), 7, 116
Nasser, Gamal Abdul, 150
Naxalites, 249
Ne Win, 191
Nehru, Jawaharlal, 19, 39–40, 74, 109, 117–22, 129, 130, 166, 177, 246
Nepal, 7, 108–9, 152, 191
New Zealand, 18
Niger, 154
Nikaido, Susumu, 228
Nixon, Richard, 13, 205–15, 219–22, 232–3, 235, 249, 250
North Kalimantan, 175
Northeast Frontier Agency, 108–109, 121
Nuclear weapons, 5–6, 66, 76, 154; American threats, 82; China's hydrogen bomb, 192; China's statement at UN, 217–18; Mao's com-

ments on, 74–5, 81–2, 89–
90; related to fall of
Khrushchev, 91–5; see also
Test-ban Treaty

Ohira, Masayoshi, 228
Outer Mongolia, 241–2; see also
Mongolian People's Republic

Pakistan, 18, 108, 161, 220–1,
249; Bangladesh war, 222–
227
Palestine, 150, 175
Pathet Lao, 111, 136
Peking, Treaty of (1860), 116
Peng Chen, 10, 190
People's Liberation Army, 157,
189–90
Persia, 242
Peru, 152
Pham Van Dong, 136
Philippines, 18, 43, 161, 165–6,
242, 249
Phouma, Prince Souvanna, 111
Poland, 28, 249
Portugal, 116
Portuguese Guinea, 175
Potsdam Declaration (26 July
1945), 35, 37, 48

Quemoy, 52, 55, 67, 82

Rahman, Mujibur, 226
Rogers, William, 215, 219
Rumania, 28, 144, 249
Rusk, Dean, 93

Sananikone, Phoui, 111
Sato, Eisaku, 113, 149, 227
Shen Ping, 199–200
Shimonoseki, Treaty of (1895),
116

Sihanouk, Prince Norodom,
211
Singapore, 175
Snow, Edgar, 16, 105, 210–11
Somalia, 171
South Africa, 175
South Yemen, 175
Southeast Asia Treaty Organization, 18, 106, 111, 136, 161,
222
Soviet Union, 2, 5–6, 10, 12, 19,
23–4, 26, 38, 45, 51–2,
64–70, 77, 80–6, 191–2, 207,
210, 218, 231, 233, 243–4,
247, 251; aid to CPR, 15–
16, 25, 27–9, 32–4; Bangladesh war, 206–7, 223–7;
borders, 144–5; boundary
disputes with CPR, 70, 106,
202–4; Japan, 113; Korean
war, 17, 44; Laos, 111, 138;
proposed Afro-Asian Conference (1965), 154, 174,
176; Sino-Indian war, 80–1,
108–10; Sino-Soviet Treaty,
15, 21–2, 29–31; Soviet-
Indian Friendship Treaty
(1971), 206–7; 'spies'
caught in Peking, 236–9;
UN forces in Congo, 169–
170; Vietnam, 70, 95, 101–
105
Spain, 116
Stalin, 6, 17, 21–2, 24, 27, 71–3,
92, 96
Sudan, 171
Sukarno, Achmed, 154, 184–5,
187
Sumatra, 184
Sun Yat-sen, 22–3, 25
Syngman Rhee, 41–2

Tachen Islands, 19, 55

Taiwan (Formosa), 2–4, 5, 7, 16, 18–19, 34–8, 43, 45–7, 52–8, 106, 112, 117, 147, 206, 210, 214–15, 227, 229, 231–4, 249
Taiwan Strait crisis (1955), 55, 82
Tanaka, Kakuei, 113, 227–8, 230
Tanzania, 154, 192
Test-ban Treaty (July 1963), 5–6, 69, 82–6, 97, 171
Thailand, 11, 18, 161, 163, 165
Tibet, 2, 7, 107–8, 118–25, 145–146, 160, 232, 241–2
Tientsin, Treaty of (1858), 116
Tito, 98, 157
Tonkin Gulf incident, see Bac Bo Gulf incident
Truman, Harry S., 37–8, 43, 47, 213, 235
Tsedenbal, Yumzhaagin, 92–3
Tunisia, 171
Turkey, 159
Twentieth Congress of CPSU, 65, 71–3

U Nu, 19, 119, 124, 166
U Thant, 176–7
U2 incident, 68
United Arab Republic, 110, 150, 152, 171, 201
United Nations, 27, 58–9, 191, 251; admission of CPR, 4, 16, 123, 137, 206, 210, 214–19; Bangladesh war, 223, 225–7; Congo, 97–8, 169–70; Indonesia, 185; Korea, 40, 41–7; proposed Afro-Asian Conference (1965), 176–7; status of Taiwan, 38, 46; Tibet, 107–8; 'two Chinas' solution, 206, 214–15

United States of America, 2–7, 10, 13, 15, 19–20, 24–5, 26–29, 52, 64, 66–7, 72–4, 96, 99–100, 105, 107, 150–2, 157, 167, 169, 175–6, 218, 231, 234–5, 244, 251; Communist Party of, 115–16; CPR's admission to UN, 16, 214–16; 'escalation' in Cambodia, 209; 'escalation' in Laos, 212–14; 'escalation' in Vietnam, 98, 101–4, 139–44, 184; Geneva Conference, 18, 135–7; Japan, 112–13, 146–9; Korean War, 16–17, 38–51; Laos Conference, 111, 138–41; Mutual Defence Treaty with Taiwan, 53, 55; Nixon's China policy, 205–209, 210–11, 214–15; Nixon's visit, 219–22, 250; restrictions on trade with China, 47, 56–7, 191, 209; Taiwan, 34–8, 43, 45–6, 53–8; Test-ban Treaty, 82–84, 97
Upper Volta, 154
Ussuri River dispute, 106, 192, 202–4

Vietnam, 6, 13, 18, 43, 98, 100–105, 110–11, 134–7, 141–4, 175, 181, 184, 205–6, 210–213, 220–1, 247, 251; National Liberation Front, 102; North Vietnam, 2–3, 7, 11, 95, 101–2, 141–3, 152, 181, 249; North Vietnamese Communist Party, 68; South Vietnam, 137, 142–3
Vyshinsky, A. Y., 30–1

Wan, Prince, 165
Wang Ping-nan, 59
Warsaw Treaty Organization, 98
Wu Han, 190
Wu Hsiu-chüan, 45

Yalta Agreement (1943), 5, 21,
48, 144
Yameogo, Maurice, 154
Yao Wen-yuan, 249
Yemen, 152
Yugoslavia, 98, 157, 249

Zambia, 192